# E-Mail Etiquette

# E-Mail Etiquette

## Do's, Don'ts, and Disaster Tales from  Magazine's Internet Manners Expert

### Samantha Miller

**WARNER BOOKS**

An AOL Time Warner Company

Copyright © 2001 by Samantha Miller
All rights reserved.

Warner Books, Inc., 1271 Avenue of the Americas, New York, NY 10020
Visit our Web site at www.twbookmark.com.
For information on Time Warner Trade Publishing's online publishing program, visit www.ipublish.com.

 An AOL Time Warner Company

Printed in the United States of America
First Printing: November 2001
10 9 8 7 6 5 4 3 2 1

**Library of Congress Cataloging-in-Publication Data**
Miller, Samantha
   E-mail etiquette : do's, don'ts, and disaster tales from People magazine's internet manners expert / Samantha Miller.
    p. cm.
   ISBN 0-446-67804-X
    1. Electronic mail messages. 2. Commercial correspondence.
   3. Letter writing. I. Title.

HE7551 .M54 2001
395.5—dc21

                                              2001026332

*Cover design by Mary Ann Smith*
*Book design and text composition by Nancy Singer Olaguera*

# *Acknowledgments*

First, I owe terabytes of thanks to the e-mailers—from high-tech experts and executives to accommodating friends and strangers—who generously and readily dished about their pet peeves, confessed their most embarrassing gaffes, and shared their own not-so-humble opinions about etiquette dilemmas. I am grateful as well to the many experts who helped guide me through the complex technological and legal issues that relate to the topics in this book.

I am especially indebted to *People* magazine managing editor Carol Wallace, who gave me a great gig with the "Internet Manners" column and had the initial vision for this project, for her confidence and support. A big thank-you to Kyle Smith and the phenomenal Katie Hirce for their help shaping the column every week, and to my other terrific colleagues at *People*.

Thanks also to Amy Einhorn, Sandra Bark and the rest of the Warner Books team; to my agent, Todd Keithley, for his invaluable guidance and good humor; and to my family and friends for graciously editing drafts—and for pointing out all the times my own e-mail messages were less than perfectly polite.

Finally, thank you to the *People* readers whose thoughtful, challenging, witty questions make writing about Internet manners such a blast.

*v*

# Contents

# Introduction

By all rights, e-mail should be the most polite form of communication ever invented. E-mail messages don't interrupt recipients during dinner. E-mailers can take all the time they need to compose and edit notes, so there should be little danger of blurting something foolish. No one has to worry about proper stationery or poor handwriting.

E-mail makes everything easier.

Theoretically.

As more and more of us get wired, at home and at the office, what have we wound up with? As the writer of *People* magazine's "Internet Manners" advice column, I can just look at the gripes in my e-mail in-box for a daily window onto the grisly scene: Friends seething about friends who forward too many chain letters. Employees grumbling about co-workers who claim to be too "busy" to spell-check. Frustrated e-mailers fed up with the hoaxes, scams, and spam—junk advertising e-mail—clogging their in-boxes. Every day, Netizens (citizens of the Net) face a new crop of etiquette and practical dilemmas. Is it proper to send a thank-you note via e-mail? Is it a good idea to share an e-mail address with one's spouse? How formal a tone should an e-mail message to a business contact take?

How can we make e-mail live up to its promise? That's where e-mail etiquette comes in. Don't worry, this kind of etiquette isn't about lists of arbitrary rules. You don't have to memorize how to address a viscount or where to place a fish fork. Instead, e-mail etiquette blends in roughly equal parts common sense, common courtesy, and knowledge of the Net's rules of the road—the dictates of computer technology and the culture established by everyday users.

We all slip up sometimes—and there are plenty of "do as I say, not as I do" directives in this book. (Just ask my friends about how I never change the subject of an e-mail message, so it reads "Re: 4th of July picnic" well into November.) But a good command of e-mail etiquette can go a long way toward creating better relationships—with co-workers, with clients, with friends, with relatives, and even with significant others.

In this book, you'll learn strategies for composing polite and effective personal and business e-mail, practical advice about issues such as e-mail privacy and junk e-mail, and important tips on how to guard against real Net dangers and identify hoaxes. You'll also read advice I've given *People* readers who've landed in sticky e-situations.

To round things out, I asked e-mailers ranging from high-tech CEOs to grandparents to teenagers to share the e-mail etiquette infractions that drive them nuts. You'll see them sprinkled throughout the text as "Net Peeves." Finally, to see the consequences of not minding one's e-manners, check out "Embarrassing E-Moments": e-mail gaffes that made headlines and anonymous confessions from everyday e-mailers. These also appear throughout the book.

Is it okay to ask for a date via e-mail?

What's the proper greeting for an e-mail message to a business client?

Are emoticons—you know, those sideways smiley faces like :-) and :-(—tacky or terrific?

Read on.

# Ten Principles of E-Mail Etiquette

1. Send e-mail that is clear, concise, and considerate of recipients' needs.

2. Spelling and grammar count.

3. Respect your correspondents' time.

4. Treat e-mail you receive as private.

5. Never assume that e-mail you send will remain private.

6. Don't trust any message that reads "Forward this to all your friends."

7. Read the manual—learn about your e-mail program's capabilities and the technology and culture of the Net. But don't be rude to those who know less than you do.

8. Take a deep breath before you hit "send."

9. E-mail isn't the right medium for every message.

10. E-mail *is* the real world.

# Before You Hit "Send": An E-mail Etiquette Checklist

1. Am I sending this message to the correct address?
2. Have I written a useful, descriptive subject line?
3. Is the message's format easy to read?
4. Is the message's purpose clear?
5. Have I used correct spelling and grammar?
6. Is the message's tone appropriate?
7. Could any statement in this message be misinterpreted?
8. Is there anything in this message I wouldn't want to see posted in public?
9. Am I sure e-mail is the right medium for this message?
10. Am I sure this is a message the recipient will want to read?

# 1

# E-Mail Etiquette: Basic Training

- *What kinds of subject lines are best?*
- *How should I sign an e-mail message?*
- *What's so bad about typing e-mail in all capital letters?*

You have before you a new e-mail message. Your mission: Address it properly. Enter a useful, descriptive subject line. And craft a message that's courteous and easy to read.

What could be so hard about that? Just take a look at your in-box. Busy e-mailers often ignore common courtesies like proper spelling; beginning e-mailers often aren't familiar with some of the basic rules of the road. Then there are tips and tricks few e-mailers think about—until they get fed up with other users' bad habits.

In this chapter, we'll tackle the basics of crafting an e-mail message, from "To" to "Ta-ta for now."

An e-mail message has two sections: a header, where the addresses and subject information appear, and the body, where you type your message.

The address lines of an e-mail message:

To: Where you put the e-mail address(es) of the main person or people for whom the message is intended.

cc: Where you put the e-mail address(es) of people who should receive copies of the message. (Future *Who Wants to Be a Millionaire* stumper for Generation Y: What does "cc" stand for? Answer: carbon copy. Ask your parents.)

bcc: Where you put the e-mail address of people who should receive "blind carbon copies" of the message: They get copies, but the "To" and "cc" recipients don't see the "bcc" recipients' addresses listed. "Bcc" recipients don't see one another's addresses, either. Handy in some situations (such as sending a mass mailing to a long list of recipients); a potential e-mail etiquette disaster in others (such as sending a secret copy of a message behind the main recipient's back). For much more on the p's and q's of "cc" and "bcc," see Chapter 5, "Mass Mailing minus the Mess."

## ADDRESS ANTICS

When it comes to avoiding embarrassing e-mail situations, the most important rule is probably the most obvious one: Use the right address. Never guess at a recipient's e-mail address—a change of just one letter could spell disaster. Be very careful if you're selecting recipients from a list of names in an address book or if your e-mail program automatically fills in a recipient's address once you've entered the first few letters. Always double-check the address before you send the message. And triple-check for errors when you add someone's name and address to your e-mail address book.

### Embarrassing E-Moment

"In her e-mail address book, one of my female friends (I'm a guy) accidentally assigned my e-mail address to the nickname of one of her girlfriends and the girlfriend's e-mail address to my nickname. I started getting copies of all this girl talk she and her female friends would exchange after the weekend. After a few weeks I had to write her and say, 'Sorry, this is Sean, not Christine.'"

## NEXT SUBJECT: THE SUBJECT

You can enter pretty much anything as the subject of your e-mail—but this is worth putting some thought into. Why? When your message lands in your recipient's in-box, he has only your name and the subject to consider when he decides when (and whether) to open it—and even more importantly, that's usually all he has to go on when, days and dozens of e-mails later, he's trying to find your message again in his cluttered in-box.

### Some Subject Do's and Don'ts

DO: Use a subject. Forgetting to enter a subject seems to be a plague among e-mail novices and ultra-busy executives. Either way, they should know better. (If you're responding to an e-mail with a blank subject, go ahead and fill one in.)

DO: Keep it short. A complete sentence will betray you as an e-mail beginner, and many e-mail programs cut off a subject after forty characters or so. A few words, or one well-selected one, are best.

DON'T: Start your subject with "Re:". Most e-mail programs automatically insert "Re:" when you respond to a message, so e-mailers think of it as meaning "Reply," not "Regarding." If you put in your own "Re:", your recipient won't know whether this is a new message or a response to one of his. And if he replies, you'll wind up with an unsightly "Re: Re:".

DO: Keep it specific. "Barbecue on Sunday" is better than "party." As for idle e-chatter with friends, "Hi" and "What's up?" are popular subjects for those in a hurry, but taking the time to come up with something creative or humorous will ensure that your pal opens up the message with a smile. Plus, some sneaky junk e-mailers use vague subjects like "Hi" to fool recipients into opening their messages.

DON'T: Use wacky punctuation. Don't use all capital letters, multiple exclamation points, or asterisks to make your subject stand out. It will look like one of those **GET RICH QUICK!!!** junk e-mails—or just be irritatingly hard to read. Whether to capitalize individual words is up to you—you can capitalize in the style of a book title ("Meeting with Consultants") or go lowercase ("meeting with consultants").

DO: Make your subject meaningful to you and your recipient. If the message spawns a back-and-forth conversation, both of you want to be able to identify it easily. In my job as a writer at *People*, I get scads of e-mail messages from would-be story subjects, sources, or publicists with a subject like "Story for People." Of course the message is about a story for *People*, and so are the ninety-eight other messages I got today—making it extremely unlikely I'll be able to find that message in my in-box if I need to refer to it again. Another popular subject that's even worse: the utterly meaningless "For Samantha Miller." Try something more specific.

DO: Change the subject when it needs changing. (Just like underwear!)

**When I'm sending e-mail back and forth with one person, how often should I change the subject line?**

Well, if you and your steady are discussing which wedding caterer to hire and the subject still reads "Re: Nice Meeting You," it's time to freshen it up. But using a new heading on every note can get confusing. So switch when the rest of the message no longer has anything to do with the subject—just say *non* to non sequiturs.

---

## Net Peeve  : (

Someone using the same subject more than, say, twice. Because if you save your messages and you're looking for a particular one and they all have the subject "Re: Hi," you've got to look through every one of them. And subjects that are pointless, like typing three periods, are just plain dumb. Use some imagination, folks.

---

## GREETINGS AND SALUTATIONS!

If you're not still trying to think up a hilarious subject line (if you've been racking your brain for more than five minutes you have permission to go ahead and use "Hi"), the next e-mail etiquette challenge is how to start off the message itself.

To greet or not to greet? Many longtime Net users eschew greetings in e-mail, preferring to launch into their message without any ado. It's clean, neat, and stylishly minimalist—and, like a little black dress, it's appropriate for almost every occasion. Consider converting to this camp—it sure makes life easier.

However, greetings can help start things off on a friendlier—or a more formal—note. Let's start with the office situation.

### What's the proper salutation for business e-mail?

In today's khaki-clad office scene, we're almost all on a first-name basis, so inter-cubicle missives can start with a cheery "Hi, Bob!", "Bob:", or nothing at all. The same goes for outside contacts you're already acquainted with, unless you're a peon and they're big cheeses ("Dear Mr. Gates:"). Don't know your recipient? Stick with "Mr." or "Ms." Traditionalists won't bristle, and whippersnappers will be tickled.

E-mail is less formal than a snail-mail business letter—and it's automatically stamped with a date and return address—so there's no need for inside addresses, the date, or any of that other stuff your high-school English teacher taught you must top a business letter. However, standard business-letter etiquette does apply to the greeting itself, if you're introducing yourself to someone or have another reason to be formal. Use titles where appropriate and a colon at the end:

Dear Mr. Jones:

Dear Ms. Jones:

Dear Dr. Jones:

Dear Rev. Jones:

Dear Senator Jones:

Dear Mr. President:

If you subsequently reach a first-name basis with the recipient, you can begin with "Dear Susan:" or "Susan:". (Please don't try this for heads of state.)

What if you're e-mailing a group of people, or a person whose identity you don't know, such as a customer-service representative for a shopping Web site? The simplest solution is to join the minimalist team and skip a greeting. If you're a die-hard traditionalist, for groups you may use "Ladies and Gentlemen:" or describe the recipients: "Dear Professors:" or "Dear Acme employees:".

For mystery individuals, you may opt for the ultra-formal "Dear Sir or Madam," the tried-and-true "To whom it may concern," or a title such as "Dear Webmaster." Less formal, but admirably all-purpose: "Greetings," "Good day," or even "Hello."

DO: If this is the first time you're e-mailing someone, once you've deployed the formal greeting use a few sentences of the message to introduce yourself. Indicate your name, your company, your job title, and a few pertinent details about who you are or why you're writing (i.e., "I enjoyed meeting you at the trade show last week" or "I'm a resident of your congressional district and I have a pothole on my block that could swallow a Humvee.").

DON'T: Be too informal when e-mailing a business contact you don't know. Plenty of e-mailers (perhaps even a majority) use first names in this situation, and plenty of recipients see nothing wrong with it, but you never know when someone will take offense. Plus, starting things off with a respectful, businesslike tone can't hurt your interests. And for Pete's—or, rather, Peter's—sake, don't use a nickname for your recipient unless he or she has invited you to do so.

When you're sending e-mail to friends, the rules loosen up considerably. Whether to use a greeting, and what greeting to use, is a matter of your own personal style. There's the time-tested

("Dear Mom"), enthusiastic ("Hi there!"), literary ("Greetings and salutations," as Charlotte of *Charlotte's Web* preferred), cinematic ("Yo, Adrian!" as Rocky might have e-mailed), and myriad more options.

DO: If you're e-mailing your significant other, a quick "My darling" or "Pookie" might help set a romantic mood—assuming Pookie isn't the cat's name.

## THE BODY OF THE MESSAGE

E-mail isn't as formal as a letter. Nor is it as casual or fleeting as a phone call. The exact format and tone of your message, of course, depend somewhat on the situation—a message to your boss will look different from one to your main squeeze. (If the boss *is* your main squeeze, better get separate accounts for your personal and professional e-mail to keep those memos and mash notes separate.)

Some basic rules, however, almost always apply:

DO: Keep the basic format clean and easy to read. Break for paragraphs frequently (think of a newspaper article) and double-space between them. Don't use tabs or spaces to indent each paragraph—keep them flush to the left. Tabs frequently get garbled by recipients' e-mail programs, and blocks of text, flush with the left-hand margin, look cleaner anyway.

DON'T: Double-space after a period. This went out with the typewriter.

DO: Keep business e-mails short—or as short as possible, anyway. If one sentence accomplishes the mission, there's no need to pad with small talk.

Among friends, anything goes—as long as everyone's happy. Some people like to craft lengthy dispatches, others one-line zingers. If you're a haiku type who's pals with an epic poet, find a happy medium, or learn to live with each other.

## Net Peeve :(

Long e-mails. Living in Silicon Valley, you get used to being very concise. People outside of Silicon Valley take twice as much room to say half as much. If I see more than two paragraphs, I stop reading and save it for later.

**I have a friend I keep in touch with online. I have so much to say. Is it okay to write a very long e-mail?**

Your friend ought to be delighted. If you're worried about sending her on a guilt trip, add a P.S. assuring her you don't require an epic-length reply.

DO: Spell-check. Or better yet, learn to spell—it's never too late. Atrocious spelling seems to have become a perverse point of pride among some ultra-busy types—it shows they're busy VIPs, you see—but many fed-up e-mailers single it out as one of their primary Net peeves. A typo here and there is no sin, but heedless sloppiness will make your message difficult to read, while your lack of common courtesy will come through loud and clear. Be extra careful with common mistakes the spell-checker won't catch, like "its" versus "it's" and "affect" versus "effect," or risk losing esteem in the eyes of a recipient who—bless him or her—cares about literacy.

**Is it okay to send e-mail full of spelling errors?**

look over emale before u sned it. its only commn curtesy. How annoying was that to read? Very—which is why the "I'm so busy I can't take time to spell-check" attitude has got to go. It's rude to recipients. They're busy too.

DO: Feel free to use common abbreviations or acronyms—if you're sure your recipient will understand them. Common Net acronyms like BTW (by the way), IHMO (in my humble opinion), and ROTFL (rolling on the floor laughing) can indubitably be useful, and most professions evolve their own patois of abbreviations and TLAs (three-letter acronyms). Such shorthand is perfectly polite in informal e-mail—as long as you know recipients speak the lingo too. Using lingo to show off in front of a Net newbie or someone outside your field is rude—and so is making fun of anyone for not understanding it. For a Net-lingo guide, see Appendix A.

**When I play online games, people send me chat messages like "a/s/l" or "gg." I don't know what they mean. What should I do?**

Abbreviations and acronyms are part of the fun of the Net. Next time you're befuddled, just ask the person you're chatting with—it's not impolite of your fellow players to use lingo, but it would be very rude for them not to let a newcomer in on the code. (By the way, "a/s/l" means "age, sex, location" and "gg" means "good game" or "gotta go.") Shy? Try a Net-slang dictionary such as netlingo.com.

DON'T: Use all capital letters for the body of the message!

**Why is it bad to type in all capital letters? What about all small letters?**

Net tradition dictates that all caps denotes shouting: PIPE DOWN! As for the e. e. cummings mode, it's fine for speed in chat rooms, but ease up on the accelerator for e-mail.

Internet newcomers sometimes gripe about the all-caps-equals-shouting rule, but it's one of the Net's longest-standing traditions. (It's so deeply ingrained that I want to cover my ears when I read a message in all caps.) Violate it in the presence of Net veterans and you'll likely see some REAL SHOUTING in your in-box.

Interestingly, when I answered the above question in my column, I heard from quite a few older readers protesting that those with impaired vision found messages in all capital letters easier to read. "MY EYESIGHT IS TERRIBLE AND BEING ABLE TO SEND AND RECEIVE MESSAGES IN ALL CAPS HAS HELPED ME TREMENDOUSLY," wrote one. "I MEAN NO OFFENSE TO ANY-ONE BUT IT CERTAINLY HELPS THE EYESTRAIN."

Commented another reader:

Since the Internet is so new I wonder who decreed that writing in caps is like shouting—just some ole duff having a bad day? I would like to say a few words for the use of all caps so people won't be so hard on others. For those recipients who have visual impairment CAPS can be help-ful. For some who are writing who have an impaired shoulder or hand CAPS is so much easier. So maybe it should not be such a big issue. Maybe we should tolerate caps and not make those who are using them have to apologize for it and have to explain about a disability. Maybe we all need to chill out some more.

If consenting adults want to correspond in all caps, who am I to say no? However, most e-mail programs—as these readers may not have realized—let users increase the type size of e-mail they read. You can usually find this option in the program's Preferences or Settings menu. For someone with impaired typing skills, why not use all lowercase letters?

Why this antipathy toward capitals? Besides irritating Netizens trained to recognize them as shouting, messages written in all capi-tal letters are also harder to read—capital letters' shapes, less dis-tinctive than those of lowercase letters, make it more difficult for our brain to recognize words. Studies estimate that we read text written in all capital letters about 14 percent more slowly. Compare how fast you can skim a message in all caps to one in lowercase letters.

**I realize it is considered rude to use ALL CAPS, as it denotes shout-ing. But what if I really want to emphasize a word?**

True, writing a message entirely in capital letters will make recipients run for earplugs, but if something really makes you wanna shout, it's usually fine to capitalize an individual word or phrase. A lower-volume way to kick a word up a notch: Surround it with asterisks. Now *that's* easier on the eardrums.

**My boss always e-mails me in giant capital letters. Since he yells 95 percent of the time anyway, this is no big surprise, but it's REALLY starting to bug me. I've asked nicely, shouted back in a bigger font; NOTHING works. He knows it's impolite and does it anyway. What can I do?**

Try explaining that people read text written in caps more slowly. (A study has proved it.) So he's sapping employee productivity, at least by a few milliseconds per message. If appealing to the bottom line doesn't end this capital punishment—and "I QUIT!" isn't an option—you may be able to edit him down to size. Microsoft Outlook, for example, offers a "change case" option when you're in message-editing mode. Or copy his messages into your word-processing program and reduce them there.

DON'T: Use formatted text—such as italics, boldfacing, underlining, or multiple colors or fonts—when sending a message to someone who might use an e-mail program different from yours. Because e-mail programs handle text formatting differently, a message that looks like an exquisite work of typographical art to you may turn into garbled gobbledygook on the screens of recipients whose e-mail software can't understand your software's formatting method.

If you can't live without boldfacing or bullet points, you must use a formatting method your recipient's e-mail program can read. The latest versions of most popular e-mail programs, including Microsoft Outlook and Outlook Express, Qualcomm Eudora, Netscape Mail, and (at long last) America Online, can read and write text formatted using HTML, the language in which Web pages are written. Most of these programs let you choose whether to send individual messages, or all messages, in HTML or in plain text. Some even include a handy feature that lets you designate which people in your address book should be sent formatted messages and which should always receive plain text.

Who still requires plain text in this day and age? Some bare-bones e-mail programs, as well as older versions of the programs listed above, can't read HTML. (Users of such programs will see code such as "<FONT FACE="Helvetica">" littering messages.) And some users simply prefer reading e-mail without any formatting fripperies. If one of your correspondents requests plain-text e-mail, honor his wishes by forgoing formatting. And always use plain text when e-mailing a new contact or a mailing list.

Some programs offer e-mailers a bigger bag of stylistic tricks by using more complex methods to encode messages' formatting. For example, Microsoft Outlook lets users create messages using plain text, HTML, Microsoft Word, or Rich Text Format (a method of encoding formatted text and graphics). Such options are safest if you're communicating with people you're certain use the same e-mail program you do, such as co-workers. Otherwise, stick to plain text or HTML.

DO: Use restraint with formatting in business and personal e-mail. It can look silly or fussy in casual memos, and even when you intend to create a message pretty enough for the printer, it's easy to overdo it. Go easy on the boldfacing, italics, and Technicolor text. And don't use more than two fonts—it's a fashion "don't" as gauche as mixing polka dots and paisley.

---

### Net Peeve  :(

When people fool with their fonts and background colors so much you can't even read their e-mail. One guy I know sends me e-mail in really small pink letters on a black-grid background. It's completely illegible!

---

So you've sworn off fancy formatting. Then how do you emphasize a word? Some e-mailers embrace substitutes such as *asterisks* to highlight a word you might otherwise boldface and a version of _underlining_ for phrases such as book or movie titles that they would usually italicize or underline. But these fudges aren't strictly necessary. You can use quote marks or context to explain anything apt to cause confusion ("I saw 'Laura' last night" or "I saw the movie Laura last night" will show you're not talking about your aunt).

DON'T: Similarly, don't use special characters like accent marks or symbols (£, ®) unless you're sure your recipient's e-mail program can read them. The plain text that all e-mail programs can read includes only the characters you see on a standard computer keyboard: letters, numbers, punctuation, a few common symbols. Anything else might get garbled in transmission. Again, you're probably safe if your recipient uses the same e-mail program you do. But in addition to differences among e-mail programs, Macintosh and IBM-compatible computers have problems translating each other's character codes.

So if a character takes more than the "shift" key to create, it's best to avoid it in plain-text messages. You can write out equivalents to symbols: Coca-Cola (tm); 15,000 pounds or GBP 15,000. If accents and foreign-language characters are crucial to your message, send them as an attached word-processing document.

One little set of symbols that can cause big-time aggravation: "Curly" quotes. Some e-mail programs have difficulty reading them—and there's nothing worse than reading a long message where every quote and apostrophe have been turned into "?"s. Make sure your e-mail program is set up to use straight quotes, and watch out when you're pasting from a word-processing program that uses curlies. Some e-mail programs can be set up to de-curl quotes automatically before sending a message.

---

## Net Peeve  : (

Using too many exclamation points. Your e-mail sounds like a Valley Girl. And they're also bossy. "Laugh now! I'm being funny!! Really funny!!!!"

---

## SIGN-OFFS

### How should I sign e-mail?

Like TV news anchors, Netizens love signature sign-offs. Hippies use "Peace"; gen Y, "C-ya L8R"; acronym addicts, "TTFN." ("Ta-ta for now.") Some savvy users scorn cutesiness and simply sign their name or initials. I say creativity is no crime, but be original—or you'll look as pretentious as non-Italians who double-cheek kiss a ciao.

For personal e-mail, signing with your first name or initials is fine. A sign-off like "Love," "Cheers," or "All my best" is optional. In fact, to ardent e-mail minimalists, signing your name is unnecessary on a message to someone you e-mail frequently. (An exception: If you share an e-mail account—with a spouse, for instance—always sign messages so readers know which person they came from.)

For business e-mail, use a standard sign-off with your full name—a sign-off such as "Sincerely" or the less formal "Cheers" or "Best wishes" is optional—followed by your contact information. (Like your business card: name, title, company name, address, e-mail address, deluxe assortment of phone, fax, cellular, and pager numbers.) It'll be easy for your recipient to copy your 411 into her Rolodex or address-book program—and if she forgets, it'll be at the bottom of every e-mail you send her.

---

### Net Peeve : (

When you don't put your contact information into your signature file. That's just a courtesy. I use my old e-mail as my Rolodex.

---

### Signature Files

Most e-mail programs let you create a customized "signature" file that's automatically appended to every outgoing message. (Some let you create several, so you can have different ones for business and pleasure.) This is great for business e-mail—create a signature with your contact information, and you'll never have to type it again. As usual, stay away from any fancy formatting.

> Jane Smith, CEO
> Acme Anvils Corp.
> 76 Main Street
> Toontown, CA 99999
> (301) 555-1234
> (301) 555-1235 (fax)
> jsmith@acme.com

Or a more compact option, if you rarely use snail mail or faxes (and are willing to put up with the inevitable "Hi. Can I get your snail-mail address?" notes):

> Jane Smith, CEO
> Acme Anvils Corp.
> (301) 555-1234

Some users might also want to insert a short (and I mean short!) self-promotional plug:

> Visit us at acmeanvils.com

or

> Look for my new memoir, Heavyweight: A Life in Anvils, coming in January

Do you need a signature file for personal e-mail? Not really, since your friends presumably already know how to get in touch with you. But some users enjoy creating a signature with a favorite quote, high-school-yearbook-style (one can get a glimpse into a user's personality by looking to see if she's picked Ayn Rand or "All you need is love"), or other informational tidbit: A minister might throw in his upcoming sermon topic; a sports nut might list his home team's latest record. These tidbits are fine in personal e-mail. (They're not appropriate for business e-mail.) Just keep them short—two lines maximum. Whatever you do, don't put a picture in your signature, whether an actual photo or a graphic created from keyboard symbols. They're annoying—and beyond tacky.

**I'm job-hunting. May I put a link to my résumé (it's on the Web) in my e-mail?**

All's fair in love, war, and the rat race. A short P.S. (not lengthy wheedling) won't bug anyone—and it might help you network. Just don't post anything online you don't want the whole world (or your current employer) to see.

---

### Net Peeve : (

Signatures longer than the body of the e-mail.

---

### Net Peeve : (

I'm in contact with a lot of creative people, and they put a quote at the bottom of their signature—something from Thoreau or whatever. It's great for the first two e-mails you get, but if you don't change it, that's really lame. At least change the quote every couple of months.

---

### Net Peeve : (

People whose automatic signatures at the bottom of e-mails say something horribly outdated. People graduate from college and get a job, but their signature lines say they're still in college.

---

## IMHO (In My Humble Opinion): Over-Emoting?

Why, oh why, do :-)s make so many people :-(?

Translation: Why do e-mail smiley faces, aka emoticons, make so many people unhappy?

Boy, do some people hate smileys. Irritating, they call them. Juvenile. Unprofessional.

I'm taking a stand. Etiquette smiles on smileys. Well, some of the time, anyway.

In the sterile world of e-mail, where you can't see a correspondent's face or hear the tone of his or her voice, it's dangerously easy to misinterpret messages. Almost every e-mailer can tell a tale of a joke that a recipient took seriously or sarcasm that got mistaken for brusqueness. That's where emoticons—used properly—come in. Emoticons give senders a shorthand way to express their feelings and make sure misinterpretation-prone messages or comments are understood in the sense they were intended. A basic portrait gallery of emoticons (tilt your head to the left to read):

| | |
|---|---|
| :-) | Smiling: "I'm happy about this" or "I'm just kidding" |
| ;-) | Winking: "I'm being flirtatious" or "I'm joking" |
| :-D | Laughing: "That's funny!" |
| :-P | Sticking tongue out: "I'm being silly" or "Nyah, nyah!" |
| :-( | Frowning: "I'm sad about this" or "I sympathize" |
| :-] | Smirk: "I'm being sarcastic" |
| :-\ | "I'm skeptical" or "I'm perplexed" |
| :-\| | Apathy: "I don't care about this" or "No comment" |
| :-o | "I'm shocked!" or "I'm yelling!" |

Variations are myriad (noses, for example, may be left out at the user's discretion). Creative e-mailers have devised scores of smileys, most more silly than useful. For example:

:*)        "I'm drunk"

-:-)       A punk rocker

*****:-)   Marge Simpson

5:-)       Elvis

%-~        Picasso

*<|:o)>    Santa Claus

:-{8       Person who is unhappy with the results of her breast-enlargement surgery, according to humorist Dave Barry

Such over-the-top creations, of course, are part of why many Netizens revile smileys. Another strike against smileys is their overuse. Some e-mailers sprinkle emoticons throughout their messages like middle-schoolers dotting their *i*'s with smiley faces. No wonder smiley-haters slam them as childish.

But even adults should learn to live with—and even love—smileys. Anyone who's ever had a flip e-mail comment misinterpreted knows that smileys guard against a very real problem.

"I wish you'd start using subject lines in your e-mail" comes across as testy, while "I wish you'd start using subject lines in your e-mail. :-)" softens the comment, showing you're saying it with a smile on your face. "Another brilliant idea from the boss. ;-)" implies you're not exactly about to nominate him for a MacArthur genius grant. "I've really screwed it up this time :-(" suggests that the sender is genuinely upset, not joking. Smileys can make the difference between giving a recipient a giggle—and getting a reply saying "Are you okay?" or "Up yours!"

Finally, consider this: Smileys make the e-mail world safe for sarcasm, humor, and irony. And a world without sarcasm, humor, and irony wouldn't be worth living in.

Help emoticons make it back into etiquette's good graces by exercising restraint:

• Use them only when necessary, directly after comments that require them. One per e-mail is plenty; two is pushing it. (If you're in a silly or sarcastic mood, readers will quickly get the picture.) Three or more will make readers think you're still in fourth grade.

- Steer clear of "creative" emoticons. Using a smiling vampire rabbi emoticon doesn't tell readers anything—except maybe "I'm a major nerd."

- Don't use emoticons in every message you send or in your signature. They're a tool, not a fashion statement. Smiley addicts are as annoying as people who tell everyone they meet, "Have a nice day."

Today, you can often send smileys right-side-up: Several e-mail programs offer graphical versions of emoticons—variations on the familiar yellow smiley face—that users can insert into e-mail. Some even automatically turn typed smileys into graphics. These high-tech smileys are nifty, but somehow I think the old-school style is more charming.

---

## Net Peeve :(

People who use elaborate emoticons like a smiling rabbi. That's ridiculous. Or people who use eighteen of them in one e-mail. That's ridiculous too.

---

### Emoticons at the Office

Okay, smiley-haters might grudgingly admit, go ahead and use smileys in personal e-mail. But shouldn't we draw the line at work?

In fact, emoticons should be perfectly acceptable in informal messages between co-workers. Office e-mail is just as likely to be misinterpreted—and misinterpretations can be even more danger-ous at work. As long as workers follow the rules above, there's no reason the occasional smiley should be seen as unprofessional.

For smiley skeptics who just can't bring themselves to use the things, there are alternatives. One somewhat more professional-looking option is to use asides or abbreviations (traditionally set off within pointy brackets) to indicate emotions or actions:

<grin> or <g>

<sigh> or <s>

<jk> (just kidding)

LOL (laughing out loud)

Another alternative: Write out exactly what you're trying to convey with an emoticon. Use phrases like "And I say this with a smile on my face" or "I'm just being sarcastic. Thanks for letting me vent." They're not particularly punchy, but they do the trick.

In more formal business e-mail situations, of course, it's best to steer clear of jokes, sarcasm, or anything that could be misinterpreted, smiley or not. If you're considering using a smiley, something's wrong.

**Survey Says**
*63 percent of workers say they like smileys.*

*Source: Vault.com*

### Embarrassing E-Moment

For want of a smiley, a kingdom was lost?

A chilly e-mail exchange helped fuel a bitter feud between Rob Glaser, the CEO of RealNetworks, and his former employer Bill Gates. Glaser, a former top Microsoft executive, had been asked to testify at a Senate Judiciary Committee hearing investigating software-industry business practices. Glaser believed that Microsoft had been using its monopoly power to try to damage his company. But before heading to Washington, Glaser sent a polite e-mail to Gates requesting a meeting to talk the problem over:

"Bill. Hope all is well with you and your family," Glaser wrote, according to *USA Today*, explaining that committee chairman Senator Orrin Hatch had persuaded him to testify. "I'm very interested in understanding your perspective on the matters that Hatch is likely to want me to talk about, and I'm happy to share with you in advance what I'm likely to say in my testimony. Please let me know if it would work out for us to talk soon."

In his reply, Gates declined to meet. "While you are in Washington," he wrote, "I suggest you visit the National Gallery and the Smithsonian."

Glaser thought Gates' reply was cold and flip. "The nature of e-mail is you can't see somebody's face," he told *USA Today*. "I wouldn't look at [the e-mail] and say he felt really bad about it." He said the e-mail helped him make up his mind to denounce Microsoft. Would a smiley face have saved Gates from Glaser's damaging testimony? We'll never know.

# Replying Right and Coping with E-Mail Overload

- *How long is it polite to take to reply to e-mail?*
- *How can I find out if someone received my message?*
- *Help! I can't cope with all the e-mail I get!*

No matter how much e-mail you get, it's too much. Ask almost any e-mail user—from an ultra-wired executive bombarded with hundreds of messages a day to a Net newcomer grandmother fending off a grand total of five a week—and you're apt to hear complaints about how overwhelmed he or she is in coping with the onslaught and how stressed out it makes him or her feel.

The reason behind all this is simple. Someone who gets a few e-mails a day probably considers each one akin to a personal letter. She takes a while to mull over her response, carefully chooses the right words to express it, maybe thinks up a creative or funny greeting. When someone gets a few dozen e-mails a day, responses get shorter and shot from the hip: "OK." "Let's do it." When that few dozen becomes scores, messages wind up deleted, ignored, or lost in the shuffle—often along with any effort at proper etiquette.

What's more, we're all a few steps behind in adjusting our attitudes to the amount of e-mail we get. We all think we should be responding to more messages, replying more promptly, crafting more polished responses. This isn't entirely unhealthy; many e-mail users should indeed be paying more attention to all of the above (or at the very least, taking the time to spell-check). If a little guilt is what it takes, so be it.

But the best way for us to become more efficient about coping with the in-box crunch is to be considerate of our recipients. That means understanding how busy recipients are, and therefore making our messages easy to read and respond to. It also means taking time to make our e-mail messages and replies considerate of others even though we're busy ourselves.

One of the handiest features of e-mail is the ability to include a copy of a message, or a few choice quotes from the message, when you reply to it. Of course, this feature is only handy if you use it—and use it right.

How do you quote a message? Most e-mail programs can be set up to automatically insert a copy of a message you're replying to into the body of your reply. (AOL e-mail users can accomplish this by highlighting the portion of a message they wish to quote before hitting "reply.") You can then choose to leave the entire message or delete some or all of it. Programs often set off the quoted text with ">" characters. They may also add a line introducing the quote such as "On July 4, 2002, Samantha Miller wrote:".

When should you quote a message in your reply?

- When you're answering a question asked in the e-mail

- When you're responding to, commenting on, or arguing with a point raised in the e-mail

- Whenever you think it would be helpful for the recipient to be able to refer back to his or her original message

## Net Peeve : (

You write a simple e-mail asking a simple question and a week later you get an e-mail from the person that says "Yes, the second one sounds good." And by that time, you have no clue as to what they're talking about. People need to either quote the original e-mail or write the question in the answer.

## TO SNIP OR NOT TO SNIP?

If you think those situations sound like they cover almost any e-mail reply, you're right. It's almost always a good idea to include quotes from a message you reply to. However, it's sometimes cumbersome to quote an entire message, especially a long one. In that case, pare the quote down to the relevant parts: the specific question you're answering, the first paragraph of a long saga, the few sections of a long report you plan to offer suggestions about. If you're doing a lot of selective quoting, avoid confusion by typing "<snip>" or "[ . . . ]" where you've chopped out chunks of verbiage. For example:

```
From: Susan Jones <sjones@xyz.com>
To: Jane Smith <jsmith@zwx.com>
Subject: Re: weekend plans

On Dec. 1, 2001, Jane Smith wrote:
>Do you want to catch a movie Saturday?
Yes, I think I'm free. I'll call you in the
afternoon.
>By the way, my daughter did the cutest
thing today.
<snip>
That's adorable. E-mail me a photo!

Sue
```

## Net Peeve :(

I get a lot of e-mail, sometimes hundreds a day, and I'm ultra-efficient about responding to them. But what really makes me crazy is when people e-mail me without quoting from my previous e-mail to them. So I end up with e-mails that say things like "Looking forward to the details" or "I know what you mean" or "Please send it to me." Help! What are they talking about? Then I have to e-mail them back and say "I get a lot of e-mail. Can you please remind me about our conversation?" and it looks like I'm not paying attention. If they'd only include some relevant snippets of our previous e-mail correspondence, I'd be happy as a clam. And NOT the whole thing, just a few sentences that pertain to the response. Otherwise, I've got an e-mail the size of *War and Peace.*

If you're quoting an entire message or a single snippet, type your response above it, at the beginning of the message body. This is Net custom for good reason: If the quoted message comes first, the recipient may not realize he needs to look below it for the response. And once several rounds of back-and-forth have taken place, you'll be able to scroll down to trace the conversation's history in reverse chronological order.

## Net Peeve :(

When someone answers your e-mail by return reply and puts his comment below your message, so you have to look at the entire message before you realize it's an answer to your e-mail.

If you're using several snippets requiring separate responses, you can insert your answers after each quote. (But try to avoid this clunky-looking structure in personal e-mail—you'll sound like a nitpicky politician issuing a point-by-point response to an opponent's nine-point plan.)

---

## Net Peeve : (

When I e-mail somebody with multiple questions and they answer simply "Yes" or "No" without specifying to which question they are responding. First of all, this inappropriately minimalist missive makes painfully clear that you did not read the whole e-mail, as if it didn't hold your interest after a certain point, which is perfectly fine, but don't expect me to put much thought or wit into future communications. Second, I gotta e-mail you again to clarify your answer. For example:

*My e-mail:* Hey, Jervis. Where do you live, and what time should I show up for your fetish product party?

*Reply e-mail:* Yes.

---

Must you always quote a message when replying to it? Quoting is almost always a good idea. But you can summarize a message or question in your own words if you prefer. If your reply really has nothing to do with the message you were sent, it's probably time to create a new subject line and make it a new message entirely.

How long is too long? After several rounds of exchanging e-mail back and forth, quoting each time, an e-mail dialogue can become longer than an epic novel. If publishing it as "The Story of a Friendship, Told Backwards" isn't quite your aim, know when to say when. Once you've moved on to a new topic, or once the information from earlier conversations ceases to be relevant, take your pruning shears to the old growth.

## Embarrassing E-Moment

An indiscreet e-mail exchange caused trouble for Florida governor Jeb Bush during the 2000 presidential election recount controversy. When Bush got a report that someone was calling voters and urging them to complain to the governor's office about disallowed votes, George W.'s little brother forwarded the information to aides via e-mail, writing: "This is a concerted effort to divide and destroy our state." His communications director, Katie Baur, replied: "Ve have our Vays also. . . . I'm working on this." No one thought the phony accent—or the implication that Jeb Bush's office might be trying to help W.—was so funny when newspapers printed the messages.

How long does a reply have to be? Some e-mailers get annoyed if correspondents reply by quoting their message and simply typing "Yes" or "OK." While you could make the case that such quick-and-dirty responses are exactly what e-mail was designed for, one-word replies can come across as overly curt. You don't have to write in complete compound sentences, but try throwing in a few extra words to avoid the appearance of brusqueness. Instead of "Yes" in response to a question about whether you're coming to a meeting, try "Yes, I plan on attending." Instead of "OK," try "Great idea! Let's do it."

**When someone e-mails me a thank-you note, must I send a "You're welcome"?**

Your mother always made you say it, even if you were never quite sure what it accomplished. We're going to take a bold stand: The "You're welcome" rule is hereby abolished for e-mail. Those extra messages just clutter in-boxes—and can turn into an aggravating game of social Ping-Pong: "Thank you." "No, thank *you*."

## A QUESTION OF TIMING

And now we come to one of the great dilemmas of e-mail etiquette: how long one ought to take to respond to an e-mail message. Minutes? Days? Weeks? You'll meet people—quite possibly all within your own family—who practice each of the above.

No one guideline can fit all. After all, some business users are constantly online, while many home users check their e-mail once a day or less frequently.

**How long should I wait for someone to respond to an e-mail?**

First, consider your correspondent. E-mailers tend to fall into three groups: those who would happily implant a modem in their brain, those who check mail daily, and those who regard booting up the computer as a once-in-a-while adventure (Hi, Mom). As a general rule, wait a few days, then zap 'em a reminder. After a week, pick up the phone.

People's habits vary widely: Some people return e-mail like Martina Hingis returns serves, and some take forever. But how long *should* one take to respond to an e-mail?

- At offices where all employees are constantly online, e-mail messages from co-workers usually call for the quickest replies. After all, there's no excuse: Your co-workers know you're there and know you're online. Plus, in most workplaces, interoffice e-mails tend to be sent with the expectation of a swift reply. Unless the message requires doing research or accomplishing a task before replying, try to respond pronto— or by the end of the day if the message is obviously not urgent.

- As for work-related messages you get from contacts or clients outside the office, unless the message is urgent, taking a few business days to respond is fair. Even though e-mail is an instant medium, you have a right to tackle more pressing priorities first. After a few days to a week, the sender is within his etiquette rights to bug you with a follow-up note or phone call.

- With personal e-mail, the trick is to establish an m.o.— whether it's always answering by the end of the day or usually taking a week to reply—and stick to it. Your friends will get to know how long it takes you to reply to e-mail and adjust their expectations accordingly. Once you've settled into a pattern that suits your lifestyle, it would be futile—and rude—for your friends or relatives to try to alter your habits. Your mom checks her e-mail only once a week? Live with it.

### Survey Says

*9 percent of U.S. Net users say they check their e-mail hourly.*

*29 percent check it several times a day.*

*38 percent check it about once a day.*

*17 percent check it several times a week.*

*6 percent check it about once a week.*

*1 percent check it less than once a week.*

*Source: UCLA Center for Communication Policy*

---

### Net Peeve : (

When people don't give me enough time to respond. They'll write, "Didn't you get my e-mail?" Especially when you're dealing with a busy person, give them three to five days.

---

**Is it poor manners to keep e-mailing someone who doesn't ever e-mail back?**

Could the address be wrong? Could your target be taking a break someplace without e-mail, like the *Big Brother* house? If not, and he or she is perfectly capable of replying but doesn't, take the hint.

I found a celebrity's personal e-mail address listed on the Net. I wrote a message but never heard back. How can I be sure she got it?

The Web teems with lists of stars' purported private addresses—most out-of-date or plain wrong. Even if you didn't get a bum steer, face it: Your idol is about as likely to write back as Warren Beatty is to get carded buying beer. (Would you return calls from a stranger who dug up your unlisted phone number?)

Instead, play nice. You can often zap celebs a note at their official home pages—many, like Cindy Crawford, post replies to fan e-mail—or, for TV actors, their shows' sites. Still no response? Seek out their snail-mail addresses—or more plugged-in stars.


## SORRY, WRONG ADDRESS

What should I do if I get an e-mail message that's obviously been sent to the wrong address? Should I write back and tell the sender?

When we pick up an errant phone call, we have little choice but to tell the caller—the only etiquette concern is whether we're saintly enough not to get snappish when the call comes at 2 A.M. With e-mail, yes, it's courteous to let someone know his message has gone awry. Reply with a quick "Sorry, wrong e-mail address" note, quoting the entire message in case the sender didn't keep a copy himself. And try to read only enough of the message to determine it wasn't meant for you.

### Embarrassing E-Moment

"I started getting these e-mail messages from a woman who was obviously having an affair. They were all about meeting places and such. After I got several of these messages, I wrote to her and told her, 'Wrong e-mail address.' It turns out my domain name was one letter different from that of the company this woman's lover worked at. Eventually I wrote to the company and told them about the confusion, without mentioning these particular misaddressed e-mails. They changed their domain name."

## COPING WITH THE IN-BOX CRUNCH

I remember a TV commercial that showed a tennis pro expertly returning one ball after another as an unseen opponent whaled them at him faster and faster. Then all of a sudden, about 500 balls whizzed over the net, and all the ace could do was duck. For some reason, this image often pops into my head when I confront my e-mail in-box in the morning.

The following organizational tips and tricks can't make the onslaught disappear, but they can help you cut down the clutter— and diminish the stress of an overloaded in-box.

- Always read and answer the most recent messages in your mailbox first, especially when you have a lot piled up (like when you come back after a vacation). That way you won't wind up responding to an outdated message or getting into a lather about a problem that's already been solved. Plus, it maximizes your appearance of promptness: At least you'll be returning *some* e-mail quickly.

- Deal with non-urgent messages all at one time. It could be just after lunch, before you leave work, or during *Letterman*, but set aside a time to sort through and reply to the day's missives. Dealing with each message as it comes in—or letting e-mail suck up any spare moments you find during the day—can be distracting.

- Delete or file messages you have already dealt with. Most e-mail programs let you move messages from your in-box into other folders you create. When you're through with a message for the time being but don't want to delete it, cut down on in-box (and psychological) clutter by filing it into a folder.

- Take anti-spam measures. Unsubscribe from mailing lists you signed up for but rarely read; learn how to cut down on unsolicited advertising e-mail in Chapter 11, "I Do Not Like That Spam I Am."

- Take advantage of filters.

## FILTERING FOR FUN AND PROFIT

Coffee and cigarettes aren't the only products that come with filters. Filters also work wonders for another addiction: e-mail. Filters let you instruct your e-mail software to automatically sort your incoming messages into separate folders. For example, filters can flag messages from specific senders, messages with certain words in the text, or messages addressed directly to you rather than to a group of recipients. This helps you read, organize, and store your e-mail efficiently: You can route all messages from your boss to one folder, messages mentioning a project you're working on to another, while messages from a hobby mailing list you subscribe to can go to a third. You can even choose to route certain messages directly to the trash. The possibilities—and the number of stressed-out brain cells you'll rescue—are nearly endless. Most popular e-mail programs, including Microsoft Outlook and Outlook Express (which call filters Rules), Eudora, MSN Hotmail, and Yahoo! Mail, though not America Online's e-mail, offer a filtering feature. Look for Filters, Rules, or Options on your program's menu.

A creative e-mailer with a good command of logic can devise all sorts of handy filters. A few more useful filters:

- Separate internal office e-mail from outside mail. Filter messages from senders whose addresses don't include your company's domain name into an "Outside Mail" folder.

- Separate mass mailings from messages addressed directly to you. Route messages that don't include your e-mail address in the "To" field—meaning the sender cc'ed or bcc'ed you or used a group nickname—to a "Mass Mailings" folder.

- Route messages from specific mailing lists to their own folders by setting up filters that look for the lists' "From" addresses.

- Create a separate folder for family e-mail by creating a filter that looks for your relatives' return addresses.

Filters take time to set up, but you'll wonder how you lived without them. I think I'll look into getting Lloyd's of London to insure my elaborate scaffolding of Eudora filters for $1 million.

> **Survey Says**
> *A 2000 survey of Pitney Bowes showed that American employees send or receive an average of 50 e-mails a day. They also deal with 48 phone calls, 21 voice mails, and 6 cell-phone calls.*

**If a friend sends me e-mail and later we instant-message with each other, do I still have to reply to her e-mail?**

If your instant-message tête-à-tête covered whatever topic she e-mailed you about, then no. But to avoid any mix-up over whose turn it is to write, send the ball back to her court with a "nice chatting with you" note—or some great dish you forgot to share.

## BE A COURTEOUS SENDER

Sending e-mail to an ultra-busy person? Help him or her achieve a state of serenity (well, become marginally less frazzled, anyway)—and increase your chances of a prompt reply—with these tips:

- Use a good subject line. Make it descriptive and meaningful to the recipient—something more specific than "Idea" or "Your request."

- Keep the message short. Skip the small talk; get right to the point.

- If the e-mail makes a request, explain it clearly. Do you need the recipient to reply, and how quickly? Carry out some task? Forward the message to someone else once she's looked it over? Don't bury your request in the middle of a paragraph. Make it a separate, easy-to-spot sentence at the beginning or end of your message. (Don't forget to say "please"!)

- If the message requires no action, make that clear too: the phrase "just FYI" usually does the trick. (Some e-mailers have rallied to introduce the acronym "NRN," for "no reply necessary," but it doesn't seem to have caught on widely.)

- Include your contact information. Especially with business e-mail (but with friends too—they might be on the road and not have your number handy), supply recipients with your full name and phone or fax numbers in case they find it easier to get back in touch with you another way.

- Keep the frivolous e-mail to a minimum. The frazzled high-tech honcho in your life might appreciate the occasional gossip dispatch or funny forward—think once a week or so—but not a daily barrage of cluttergrams.

## PRIORITY MAIL?

Many e-mail programs let you tag a message you send with a "priority" such as "high," "low," "urgent," or "bulk." Are these useful? In my experience, no—because messages senders think of as "urgent" often tend to be anything but to recipients. (And good luck getting junk e-mailers to tag their messages "bulk.") But if a group of correspondents—within your office, for example—decided on a scheme for prioritizing messages and stuck to it, they could turn the priority tag into a handy way for recipients to assess messages instantly.

## I PRY

"Did you get my e-mail?" More and more e-mail users don't even have to ask. E-mail is turning into a control freak's dream: It's often possible to find out whether, and exactly when, a recipient reads a message. Such features can be incredibly useful to senders—and disturbing to recipients who value their privacy. (Is it a good idea for your mother to be able to find out that you opened her e-mail at 3 A.M.—or, worse, that you've been ignoring it? I think not.)

There are two ways senders can spy on the fates of their messages.

*Return receipt:* On many closed e-mail systems (such as those within offices), senders can choose to be notified automatically via e-mail when a recipient receives a message (often called a "delivery receipt") or when she opens it (often called a "read receipt"). For messages sent over the Internet, however, such receipts often don't work. Read receipts aren't usually supported over the Net, and delivery receipts guarantee only that a message made it to the e-mail server maintained by the recipient's Internet service provider. But before you sigh in relief: Some companies now track which recipients open their marketing messages by including a graphic that HTML-enabled e-mail programs (programs that can read the language used by Web sites) must download from the company's Web site, which registers the visit.

*Message status systems:* Some closed e-mail systems, including America Online's and some offices' internal e-mail systems, let users see a list of e-mails they have sent to others on the same system and their status: whether they've been read, what time recipients opened them, even whether recipients deleted them. (On AOL, go to your "Sent" mailbox, then click on "Status" to check on any message.) Such features aren't always foolproof, as I learned when I answered the following letter in my *People* column:

**On my e-mail system you can see what time someone read your message or if they deleted it without reading it. When people have deleted mine, I e-mail asking why. Am I doing the right thing?**

The I-pry feature offered by some services is handy, but it opens some shaky etiquette ground. To be polite, pretend you never checked up and work an innocent mention into a later conversation: "Oh—didn't you get my e-mail?" Save the confrontational note for a last resort—and first think about why you're being ignored. Could you have forwarded one too many dumb jokes?

I immediately got a dressing down from dozens of people who pointed out that the poor reader might not have been getting the cold shoulder: If a recipient read the message in the Microsoft Outlook e-mail program's "preview" mode, then deleted it, the message would still show up as "deleted without reading." (In my defense, I should point out that this quirk is Microsoft's fault, not mine.)

### Etiquette for I-Spy Fans

Love 'em or hate 'em. these e-mail tracking features are here to stay. How to deploy them without irking fellow Netizens who value their privacy? Try these guidelines.

- Don't use return receipts on personal e-mail—or even on business messages where there is no clear reason to. Recipients may resent the intrusion—and begin to think you have a Big Brother complex.

- Even if you know exactly what time recipients opened your e-mail, allow them a reasonable length of time to respond: a few days for non-urgent business e-mail, more for personal e-mail. Don't expect them to drop everything to reply to your message immediately.

- Don't compulsively check on the status of your messages. It's tempting, but it's not productive, not healthy, and generally only leads to trouble.

Some closed systems, including AOL's, allow users to "unsend" messages recipients haven't read yet. This feature can be a lifesaver for the gaffe-prone (the sooner programmers figure out how to make it work for all Internet e-mail, the better). But don't let this safety net make you reckless. Somehow, the not-ready-for-prime-time messages turn out to be the ones recipients open immediately, before you have a chance to snatch them back.

## MANAGING MULTIPLE MAILBOXES

---

### Net Peeve : (

People who have three or four different e-mail addresses, so you're never sure where to send something to, or if they'll get it.

---

If you're a high-tech type nowadays, you've got a work e-mail address or two. A home e-mail address. A Web-based e-mail account or two for posting to online message boards or checking when you're on the road. Maybe an America Online account for chatting. And let's not even think about e-mail-enabled cell phones and pagers.

Keeping track of all those accounts isn't too hard for you: Most e-mail programs can be set up to check mail sent to several different addresses. But confusing your friends with an ever-changing array of addresses—a problem that can be exacerbated if you change jobs or home Internet service providers—is poor e-mail etiquette.

The polite solution? Get a permanent personal e-mail address. If you don't plan on staying with your current Internet service provider until death do you part, your permanent address can be your account at a free Web-based e-mail service like Yahoo! or MSN Hotmail. Plenty of other players are now offering vanity plates for the info highway. For example, colleges now offer alumni permanent e-mail addresses showing their school pride.

Or you can sign up for the ultimate Net vanity plate: your own domain name. Check to see if your name—or any Web site name you pick—has been dot-commed yet at any of several Web sites that oversee domain-name registration, such as www.networksolutions.com. (Alas for me, "miller.com" is taken. So is "miller-time.com.") The company through which you register your site (whether you choose Network Solutions or another registry) or that you pick to host your Web site will help you set up a matching e-mail address. Of course, you'll have to open your wallet every year to keep your domain name registered, but what cachet!

## WHAT DOES YOUR E-MAIL ADDRESS SAY ABOUT YOU?

On the Net, no one can tell what you're wearing or what you look like—but they can still make snap judgments about you. How? By looking at your e-mail address. So take care in choosing the image you project with your address—at least as much as you take picking out a designer T-shirt. Some considerations for the practical and the status-conscious:

- Your handle. Aim for one that's memorable and easy to spell. Besides being difficult to remember, a handle laden with a iot of numbers—jsmith82113@aol.com, for example—pegs you as a Johnny-come-lately to the Net. (Conversely, owning rights to a common name on a large Internet service or at a large company—being just plain "jsmith," for example—can be a subtle badge of prestige among Net cognoscenti.) Additional considerations: Women planning on carrying out activities in public on the Net, like chatting or posting to online message boards, should pick a genderless handle to avoid harassment. And cutesy handles like "surfrboy" or "diva213" might be fine for personal e-mail, but for work use something sober and based on your name.

- Your Internet service. If you're signing on from home, your e-mail address probably reflects the name of your Internet service provider (or the Web-based e-mail service you use). Is there a pecking order in ISP prestige? Not really, but some Netizens assume those who sign on through a hand-holding Internet service like AOL or WebTV to be less sophisticated Internet users.

- Your top-level domain. That's the .com, .org, .edu, or other suffix at the end of your address. While most ISP addresses end in .com or .net, a few suffixes convey information about the user: .edu belongs to U.S. institutions of higher education, .org to nonprofit organizations, .mil to the U.S. military, and two-letter country codes (see Appendix B) to overseas companies and institutions.

## DOT-COM DETECTIVE WORK

Where'd that e-mail message come from? Even if you don't recognize the sender's handle, you can learn a little by examining his or her e-mail address closely. Most e-mail addresses look like this:

handle@domain.suffix

The domain name in most e-mailers' addresses reflects the Internet or e-mail service they subscribe to—such as AOL, Earthlink, or MSN Hotmail—or the employer, school, or other organization through which they access the Net. Some Netizens sign up for their own domain names (registering one costs about thirty to fifty dollars a year) so they can create personal Web sites and matching e-mail addresses, like jane@thedoefamily.com.

Want to find out who owns a domain name? Whether you're checking up on a mystery e-mailer or dying to know who beat you to millertime.com (some sneaky Miller in California, apparently), you can do something called a WHOIS search, which supplies the name, address, and phone number of the person or organization that owns a domain name. Some sites currently offering WHOIS searches:

www.allwhois.com

www.easywhois.com

www.networksolutions.com/cgi-bin/whois/whois

www.webmagic.com/whois/index.html

Remember, WHOIS doesn't tell you who an e-mailer is, just what company or person registered the domain name through which he gets his e-mail service. And don't use this information, which those who register domain names are required to supply, to invade anyone's privacy. It's not an invitation to call someone up and say you love—or hate—his site. If you need to get in touch with the proprietor of a Web site, first check the site itself for contact information. If you have a problem with e-mail coming from a certain domain name, your first move should be to report the problem to that Internet service provider's abuse e-mail address: usually "abuse@" the ISP's domain name.

Sometimes you'll see e-mail addresses with additional words, set off by periods, before the domain name: someone@cyber.law.harvard.edu, for example. Only the suffix and the phrase immediately preceding it—in this case, "harvard.edu"—is the domain name. The other stuff probably refers to parts of the domain-name owner's internal network.

## BEYOND DOT-COM: TOP-LEVEL DOMAINS

The final part of an e-mail address, known as the suffix or top-level domain, can also supply information about its origins. While .com domains can belong to any business or individual around the world, others such as .edu and .gov are restricted to certain types of owners. In addition, every country has its own two-letter suffix: An e-mail address ending in .uk comes from the United Kingdom; .de from Germany. Some U.S. e-mail addresses, including those used by state and local governments and elementary, middle, and high schools, use the .us country code.

The original top-level domains:

| | |
|---|---|
| .com | denotes commercial sites and addresses |
| .edu | U.S. educational institutions |
| .org | non-profit organizations |
| .gov | U.S. government |
| .net | general commercial use |
| .mil | U.S. military |
| .int | international businesses and organizations |
| .nato | NATO |
| .arpa | ARPANET (a precursor to the Internet) |

In November 2000, the governing body for Web addresses approved seven more top-level domains:

| | |
|---|---|
| .biz | general commercial use |
| .info | general commercial use |
| .name | for individuals to register their own names |
| .pro | for professionals such as doctors and lawyers |
| .museum | for museums |

.aero            for the airline industry

.coop            for cooperatives

And there are the country codes. Just because a Web or e-mail address sports one of these suffixes, though, doesn't mean the user necessarily hails from overseas: Some small countries—like lucky Tuvalu, which was assigned the .tv suffix—boost their bottom lines by selling domain names within their country codes. In addition, some junk e-mailers route their spam through overseas computers (or forge foreign addresses) to skirt U.S. law. See Appendix B for a complete list of country codes.

**"E-mail address" is such a mouthful that I ask people for their "eddress" pronounced "ee-dress," instead. What do you think?**

Without pronunciation tips, "eddress" looks like what a cockney would call Cher's Oscar headgear. Since "e me" is short for e-mail me," how about a push for "What's your e?"

*3*

# Best Foot Forward

- *When is it okay to forward a personal message?*
- *How can I get friends to quit forwarding me chain letters?*
- *Can forwarding messages violate copyright law?*

In e-mail, the "Forward" command is one of the most dangerous there is. (Up there with "Reply All," anyway.) It's what makes those annoying chain letters possible. It's what makes it possible for your girlfriend's fifteen best friends to wind up giggling over the sappy love poem you sent her. It's what virtually guarantees that the profanity-laced rant about a world-class jerk of a client you sent to a co-worker will, accidentally or on purpose, wind up in that client's in-box.

But forwarding can also, of course, be invaluable. Sharing information at the touch of a button is what e-mail is all about. At work, it's nice to be able to zap a co-worker's twelve-point proposal over to the legal department or pass along the boss's marching orders. At home, you might forward on an invitation to a come-one, come-all party or information about your favorite band's next gig. You may also enjoy swapping those humorous, weird, wacky, or touching tidbits that float around the Net; some fed-up e-mailers detest such clutter, but others will defend to the death their right to giggle.

In terms of etiquette, there are two distinct types of forwarding to address, each with its own pitfalls. One is the forwarding of personal messages: letters from friends, business memos, any correspondence not obviously created for a world audience. The other is that burgeoning international pastime: passing along jokes, wacky news stories, rumors, chain letters, and similar Net flotsam and jetsam.

## FORWARDING PERSONAL MESSAGES

When is it okay to forward a personal message? Not as often as some people think—or as often as many people do. Use a lot of caution when forwarding a personal e-mail. A general rule: Unless the sender explicitly gives you permission in the message to forward it—or it's absolutely evident it's meant to be passed along—contact the sender and get his or her consent before forwarding it.

It's pretty obvious that forwarding a truly personal note, like a letter from a relative or a romantic note, without permission is an etiquette violation. (Those of you who assemble a virtual focus group of friends to analyze every missive from a new beau, go back to junior high school!) But less emotional e-mail, from office memos to dashed-off tidbits, warrants caution too. There could be lots of reasons, including some you can't guess, why a sender might not want others to see a message. The person who sent you the message was writing it for your eyes, and may not have been thinking about how its contents or tone might affect others. (The boss might have asked you to "run this by that idiot consultant when you're done," but you'd better not forward the message to him verbatim.) The sender might not want his e-mail address falling into the hands of strangers. Or, unbeknownst to you, he might be keeping certain aspects of his political, cultural, or sex life secret from other slices of his social circle. The point is, you never know, so even if a message looks innocuous, it's best to check before sending it on.

**I plan to invite several friends to a party via e-mail. Is there a nice way to ask them please not to forward the invitation?**

If you're past frat-party age, your friends should know that an invitation is meant strictly for its recipient. Others (dates, kids, thirsty moochers) get to tag along only if the invite so specifies. Of course, just one clueless blabbermouth can turn your soirée into Woodstock. Don't issue any nasty warnings, just be crystal clear about the purpose of the party and who's invited. They'll get the picture.

**TIP:** Make sure the entire message is fit to forward—including any earlier back-and-forth conversations that might still be attached to the bottom of a long e-mail. All sorts of unpleasant surprises might lurk in your e-mail's nether regions.

### Embarrassing E-Moment

"I forwarded an e-mail to a friend, not realizing that a back-and-forth conversation with another friend about plans to go out Friday night was at the bottom of the e-mail. Later, I got nailed fibbing to the first friend that I was staying home on Friday (the second friend and I hadn't wanted to invite her along)."

On the flip side, when you're writing e-mail, always keep the possibility that it might be forwarded in the back—or, even better, in the front—of your mind. Not everyone is particularly cautious about following these rules. And sometimes even the most conscientious of us get lazy or distracted and forward something we shouldn't. So—and I can't say this too many times—don't write anything in e-mail you wouldn't want your boss/employees/clients/spouse/kids/mother-in-law/best friend/worst enemy to see.

### Embarrassing E-Moment

"Shortly after they announced that the dot-com boutique I used to work for was going out of business, one of my co-workers got an e-mail notice from one of the company's co-founders saying that the next planning meeting for the Jewelry and Accessories section was canceled. My co-worker wanted to forward us the notice, with a note saying that the co-founder was a jerk. She hit the button—and sent it right back to the co-founder. The only good news? She couldn't possibly get fired."

## FORWARDING MESSAGES THAT AREN'T PERSONAL

E-mailers' number-one etiquette gripe? That's easy. From high-tech honchos to college students, the people I quiz about their Net peeves overwhelmingly cry out: "How can I politely ask my friends to stop forwarding me dumb stuff?" Indeed, many Netizens reserve their bitterest rancor for messages whose subjects start with the telltale "Fwd"—those jokes, chain letters, and other choice tidbits that get passed endlessly around and around the Net.

The trouble is, there seem to be just as many Net users who love to forward. Hey, being able to communicate information, or share a laugh, at the click of a mouse is what the Net's all about, right? And what's the big deal? If someone doesn't want to read a forwarded message, it takes only a second to delete it.

When these two factions clash—and they often do, since Murphy's Law dictates that the most irritable anti-forwarder will wind up with the most fervent forwarding fanatics among his friends and relations—you've got an etiquette crisis of epic proportions. Fed-up recipients silently seethe—or struggle to find a polite way to tell their pals to knock it off. Senders wonder why their friends never write back anymore—or have their feelings hurt by brusque cease-and-desist pleas.

Some people would welcome a complete ban on forwarding. But I think it's fine among consenting adults (or kids) who make the effort to forward responsibly: to respect friends' time, to steer clear of forwarding specific types of messages, and to take a few simple steps to avoid some of the practices that other users find most irritating. Of course, such a solution also calls for some frank communication. If you just can't abide another "Fwd: Why Cucumbers Are Better Than Men" in your in-box, don't be afraid to ask friends for a forward moratorium. If you get such a plea, don't take it personally. Just strike that person off the forward list.

### How do I get my friends to stop e-mailing me lists of jokes?

Would-be Jay Lenos, listen up: This seems to be readers' top e-etiquette peeve. As for those of you who don't like being drafted into Open Mike Night, begin by trying a polite "Thanks, but no thanks." If that doesn't work, say you just don't have time. Worried about being rude? How rude are your so-called friends to clog your in-box in the first place?

The consenting-adults rule has one big exception: Chain e-mail has no place at the office. Forwards are a waste of time, which is fine if your time is your own, but is not while you and recipients are on the clock. Captive co-workers who find forwards offensive or irritating may not feel as free as your friends to tell you to quit it. (Or they may feel more free—watch out.) If a co-worker, or someone monitoring company e-mail (see Chapter 12, "Spy Games: E-Mail Privacy"), considers a message offensive, you can quickly land in very hot water. And many companies have policies forbidding any chain e-mail. So just don't do it. If you want to swap messages with a colleague, ask for his or her personal e-mail address, and use yours, too.

Posting jokes or similar forwarded messages is also a major violation of etiquette on many e-mail mailing lists, where messages that veer off the designated topic of discussion tend to spark a furor. Fellow members of your book club or professional organization didn't sign up to hear the riddle of the day or the latest political rumor. More freewheeling mailing lists, or groups dedicated to subjects such as humor or politics, might be more welcoming, but wait until you've been a member for a while so you know what sort of messages are condoned.

Why do forwarded messages bug so many people so much? After all, how long does it take to delete a few dumb jokes or trite tidbits from well-meaning friends? In fact, I believe, the waste-of-time and mailbox-clutter factors aren't what really get most users hot under the collar. Let's look at some of the gripes about forwards and ways to rectify the problems.

GRIPE: Dashed expectations. Many users have such spite for forwarded messages because of the way forwarding tends to replace more personal communication. Does this situation sound familiar? You see a new message from an old friend. Excited, you click it open—and it turns out to be a list of haikus about *Star Wars* that was sorta funny the first time you saw it . . . two years ago. The let-down adds an even bigger irritation factor to the message.

SOLUTION: Give your forwards a personal touch. Preface the message with a greeting and a few pleasantries, then perhaps a news tidbit about yourself or an explanation of why you thought the recipient would enjoy this message. That way the forward implies, "Thinking of You," not "I Don't Think Much of You." (Recipients: Be sure to delete any such comments if you send the message on to others.) And don't let communication with a friend deteriorate to nothing but forwards; occasionally, send a personal message without a joke attached.

**What should I do if someone responds to a forwarded joke with a note with news about a very serious health problem? We don't usually communicate otherwise.**

Sounds like this person may be crying out for a connection more meaningful than joke-swapping. Respond with a personal note expressing sympathy and support. Then let this person make the next move—you'll figure out whether the best prescription is to build a cyber-friendship, offer real-world help, or just remain a loyal laughter provider.

---

### Net Peeve : (

"Those folks that leave all those >>>>> when forwarding a joke or chain e-mail message. Or those folks that leave the whole damn history when forwarding an e-mail. You get hundreds of lines before you actually get to the good stuff, only to find out it is not good."

---

GRIPE: Clutter at the top. Too often, recipients have to slog through pages of other people's e-mail addresses and comments before reaching the payoff.

SOLUTION: Pare before you share. Sure, it's fun to see where a joke has been, but most people hate paging through all that gobbledygook—and fear (justifiably) that forwarding could land their own address in the hands of spammers or scammers. In some e-mail programs, you can simply highlight all the extraneous gunk and delete it. (To be extra considerate, you can clean up the message by removing those long rows of ">>>>>"s, too.) In others, including America Online's, messages must be forwarded as is. But there's still a solution: Highlight the pertinent part of the forward, copy it, and paste it into a new e-mail.

GRIPE: Your recipient has seen that message a hundred times before.

SOLUTION: Don't forward indiscriminately. If you've seen the message—or something similar—before, your recipient probably has too. If you know an intended recipient is a major Nethead, don't think twice; odds are he has already seen anything you beam his way. And odds are he has ceased to be amused by forwarding in general, so lay off.

**How do I politely tell people that the e-mail they forwarded to me was the message I sent them?**

When this happens, you know your e-circle's joke-forwarding is out of hand. (Somehow I doubt we're talking about urgent business memos.) Respond with a chuckling "Guess what happened?" note. Whether to add a hint about cutting back on the forward flurry is up to you.

GRIPE: Forwards that recipients find useless, offensive, or just not funny.

SOLUTION: Put some thought into the process: Instead of forwarding something to everyone you know, send it only to people who you think will find it fresh, funny, or useful. Don't try to convert people via e-mail—forwarding a political or religious message to someone who may not share your beliefs is highly impolite. (And never make assumptions about someone's political or religious beliefs. Your circle of liberal friends may hide more than a few closeted Republicans, or vice versa.) Debate is healthy, but do it in person.

---

## Net Peeve :(

My pet peeve is when people I usually find credible write "very funny—worth reading" or something similar in the subject line just to make sure I read the e-mail—and the e-mail is (a) not funny, (b) irrelevant, and (c) a total letdown!

---

As for off-color jokes, save 'em for happy hour. Nothing against a good dirty joke, but spreading them by e-mail is simply too risky. Not only might your recipient find the gag more offensive than funny, but any number of disasters could happen: You could send it to the wrong address. You or your recipients could find yourselves in deep doo-doo if the joke passes through anyone's office computer. And if your recipients pass the joke on, it could live on in cyberspace forever—with your e-mail address attached.

**One of my friends e-mails me lots of inflammatory political propaganda. How can I ask her to stop shoving it in my face?**

It's tough staying friends across political lines, so bully for you (hope you don't debate over dinner). But it sounds like this relationship may not last until Election Day if you don't lobby for change. Explain to your pal (in person if possible) that you feel your friendship is more important than your differences, but that you would rather not get daily reminders of the second. And then hope your idea wins a landslide of support.

GRIPE: E-mail hoaxes.

SOLUTION: Don't forward them! See Chapter 9, "E-Mail Hoaxes," for tips on spotting and stopping the spread of these annoyances: useless petitions, phony freebies, fictitious cancer-stricken kids, and more.

GRIPE: Chain letters—the sort that promise you cash or good luck if you forward them and horrible fates if you "break the chain."

SOLUTION: Never forward them. It doesn't matter whether you believe this kind of stuff or just think it's fun to play along. Forwarding a chain letter is rude, unclassy, and downright idiotic. Chain letters that involve money—of the "send $5 to the person at the top of the list" variety—are illegal, online or off. Most Net users wouldn't mind if the stockade were reinstated as punishment for those who unleash any chain e-mail messages, too.

---

## Net Peeve : (

Superstitious spam. "Happy thoughts" spam.

---

**Survey Says**
*Asked what type of forwarded message they would be most likely to pass along, 48 percent of workers said none, 27 percent said warnings about scams or viruses, 13 percent said political messages or petitions, and 12 percent said shopping deals or promotions.*

*Source: Vault.com*

---

## Net Peeve : (

When someone sends me a forward just so they can get their wish, win (yeah, right) money, or not have bad luck. If I actually had everything happen to me that those letters promised, I would

have been killed about 27 times, lost out on over 3 million dollars, had as much bad luck as breaking a mirror 14 times, and
missed my true love 42 times—and I would have given up more
wishes than Aladdin could have hoped for.

---

**If someone forwards me a joke, need I send a reply?**

Usually, no. Thank-yous aren't required, since a frequent for-
warder probably can do without a bunch of "Gee, thanks" or "Got
it" replies stacking up in his in-box. However, if you truly found
the forward unusually hilarious or useful, you could relay your
thanks (tell the sender you were ROFL, rolling on the floor laughing). Another reason to reply: If you prefer not to get forwarded
material, you should speak up and ask the sender for a cease-fire.

---

### Net Peeve  : (

Those weenie poem forwards about friendship and love. And the
ones with the pictures that appear when you scroll down. I
would rather not hear from you at all if all you're going to do is
send forwards.

---

## COPYRIGHT: IT'S NOT JUST THE LAW, IT'S GOOD MANNERS

A friend e-mails you an article copied from the *New York Times*
Web site. "Thought this might interest you," he writes. Since the
article is copyrighted, has he violated the law? And, law aside, is
this improper e-mail etiquette?

Copyright law is complicated, and it doesn't always serve up
a clear yes or no as to what's kosher. But it's well worth understanding some basics and doing your best to follow its guidelines.

Not just to stay out of trouble—you're pretty unlikely to get hauled into court simply for forwarding copyrighted material for personal use—but because copyright law exists to protect the owner of written material from the harm unauthorized copying can do. Since not hurting others is what etiquette is all about, that makes following copyright law good manners.

The first rule of copyright might come as a shocker to some:

- *Pretty much everything a person writes, online or offline, is copyrighted as soon as he or she writes it down:* an article from the *New York Times*, a love poem to Sarah Michelle Gellar posted on some guy's *Buffy the Vampire Slayer* Web site, your last posting to a mailing list, a business memo, or a letter to a friend. You don't need to attach a copyright notice for material to be copyrighted. (Although it can help if there's ever a dispute: If you post a written document, photograph, or computer program in public and want to deter redistributing, it's a good idea to attach a copyright notice: The word "copyright" or the symbol ©, your name if you are indeed the copyright owner, and the year of first publication of the document, i.e., "Copyright 2001 Samantha Miller.") You may not own the copyright to everything you've written, however; if you created something at work, your employer probably controls it.

  Making a copy of anything copyrighted may infringe on the rights of the copyright owner. Obviously, there are plenty of exceptions—or else you wouldn't even be able to quote a friend's e-mail when replying to it. Copying is kosher if:

- You're copying facts. If CNN.com reports that the prime minister of Russia has had a heart attack, or the results of a study into Americans' favorite ice cream flavors, the facts of the matter are in the public domain. But copying CNN's wording—or swiping its spiffy bar graph—is still a no-no.

- The copyright owner explicitly authorizes you to make copies. Some Web sites or e-mail newsletters (like some joke-of-the-day services) include a tagline saying readers may redistribute an article or message as long as they leave it unchanged. That usually means not deleting information identifying the source and author of the material.

- The copyright owner gives you "implied license" to make copies. This is one of those annoyingly vague legal concepts dealing with what a "reasonable person" would assume. If you send a message to an e-mail mailing list, other users assume it's okay to include a copy of the message (or a portion of it) when they reply, because this is the customary (another favorite legal term) practice.

- Fair use. Many instances of copying are protected by this doctrine, which weighs a copier's free-speech rights against the interests of the copyright holder. In determining whether an incident of copying constitutes fair use, the law considers several questions. Beware: None of these guidelines automatically means something is or isn't fair use. The law looks at the big picture, and it's hard to predict where it will come down in an individual case.

According to the fair-use doctrine, copying is more likely to be considered fair use if:

- You copy only a small part of the work. A few sentences or paragraphs from a longer work are generally regarded as okay; there's no rule establishing a certain percentage of a work as a ceiling.

- You copy the material for purposes of criticism, comment, parody, news reporting, teaching, scholarship, or research.

- You add a lot of new material to the work.

- You copy a work that is mostly fact.

- You copy a work that has been published widely.

- Your copying doesn't potentially affect any profits the copyright owner could make from the work (by selling advertising on its Web site, for example, or charging subscribers to see it).

Copying is less likely to be considered fair use if:

- You copy the entire work.

- You copy it for commercial purposes—that is, you make money from it.

- You don't add anything new to the work, just excerpt it.

- You copy a work that is fiction or opinion.

- You copy a work that had been sent only to one or a few people, like a personal e-mail.

- Your copying affects the ability of the copyright owner to make money.

So how does all this affect an article copied from the *New York Times* site? That likely wouldn't be considered fair use—your friend copied the article in its entirety, didn't add anything to it, and his forwarding it to you hurt the *Times*'s ability to make money from it by selling advertising, whose rates are based on the number of people who visit its site. (Find it hard to muster pity for the *Times*? Think of smaller sites whose very survival depends on keeping their readership numbers up—or writers whose jobs depend on the number of readers their articles attract.)

In fact, several news publishers filed a copyright-infringement lawsuit against a political Web site where members would post full copies of news articles and comment on them. A federal judge found for the newspapers, ruling that full-text copying of the articles, even to discuss them publicly, was not fair use.

---

### Embarrassing E-Moment

"Wear sunscreen." "Do one thing every day that scares you." "Keep your old love letters. Throw away your old bank statements." In 1997, e-mailers went wild for a witty, wise advice treatise identified as an MIT graduation speech by author Kurt Vonnegut. Only hitch: The essay was actually a *Chicago*

*Tribune* piece by veteran columnist Mary Schmich. "I thought it was funny—at first," Schmich told *People*. But as hundreds of calls and e-mails streamed in—some accusing her of plagiarizing Vonnegut (who never spoke at MIT) or vice versa— "I just panicked," she said. "I flashed on my life as a bad movie of the week, my whole career being destroyed, being completely trapped in this and not being able to prove that I didn't steal Kurt Vonnegut's speech." When the snafu was cleared up, Vonnegut (whose own wife was among those who forwarded the e-mail) told the *New York Times* he "would have been proud had the words been mine." And a lot richer: Baz Luhrmann turned the essay into a radio hit called *Everybody's Free (To Wear Sunscreen)*.

If you want to share a news article or other copyrighted material with friends, there are a couple of polite—and lawyer-proof— solutions. Many news sites have added an "e-mail this article to a friend" feature. You click the link, give your and your friend's e-mail address, and the site sends off the article (and chalks up another reader). However, you may not be comfortable giving the site your and your friends' addresses (some, but not all, sites promise not to track e-mail addresses collected this way). The solution many e-mailers have settled on is to send a short excerpt from the article—the headline and first two paragraphs, perhaps— followed by a link to the Web site. Or just e-mail the link, but be sure to explain to your friend what the link leads to and why you think the story would interest him or her.

How to e-mail a link: Ever get an e-mail message that contained the address of a Web site and you could click right on the address to go to the site? Some e-mail programs automatically recognize Web site addresses in the text of a message and turn them into links. The trick: Most recognize Web addresses only if the sender includes the http:// at the beginning of the address. If you're sending the e-mail, you can copy and paste the address straight from your Web browser, or type in the http:// yourself.

## Net Peeve  : (

I work with students, and I think this is a generational thing:
They'll send me an e-mail saying "check this out," and then just
list a Web address. I don't want to take the time to visit the site
to find out what it's all about.

Let's look at a few other copyright-related situations.

You subscribe to a free "joke of the day" e-mail newsletter from
a humor Web site. Is it okay to forward it to other people? Probably.
If the site sent it to you free, that suggests implied license to send
it to others. Check the message to see if it includes any explicit
instructions about whether copying is allowed. To follow the law to
the letter, you should send it on intact—including any advertising
or information about the site it came from—or you'll be interfering
with the copyright holder's ability to make a buck.

Someone on your e-mail discussion group for *X-Files* fans
writes an incredibly funny rant. Is it okay to forward it to a bunch
of your friends—or post it on your sci-fi Web site?

Answer: Maybe. Legally, it depends on how large and public
a forum the discussion group is considered, whether your purpose
in copying the work is seen as commercial or commentary, and
many of the other factors outlined above. The court of etiquette
has a clearer ruling: E-mail the writer and ask. She will probably
(though not necessarily) be flattered, and it's courteous to let her
know her work is being appreciated.

### Embarrassing E-Moment

Kurt Vonnegut isn't the only genius who's gotten his name mistakenly attached to a piece of e-mail flotsam. A humor piece
called "Women Speak in Estrogen and Men Listen in
Testosterone" (sample: "Women love cats. Men say they love
cats, but when women aren't looking, men kick cats") has been
making the rounds for years misattributed to cartoonist Matt

Groening, the creator of *The Simpsons*. Although Groening disavowed having written the piece in several interviews, it's been attributed to him even in newspaper articles. The real author? *Chicago Sun-Times* columnist Richard Roeper (Roger Ebert's TV sidekick), who wrote the piece back in 1986.

## MAKING FORWARDING WORK FOR YOU

Think of e-mail as a cocktail party, and you're going for a gold medal in savvy schmoozing. (Go ahead, mix yourself a martini—just watch out for the keyboard. Computer equipment does not hold its liquor well.) You work the room, renewing ties with friends you haven't seen in a while and cultivating bonds with newer acquaintances. You dish out carefully chosen tidbits you know each friend will enjoy: the latest tech-world joke for one, news about the next *Star Wars* movie for another, a reference to a provocative op-ed article for your favorite policy wonk. You don't ignore the importance of more personal talk. You don't monopolize conversation. You don't plant yourself in front of a group of partiers and tell jokes until they flee to the bar. If the friend you thought was *Star Wars*–obsessed just nods politely and scans the room, spinning his head like R2D2, you change the topic. E-mail—and yes, the occasional well-placed forward—can be a valuable networking and socializing tool. Just be sensitive to your targets' sensibilities—and don't overdo it.

## IMHO (In My Humble Opinion): Making E-Mail Software More Mannerly

E-mail etiquette's woeful state isn't entirely the fault of us Netizens. Technology deserves some of the blame: Often confusing to use and befuddling in their differences, e-mail programs are hardly etiquette-friendly. What's more, software misses some golden opportunities to help make the Net a more mannerly place. So listen up, programmers—here are ten ways e-mail programs should maximize their politeness potential:

1. Warn users before they send e-mail to a large group of recipients. Something like "You are about to send this message to forty-eight people. Do you really want to do this?" would save many e-mailers from embarrassing slips—and perhaps dissuade those who mass-mail trivial messages.

2. Warn users if they're about to send a message without a subject line. Some e-mail programs already do this, and more should.

3. Make the "bcc" (blind carbon copies) feature easier to find. Some e-mail programs hide—or don't offer—this handy addressing option.

4. When users forward e-mail, make it easy for them to delete the addresses of previous senders. When we want to pass along a joke, we don't want to burden recipients with a long stretch of addresses to slog through—or to circulate our and our friends' addresses throughout cyberspace.

5. Warn users when they're about to send a large attachment with a note something like this: "This attachment will take eight minutes to download via a 56K modem. Would you like to compress it, cancel it, or send it anyway?"

6. Don't allow users to enter subject lines too long for recipients' e-mail programs to display. Many e-mail programs show only the first forty or so characters of a subject line, yet e-mailers are often permitted to write longer ones that get cut off—or mistakenly enter their entire message in the subject field. Why not restrict subjects to forty characters in the first place?

7. Take into account the recipient's e-mail system. A program might automatically switch a formatted message into plain text if the recipient's e-mail software can't handle graphics, or warn a user before he sends a forty-page e-mail to a WebTV user.

8. Make it easier for users to increase the font size of e-mail messages they receive. Many e-mailers have difficulty reading small type, and while some programs make the options for changing font size easy to find, others bury them deep in menus.

9. Include an easy way to convert an e-mail message written in all capital letters to lowercase letters. A few programs already include this feature—a great way to muffle habitual SHOUTERS.

10. Set up an etiquette-friendly "Out of the Office" feature—one that lets users choose which senders should receive automatic notes and which (like mailing lists) shouldn't.

*4*

# Getting Attached

- *Is it rude to send an attachment without asking first?*
- *How can attachments be dangerous?*
- *What's your e-mail program's etiquette quotient?*

If most e-mail messages are slim envelopes, those that come with attachments are UPS packages—often the hulking kind that leave the delivery guy's knees shaking and you hunting for a kitchen knife to saw through yards of impenetrable packing tape.

Attachments are indisputably useful. When you want to e-mail something that's more than just plain text, you usually send it as an attachment. An attachment can be almost any sort of computer file: a word-processing document program, a digital photo or video, a spreadsheet, a computer program. The recipient gets an exact copy of the file to read, print, or work on.

## THE BASICS OF SENDING ATTACHMENTS

Every e-mail program works a little differently. Generally, from within your e-mail program, you begin composing a new e-mail message, then click a button or choose a command from the menu to tell the program you want to add attachments. The program will prompt you to pick a file or files from your computer's hard drive or a disk drive, then clip the attachments on for the ride, often using a compression program to squeeze them down to a smaller size.

When a recipient gets the e-mail, the text of your message serves as a sort of cover letter. Her e-mail program notifies her that the message carries attachments and may tell her what kind of files the attachments are. Depending on her e-mail program and how she has set it up, she can choose whether to download the attachment to her computer and, once downloaded, whether or not to open it immediately. If she has anti-virus software installed, her computer may also automatically scan the attachment for viruses.

## THE PITFALLS OF ATTACHMENTS

What makes attachments such a popular Net Peeve? They can get aggravating for several reasons:

- Their sheer size. A five-megabyte video clip (a few minutes of teensy, fuzzy action) can take several minutes to download on a 28.8 kbps modem; a PowerPoint presentation, an eternity. And for the many users whose e-mail storage space is limited, Godzilla-sized attachments gobble up valuable memory.

- Translation problems. If a recipient doesn't own the program you used to create the attachment or another program capable of reading it, or doesn't have the right program to decipher a compressed or encoded file, she may not be able to open the attachment at all. PC users e-mailing Mac users, and vice versa, are in for a particularly rough ride.

- Viruses. These nasty critters are spread chiefly through infected attachments. A few simple security measures should keep you safe (see Chapter 10, "Viruses")—but many wary users regard attachments with all the fear and loathing they'd accord a rat during the days of the Black Plague.

So until everyone can proudly claim a blazingly fast Internet connection—and until our computer programs get smarter about translating one another's files—users need to follow a few etiquette rules before getting too attached to attachments. And it's not just senders who are guilty of attachment-related rudeness. Recipients, there are rules for you, too.

## ATTACHMENT ETIQUETTE FOR SENDERS

1. Before sending an attachment, check with the recipient.

2. Explain to the recipient what the attachment is.

3. Keep your e-mail software up to date.

4. Keep your anti-virus program up to date.

5. Avoid sending attachments when they're not necessary.

Now, let's examine these rules one by one.

1. *Before sending an attachment, check with the recipient.* Tell him what format or program the file is in, its size, and why you want to send it. The recipient can then give you the go-ahead, suggest a file format that better suits him, or propose another solution ("I can't handle a file that big. Can you please print it out and mail it?").

Unless you regularly send attachments to a particular recipient with no difficulties, it's best to check each time you want to send one. You'll find out if the last one left him tearing his hair out—and the advance warning will alert him that your attachment isn't a stealth virus.

DO: Just made a new business contact or friend to whom you expect to send many attachments? Take a minute and hammer out an overall attachments strategy: Find out what kind of computer he uses, what file formats and sizes he can handle, and whether he prefers to be warned before you send an attachment. You'll save much future aggravation.

DON'T: Don't send attachments to mailing lists or large groups. You'll eat up staggering amounts of storage space and tick off everyone who doesn't need them or can't open them.

2. *Explain to the recipient what the attachment is.* Ever get an e-mail saying only "Thought you might like this"—or something equally vague like "the latest from our company"—with an attachment attached? Not only is this annoying, it's also exactly the way some viruses arrive. (If you get a message like this and you're not expecting it, delete it.) When you're sending an attachment, use the text of the e-mail as a cover letter. Describe what the attachment is, what format it's in, and why you've sent it.

---

### Net Peeve  :(

When people send me e-mail that says "see attached"—only they've forgotten to attach the attachment!

---

3. *Keep your software up to date.* Files created by ancient versions of programs or programs no longer in common use may be more difficult for recipients to open, or may not translate well. This applies to your e-mail program, too: Since software makers are constantly tinkering, having the latest version will ensure that you're sending attachments using the most accepted methods.

   DON'T: Compress an attachment unless you know the recipient has the right software to decompress it. But once you're sure, do compress it—you'll save your recipient lots of downloading time.

4. *Keep your anti-virus program up to date by visiting the maker's Web site and downloading its periodic updates.* Regularly sweep your computer's hard drive for viruses. Scan any incoming files you get. Keeping your own computer virus-free will ensure that no surprise stowaways hitch a ride on attachments you send.

5. *Avoid sending attachments when they're not necessary.* To recipients, even the least problematic attachment is still kind

of a hassle: They take an extra step to open, they eat up storage space, and they're difficult to find again in a brimming inbox.

### Reasons to Send an Attachment

- The recipient will need to open up a file in a specific program and make changes.

- A formatted document needs to arrive picture-perfect—for example, a word-processing document the recipient plans to print and distribute.

- The recipient needs a large document right away.

- The recipient will want to pass the file on to others.

But alternatives exist. Before sending an attachment, consider whether another method would make the recipient's life easier.

- Copy and paste. Sending a word-processing document that doesn't need to arrive in perfectly formatted shape? Copy the text and paste it into the body of an e-mail message instead of sending it as an attachment. You may have to take a minute to clean up any garbled formatting, but if the recipient simply needs to read the information it contains, he'll thank you.

- Putting files on a Web site or server (storage space shared by multiple users). That way, recipients can look at them at their leisure and won't have to store bulky files themselves. A chart-laden report could go on your company's external or internal Web site or your work group's server. At home, if you don't have your own Web site, several sites offer users free file storage or photo albums friends can browse.

- Sending files on disk. If you have a few days to work with, high-storage-capacity diskettes are dandy for sending files, particularly extremely large ones. Ask your recipient if he'd prefer a file on disk.

- Fax. Yeah, they're sooo twentieth century. But if your recipient is attachment-challenged, faxing is often the easiest way to send short formatted documents.

- Snail mail. Cheap and highly unlikely to involve technical problems—you can always print out a document and slap some stamps on it.

---

## Net Peeve :(

I get e-mail from Japan with attached signatures in kanji characters. My e-mail program automatically tries to download the application to show them, even when I try to stop it.

---

And a final word to attachment senders: Be considerate! Remember, not everyone has a spanking-new PC with a blazing Net connection and all the software trimmings. Some of us compute on creaky five-year-old beaters with plodding 28.8 kbps modems. Some of us don't have Microsoft everything. Some of us are paying by the minute for wireless Web connections. Some of us are on Macintoshes. So don't get annoyed when someone can't open an attachment. Find a way around it—and be pleasant about it.

**Is it terrible to send lots of pictures of my new baby boy to all my friends? I have gotten into the habit of scanning several pictures about once a month and sending them to twenty or so friends, and some of them don't respond.**

To you, of course, he's the cutest thing ever, but yes, your friends may be feeling a bit colicky amid the baby barrage. Besides the time it takes to download photos, there's the challenge of coming up with a response once they've been deployed. ("He's getting so big!") To pals who seem genuinely interested, try sending a great shot every few months, and lay off with those who've quit responding. Or you could post the photos at a site like Zing.com and let your friends browse at their leisure.

## ATTACHMENTS ETIQUETTE FOR RECIPIENTS

1. Don't get indignant about attachments you can't open.

2. Know what kind of attachments you can and can't open.

3. Be able to open as many kinds of attachments as possible.

4. Keep your software up to date.

5. Be wary of viruses.

Now, one by one.

1. *Don't get indignant about attachments you can't open.* Yes, attachment problems can be aggravating. And yes, senders don't always use good etiquette in sending them. But don't take out your frustrations by lecturing errant senders. Just explain the problem and propose a solution—whether it's "Can you please send word-processing documents as text" or "Put it in the mail"—and don't forget to say "please."

---

### Net Peeve : (

I'm a corporate lawyer and I often have to prepare very long documents for clients. I do work for some people and then try to send them the document they asked me to prepare, but I can't because they don't have the ability to accept documents as large as the ones they requested.

---

2. *Know what kind of attachments you can and can't open.* Learn about your computer's capabilities, so if someone asks you if he can send a JPEG photo or Microsoft Excel spreadsheet, you don't have to dither around. And find out if your e-mail system bars attachments over a certain size.

DO: If you have particularly unusual requirements regarding attachments—you don't want them at all due to a super-slow

Net connection, for example—do your best to let correspondents know. A good tactic: Put a line in your e-mail signature about it.

---

## Net Peeve : (

When people send me Word documents as attachments. I'm running Linux.

---

3. *Be able to open as many kinds of attachments as possible.* Particularly if you're a business user, you should be able to open files created by the most popular business software programs and other software commonly used by companies in your field. Protesting that you can't open Microsoft Word files is a little like boasting you don't have an answering machine: You might fancy yourself a free-spirited rebel, but people trying to communicate with you will just think you're a pain in the rear.

   Fortunately, makers of some popular software programs offer free "viewers" that let users who don't have the programs open, copy, and print (but not alter) files created in those programs. Two must-haves for everyone: the Microsoft Word viewer (download it from microsoft.com) and Adobe Acrobat Reader (at adobe.com), which lets you open files in PDF (Portable Document Format), another popular format for formatted text.

### How the Heck Do I Open That?

Opening an attachment is a snap if you have the software used to create it: You double-click on the file and your computer automatically selects the right application.

If you don't own the right software or another application

capable of opening the file, you can often figure out what type of file it is from its filename extension, the last few letters after the dot in the file's name. (PCs use these; Macs don't.) Why do you need to know this? It might help you find the right software to open the file yourself—or at least to explain the problem to the sender.

Some common file extensions:

.doc:                     Microsoft Word word-processing document.

.wp:                      WordPerfect word-processing document. These two popular programs can usually open each other's files perfectly. If you don't have either one, or another program capable of opening their files, try picking up a free "viewer" at the companies' Web sites.

.txt:                     A text-only document. Any word-processing program can open one of these bare-bones text files.

.rft:                     Rich text format. Plain text that preserves a few formatting frills—also easy pickings for most word processors.

.pdf:                     Portable Document Format. For text documents with fancy formatting. Pick up the free Adobe Acrobat Reader (adobe.com) to pop these open.

.xls or .xlt:             Microsoft Excel spreadsheets.

.ppt or .pps:             Microsoft PowerPoint presentations.

.jpg. or .gif:            Two types of digital pictures.

.mp3, .mov, .amp,         Music or movie files.
and many, many
more:

.zip or .sit:             Compressed files that require special uncompression programs to open (see below).

.exe, .vbs, .com, .drv, .dll, .bin, .sys, and more:   Executables and scripts—that is, computer programs that spring into action when you open them. Because of this, attachments with these extensions are the most likely to harbor viruses. Be especially careful not to open these unless (1) the sender has explained exactly what they are, and (2) you've scanned them for viruses.

There are dozens more filename extensions out there in PC-land, denoting everything from new multimedia formats to pieces of your computer's operating system. Never open any mysterious or unexpected attachments. "Gee, I wonder what this does" are famous last words.

4. *Keep your software up to date.* Since e-mail programs have gotten better at handling attachments over the years, it's worth it to spring for the latest version. And older versions of other programs may have trouble opening files created by later releases.

## Compressed and Encoded Files

Most e-mail programs nowadays come fully equipped with the Swiss army knife of tools they need to decode almost any attachment. But you may receive compressed attachments that require a special uncompression program to unsquash them. Hit the Web and pick up a program like WinZip for PCs (which opens files whose names end in .zip) or StuffIT Expander for Macs (which handles .zip files as well as its own .sit format). Or just ask the sender to zap you the file again without compression—and go get a cup of coffee while you download.

5. *Be wary of viruses.* Attachments are the way e-mail viruses spread themselves: A sender may unwittingly attach an infected file, or, in the case of some high-profile mischief-makers like the "I love you" virus, the virus itself commandeers the

sender's e-mail program and sends booby-trapped attachments to people in his address book. But don't fret: Just receiving a virus-laden attachment typically won't infect your computer. Only by opening or running an attachment do you unleash the virus. (For more on viruses, see Chapter 10, "Viruses.")

Want to stay safe? Follow these rules with attachments:

- Install anti-virus software, update it every few months, and scan all incoming e-mail attachments before opening them.

- Don't open any attachment you aren't expecting. Viruses achieve success by appearing to come from friends and by sporting tempting subject lines (like "I love you"). But if you weren't expecting the message, delete it. You can always check with the sender and have him resend it if it was bona fide.

- Pay close attention to the type of file an attachment is. Use extra caution with attachments whose file names end in ".exe," ".vbs," and other extensions that denote programs or macros (mini-programs that run within other applications) that might harbor a virus. Double-check with the sender and do an anti-virus scan before running such attachments. But remember that viruses can also hide within other types of documents. For example, word-processing files booby-trapped with malicious macros.

- Don't set up your e-mail program to open attachments automatically—have it prompt you first. If your e-mail program has an automatic "preview" function that shows you a message before you open it, turn it off.

---

### Net Peeve  : (

Please do not send me e-mails with attachments unless I've requested them or unless you have asked my permission first and specified what kind of file it is. I often have my e-mail set to automatically trash all e-mails with attachments. Why? Three major reasons: (1) Attached documents of any kind can carry computer viruses, even Word documents, which are plagued with macro bugs; (2) I'm not always on a zippy Internet connection (I recently took an RV trip across the country and had only a slow wireless connection) so those pesky attachments clog up my e-mail as it downloads to the point where I sometimes have to call my Internet service provider and ask them to delete the offending e-mail; (3) I'm on a Mac and there is no guarantee that the document will open on my computer, so it's useless to me. When someone e-mails an attachment without asking, they are wearing a sign that says "amateur Internet user" in neon lights.

---

## IMHO (In My Humble Opinion): How Software Makes Life Hard

If everybody used the same e-mail program, polite communications would be seriously simpler. Instead, it's as if we're attending a cocktail party where every guest is a native of a different country. Tongues get tangled. Conversations get mangled. Customs and cultures clash.

Citizens of the e-mail world also hail from a semi-united set of nations, full of technological and cultural differences. Some users hear "You've got mail!" at America Online; others pick up their messages through free Web services like Yahoo! Mail and MSN Hotmail. Many surf from the office, using e-mail software such as Microsoft Outlook or Lotus Notes. At home, wired types may boot up their PCs or Macintoshes, connect to any of hundreds of Internet service providers, and choose from a smorgasbord of e-mail programs such as Netscape Mail, Outlook Express, and Eudora. Couch potatoes use their remote controls to flip on WebTV. High-techsters get the latest from the geek grapevine straight from their mainframes. On-the-go road warriors squint at palmtop computers, pagers, and even e-mail-enabled phones.

As most e-mail users know too well, all of these different hardware platforms and software programs often run into problems communicating with one another. An e-mail message spiffed up with graphics or funky formatting might come out fine when you send it to a co-worker or another Microsoft Outlook user but arrive unread-able when you send it to an AOL user. PC partisans and Mac mavens sometimes have a devil of a time successfully swapping attachments.

Further complicating matters, the features that help you com-municate effectively and politely vary dramatically depending on what e-mail software you use. Want to send an automatic "Gone Fishin'" message to those who e-mail you when you're on vaca-tion? Your e-mail program may or may not offer this feature—and no two programs seem to locate it in the same menu or allow you the same options. Want to block out junk e-mail? Every service and software maker proposes a different strategy to squelch the spam.

Most of this book's etiquette advice applies to everyone, regardless of software, religion, race, creed, or feelings about Bill Gates. If anything you read here doesn't seem to compute, how-ever, remember that every e-mail program works in its own pecu-liar way—and features change with every new version. Take some time to mouse around the unexplored niches of your program's menus; browse the help files; quiz a power-user co-worker or your local technoteenager. To maximize your politeness potential if you frequently correspond with people using different e-mail software, take advantage of a borrowed computer, a free trial, or a friendly expert to get a sense of the other program's ins and outs. Think of yourself as a foreign-exchange student.

## GETTING WITH THE PROGRAMS

Between office e-mail systems, Web-based e-mail services, and home software, there's an e-mail scene to suit almost any need or taste. Here's the scoop on some of the most commonly used ser-vices and software and their manners quotients:

*America Online:* A large proportion of home users sign on through the biggest online service, known for its cheery "You've got mail!" greeting, its ease for users new to the Internet, and its hopping chat and instant-message scene. AOL uses its very own e-mail software, which is a snap for beginners but less sophisti-cated than many other programs.

POLITENESS PRO: When AOLers e-mail other AOL members, they can check whether—and at what time—their messages were read.

POLITENESS CON: Formatted messages and attachments sent by non-AOL members can sometimes wind up hard—or impossible—to read.

*MSN Hotmail and Yahoo! Mail:* These free Web-based e-mail services (and others like them) let anyone use the Web to receive and send e-mail and save it in a private account.

POLITENESS PRO: Great for people who get their Net access on public school or library computers—or those who (wisely) want to keep their personal e-mail separate from their work e-mail.

POLITENESS CON: Although these services do their best to stay one step ahead of spammers, such accounts can be magnets for junk e-mail.

*Microsoft Outlook and Outlook Express:* The communications software used by the vast majority of business e-mailers is a typical Microsoft product: big and jam-packed with more features than you could ever imagine (or need). Outlook Express, a "light" version that works in tandem with Microsoft's Internet Explorer Web browser, is still plenty handy—and pretty heavy-duty.

POLITENESS PRO: An elaborate filtering feature automatically sorts incoming e-mail into folders, or even highlights it in different colors, according to rules you set up, helping you cope with in-box overload.

POLITENESS CON: Outlook's popularity—and its feature overload—make it the primary target for virus-writing villains.

*Qualcomm Eudora:* Long a techie favorite, this e-mail program is known for its super-duper filtering system—great for those who deal with tidal waves of e-mail.

POLITENESS PRO: Its "Mood Watch" feature can warn you if you're about to send a potentially nasty e-mail.

POLITENESS CON: If you need a computer to tell you you're being rude, you're in trouble.

---

### Embarrassing E-Moment

I used to e-mail a relative from my Hotmail address. I found out weeks later that she had been deleting all my messages without opening them because she thought anything called "hotmail" must be some sort of porno spam.

*5*

# Mass Mailing minus the Mess

- *What is the proper way to send e-mail to a large number of people?*

- *What is "bcc," and why is it a manners must?*

- *How can I avert a mailing-list manners meltdown?*

---

### *Embarrassing E-Moment*

"I had been planning for a long time to get breast implants. Shortly after I got the surgery, I moved to a new job. I sent an e-mail to all of my friends and professional contacts to tell them about my new phone number and address. One of my friends sent a reply to the whole list: 'So, how are the new boobs?'"

---

Sending e-mail to large numbers of people is hazardous business. Knowing how to behave as a recipient is important, too. Some of the situations that come up (like the easy-to-miss choice between replying only to a sender and replying to an entire mailing list) seem to court disaster. And any gaffe is likely to be witnessed by the maximum number of people. (Maybe the woman who told me the anecdote above should have pretended the "new boobs" her friends asked about were her new co-workers. "Much friendlier," she could have replied. Or maybe not.)

Sending e-mail to a crowd? There are two general ways (intentional ways, anyway) e-mail reaches large numbers of readers. One is when you address a message to multiple recipients. The other is when you contribute to an e-mail mailing list—an Internet discussion group that automatically distributes messages from any one member to all the other members. Mailing lists have protocols and pitfalls all their own; we'll get to them in a few pages.

## SENDING A MASS MAILING

You're sending an announcement about a new product line to a few dozen of your company's clients. You're forwarding a joke to an assortment of friends and relatives. You're inviting a bunch of buddies to your Super Bowl party. Entering a long list of e-mail addresses in the "To:" field of your message is one way to do it—but it's far from the best way. It's impolite to make recipients page through a long list of addresses before they reach your message. And using "To:" will let recipients see one another's names and addresses, a flagrant etiquette faux pas if you're writing to people who don't know one another. Many people guard their e-mail addresses closely and would prefer not to be involuntarily introduced to a list's worth of potential buttinskis, busybodies, and annoyingly overaggressive networkers. (Glomming an address from a list of recipients is poor e-manners, but that doesn't stop many people.)

The polite solution? Get to know the difference between "To," "cc," and "bcc" and when to use which for addressing your e-mail.

*Use "To" for:* the main recipient or recipients of your message. If you have several equally important targets in mind, you may list them all under "To." But watch out! Each recipient will see the names and addresses of the other recipients—which is fine if you're getting the gang together for bowling or lassoing co-workers for a meeting, but a no-no if you're e-mailing people who don't know one another.

*Use "cc" for:* secondary recipients of your message. Think of "cc" as meaning "Just FYI": You might cc a co-worker who worked on a project with you when sending a progress report about it to your boss, or cc the boss when you're e-mailing an important message to a client. (People generally use "cc" more around the office than they do with friends.) Cc'ing someone usually implies that you don't expect him or her to reply.

*Use "bcc" for:* sending messages to people when you don't want them to know one another's identities or e-mail addresses; each "bcc" recipient will see only his or her own address on the message. This is the perfect solution for party invitations, messages to several business clients, or any message to a long list of recipients. In some e-mail programs, you may need to enter an e-mail address in the "To" field—just use your own. In other programs, you can leave the "To" field blank and recipients will see "To: undisclosed recipients" or "To: (recipient list suppressed)."

DO: For extra politeness points, list recipients in alphabetical order (or any order that makes sense—just don't list your favorite people first).

DON'T: Use "To" if your list of recipients is a mile long. It'll be a pain for recipients to page through to get to the good stuff. For several or more recipients, use "bcc" instead.

DON'T: cc your boss on every e-mail you send. You might think you're keeping her "in the loop," but you're really driving her loopy. (On the other hand, a barrage of petty cc's might be a good way to teach a lesson to an insufferable micromanager—try at your own risk.)

**I got an e-mail addressed to a list of people. May I introduce myself to other people on the list now that I know their addresses?**

Networking is a national pastime. But better ask your mutual buddy to check with the intended targets first. Many people guard their e-mail addresses as fiercely as unlisted phone numbers—or just find unsolicited e-mail creepy. The person who sent the message, however, is also guilty of a common faux pas. When sending e-mail to a bunch of people who don't know each other, use blind carbon copies ("bcc" in e-mail programs). Everyone stays anonymous, with privacy protected.

DON'T: Use "bcc" to secretly send someone a copy of a message behind the back of the main recipient. It's often impolite, and dangerous, too. All too frequently, the person receiving the blind carbon copy doesn't realize it's so secret, and blabs about the message in front of the main recipient (or, worse, dashes off a reply to him). If you need to send a covert copy of a message, paste it into a separate e-mail and add a note asking the recipient to keep it to himself.

## CC, BCC, AND AOL

The existence of cc and bcc is often news to America Online users because AOL's e-mail program, unlike most others, doesn't automatically show these options. But they're just a click away. When you're addressing an e-mail, just click on the icon that says "To." You can change it to read "Cc" or "Bcc." Additionally, you can send a blind carbon copy by entering a recipient's e-mail address in parentheses: To: (jane99@doe.com).

---

### Embarrassing E-Moment

As online fan voting kicked off to elect players for the 2001 NBA All-Star team, Dallas Mavericks owner Mark Cuban, reported *The Industry Standard* magazine, sent an e-mail to more than 5,000 friends containing a link that, when clicked, automatically filled in a ballot with votes for five Mavericks players as All-Stars. The attempt at ballot-box stuffing was bad enough, but Cuban also didn't send the list as blind carbon copies, meaning the names and e-mail addresses of well-heeled pals like NFL star Ronnie Lott, rocker Perry Farrell, and USA Networks CEO Barry Diller were on full display.

## Net Peeve : (

People who send e-mails to a mass group of friends or colleagues and use the cc function instead of the bcc function. The more this happens, the more likely you are to get spam. Plus, people will hit "reply all" and your in-box will fill up.

**Survey Says**
*51 percent of workers say they use e-mail's bcc feature. 83 percent say they would contact a person whose address they saw on someone else's e-mail distribution list.*

*Source: Vault.com*

Another polite—and labor-saving—tactic is to create a nickname for a group of recipients you e-mail frequently. Most more sophisticated e-mail programs allow you to create customized mailing lists. For example, you could create a group named "family" that included the e-mail addresses of your relatives. When you addressed a message to "family," your e-mail program would send it to the kin whose addresses you designated.

Whether recipients will see fellow recipients' names or just the group name depends on how your e-mail program handles nicknames. If privacy is a concern with your message, investigate how your e-mail program handles nicknames first, or just bcc the message to the nicknamed group.

Your company's e-mail system probably also has a few pre-set distribution lists you can employ for your messages: "senior managers," "Chicago staff," "all employees." Be careful with these. Familiarize yourself with exactly who's on a particular list (does "senior managers" go to the CEO as well as the underbosses?). To avoid message duplication, watch out for overlapping groups. And be sure to send your mass mailings to as narrowly focused a group as you can—the folks in Chicago don't need to know about the leftover pizza in Boston.

## THE REPLY-TO-ALL PITFALL

If you're on the receiving end of a mass mailing, beware of the slip that launched a thousand embarrassing e-moments: a too-hasty reply. Instead of replying just to the sender, you might be replying to the sender *and* to everyone else to whom the message was sent. Mix-ups can run from mildly irritating to your fellow addressees (for example, accidentally sending your RSVP for a party to the entire guest list) to majorly mortifying (say, RSVPing and remarking, "I can't believe you invited that jerk Howard").

Some e-mail programs are wise enough to offer users a choice between "reply" and "reply to all" (via separate buttons or an alert box when you opt to reply). Others let you set a preference for replying only to the sender unless you use a certain command, like holding down the option key when you click "reply." But it's often distressingly easy to click right into a humiliating faux pas with nary a warning.

How to stay safe? Learn exactly how your e-mail software handles replies to mass mailings and explore its settings menu for any warning features you can turn on. When you fire off a response to any message, triple-check the "To," "cc," and "bcc" address fields in your e-mail so you know exactly where your reply is headed. Watch out for e-mail addresses that represent multiple people, like distribution-list nicknames ("Sales Dept.") or addresses that direct messages to an e-mail mailing list (see the next section). And be extra alert whenever you're dealing with mass e-mailings. The gremlins of the Net just love to see users humiliate themselves in front of an audience.

### Embarrassing E-Moment

The most humorous e-mail gaffe I've witnessed occurred over my graduate program's mailing list, which went at the time to 381 master's and doctoral students, faculty, and graduates. A student sent a message saying that a particular professor's class was canceled for that day. Another student replied, thinking that he was communicating only to that original student; but, of course, Student Two replied to the entire mailing list. An interchange between the two students followed, with each apparently thinking that he was responding only to the other student, when in reality the entire list watched the interchange because the students hit the "reply" button instead of changing the address to each other's personal accounts. They were discussing how horrible and juvenile the professor and her class were, commiserating about the necessity of ever having to deal with her, generally flaming her and her family, and on and on. The interchange continued for several hours until some empathetic-but-humorless third student responded to the entire list and pointed out that the interchange was taking place in the most public venue imaginable!

## MAILING LIST MAYHEM

And speaking of humiliating yourself in front of an audience, there's no better place to do it than on an e-mail mailing list. E-mail mailing lists (often known as listservs, after a popular program used to manage them) are discussion groups set up so that subscribers who share an interest—be it battling breast cancer or watching *Buffy the Vampire Slayer*—can exchange news and views. Any message a subscriber sends to a special mailing-list address is sent on to all his fellow subscribers. They reply, creating a running conversation.

Mailing lists come in many flavors. They can be public and open to all comers. Or they can be private: restricted to employees of one company or members of a certain organization. They operate under three general structures:

- Moderated: A designated list moderator reviews each message, weeding out any errant, irrelevant, or otherwise inappropriate posting before it's distributed to the full list.

- Unmoderated: Anything goes. Any message a subscriber sends to the list automatically gets distributed to other subscribers.

- Announcement-only: A newsletter-style list in which only the list manager posts messages—subscribers don't talk amongst themselves.

Every mailing list has its own style and culture. Some stick closely to the designated topic, while others spin off on tangents at the slightest provocation. Some keep the tone of conversation formal and professional, and others merrily host raucous arguments, R-rated flirting, and scorching so-called flame wars of ad hominem insults. Some lists encourage participants to share details of their personal lives and even arrange face-to-face get-togethers; other lists' subscribers revel in keeping everyone guessing with mysterious nickname and invented identities.

### Embarrassing E-Moment

During the 2000 post-presidential election mess, a programming glitch turned *Nightline*'s mailing list—an announcement-only list where producers would brief subscribers on plans for the night's program—into an inadvertent public gripe session. The glitch allowed subscribers to send replies to everyone on the list. Voters on both sides spammed their opinions to thousands of fellow Koppel-heads before ABC shut the list down.

## JOINING THE YAK PACK

Ready to make friends, influence people, and keep your in-box hopping? You can find an e-mail mailing list devoted to almost any imaginable topic: hobbies, professions, health problems, political issues, TV shows, musicians, authors, cult idols. If you need help finding the mailing list for you, several Web sites (two to try: www.lizst.com and www.topica.com) offer directories where you can browse descriptions of thousands of available lists and get directions for signing up.

## LET'S GET IT ON

Mailing list etiquette requires careful attention to manners, mores, and some not always user-friendly technological considerations. The first etiquette hurdle is learning the proper way to subscribe to (and leave) your list. The human beings who run most e-mail mailing lists rely on special list-server software to handle the drudgery of distributing messages and keeping track of subscribers. You interact with the list-server program by sending e-mail messages to a designated administrative address (*not* the same address you use to send messages meant for fellow list members). Since you're corresponding directly with a computer, you have to send it specific commands, spelled and formatted correctly. Further complicating matters: The commands differ depending on which list-server program your list uses.

You don't need a degree in computer science, however—just an ability to follow instructions. You can usually find precise sign-on directions wherever you heard about the list: on a Web directory like Lizst or Topica, on the list's own Web site, or often at the end of any message sent to the list's subscribers. (Many mailing lists also now operate Web sites where subscribers can sign on and off by clicking a button or two—a relative snap.)

Let's say I wanted to subscribe to a (fictional) mailing list for collectors of vintage sporks called SPORK-L managed by a popular software program called LISTSERV running on computers at the Web address allaboututensils.org. To join, I'd send an e-mail message to LISTSERV@allaboututensils.org with the following text in the message body (not the subject line):

SUB SPORK-L Samantha Miller

Another popular mailing-list program is Majordomo. If the silverware folks ran a mailing list dedicated to fish-fork appreciation using Majordomo software, the process for signing up would be to send e-mail to Majordomo@allaboututensils.org with the following text in the message body (not the subject line):

subscribe fish-forks

To subscribe to private lists, or lists where subscription requests are directed to an actual human being, you can be less terse—and you should include any requested or relevant details about yourself. ("Please subscribe me to the silverware-scholars list. I'm a grad student studying asparagus tongs at Martha Stewart University.")

In any case, once you've successfully subscribed to a mailing list (some lists will first send you a message asking you to confirm your subscription; follow the instructions precisely), you'll get an e-mail message welcoming you to the list. Read it carefully and save it: It will contain instructions on how to unsubscribe from the list, as well as an introduction to the rules of the list and tips on other nifty things you can do with the list-server software.

### List Tricks

Depending on the software managing your list, you may be able to take advantage of some of these handy tricks. Check your introductory message (you saved it, right?) for details and instructions.

- Temporarily stop mail from the list when you go on vacation

- Look at a list of your fellow subscribers

- Hide your name from other members who request a subscriber list (recommended to keep spammers from getting hold of your e-mail address)

- Request a digest version of the list: Instead of reading messages one at a time, you may be able to choose to receive all of a day's or a week's messages automatically gathered into one big e-mail.

You've successfully navigated your way onto an e-mail mailing list. Ready to dish? Not so fast. Here comes the most critical etiquette tip of all for good mailing-list manners: Wait a week—or longer—before posting anything. Get a sense of the list's particular tone and culture, and you'll avoid making your grand debut with a typical newbie gaffe. Some questions to ask yourself as you lurk, listen, and learn:

- Do messages have a formal or informal tone? Do spelling, grammar, and complete sentences seem to be a priority? Do members who disagree with one another rant and rave, or diplomatically beg to differ? Is their language rated PG, R, or NC-17?

- What topics do members frequently discuss—and which ones are they sick of? Does the list have a FAQ (frequently asked questions list) or Web site you can check before introducing a topic or posing a question that may have been discussed to death already?

- Do subscribers use their own names or creative pseudonyms? Do they reveal details of their personal lives or remain mysterious?

- Are messages that stray from the list's designated topic condoned or discouraged?

- Do members often request answers to questions via private e-mail, or do discussions usually play out in front of the whole list?

- Are there particular members who seem to be gurus—or cranks?

- How often do individual members post messages?

TIP: E-mail mailing-list etiquette rules also apply to other types of Internet discussion forums, such as message boards hosted by Web sites or services like America Online. They also apply to Usenet newsgroups, the Net's hundreds of public special-interest discussion groups with names like alt.fan.barry-manilow and rec.arts.bonsai. If your Internet service provider offers Usenet access, you can participate using newsreader software included in Web browsers like Netscape and Internet Explorer. Or you can click onto a Web site that lets visitors read newsgroups, such as Google.com. Since they're open to anyone and everyone, Usenet newsgroups tend to be raucous and cluttered with spam and irrelevant postings. Check them out if you're curious, but for most topics you're more likely to find meaningful conversation on a mailing list or a message board on a Web site devoted to the topic.

Once you've soaked up a good dose of your mailing list's culture, you're ready to contribute. It's usually good manners to introduce yourself briefly in your first posting. On many lists, "Hi, I'm Sam and this is my first post" will do fine. On others—e-mail support groups for those coping with an illness, for example—you may be expected to share additional personal details. Some rules for becoming a responsible mailing-list citizen:

DO: Use a good, descriptive subject line for your messages. Fellow subscribers will be more likely to read your message and find it easier to keep track of follow-ups. Those who receive the list as a digest will see your subject line in the digest's table of contents.

DO: Quote any message you're responding to—either the full message or relevant excerpts. (Make sure you leave in the name of the subscriber who wrote the message.)

DO: Send only plain-text messages—messages with fancy formatting are likely to cause problems for subscribers using different e-mail software. Attachments are also a no-no—they'll eat up fellow subscribers' disk space.

DO: Take private conversations off the list. If a discussion turns into a one-on-one argument, romance, or bonding session, spare list subscribers by switching to private e-mail.

DON'T: Post responses reading just "Me too!" "I don't know" or anything similarly content-free. If you don't have anything to say, don't say it at all.

DON'T: Post a complaint about another user's etiquette violations to the entire list. Two annoying messages are not better than one. If you must complain about a persistent problem, e-mail the list owner privately and ask him or her to set the offender straight. (Attacking someone for poor spelling is considered especially rude.)

DON'T: Flame. In Net lingo, a "flame" is an over-the-top tirade attacking someone in a public Internet forum. This dubious tradition should have no place in polite communication. Just because you're on the Net doesn't mean your words don't wound. Flaming a fellow list member, no matter what his offense, is abysmal manners. (If you must criticize, simmer down, then e-mail the person privately and explain the problem.) And flaming an interloper, such as a spammer who's probably long gone, just creates bad vibes.

DON'T: Fall for a troll. Sometimes pranksters e-mail something obviously offensive to a mailing list just to provoke an angry reaction. (Typical strategy: telling devotees their idol "sucks," concocting a scandalous rumor about him or her, or singing the praises of his or her chief rival.) In Net lingo, this is called trolling. Don't reply.

DON'T: Send administrative requests to the entire list. Few things tick off mailing-list subscribers more than a bunch of "unsubscribe" messages (or "How do I unsubscribe?" messages) cluttering their mailboxes. Don't hit "reply" to a mailing-list message to unsubscribe—messages sent to that address go to the entire list. Such requests must be directed to the list's separate administrative e-mail address. You can find instructions for unsubscribing in the introductory message you got when you subscribed to the list, or, for a refresher, check the list's Web site or FAQ, or send private e-mail to someone in charge and ask.

**I am a member of several clubs with e-mail lists. Some members repeatedly use the lists for nonclub matters and send messages advertising the fact that their friends are having a yard sale or that someone's mother will be in New York City and needs a place to stay. This is annoying—how can I tell them to stop it?**

Most mailing lists set a policy about this sort of thing: Some ban off-topic messages, others allow them. Contact the person in charge of the list. He or she should be the one to determine if the list is being abused and to reprimand the scofflaw. (If you don't have a clear policy, members should vote on one.) Don't upbraid the offender yourself. Mailing-list squabbles can quickly get nasty enough to turn your next get-together into *WWF Smackdown!* And definitely don't e-mail the whole list to complain; that's a Netiquette no-no of the first degree.

## MAILING-LIST MELTDOWNS

Mailing lists occasionally host some of the most spectacular demonstrations of the consequences of poor e-mail etiquette—the result of multiple manners mistakes piling up on one another.

It's the e-mail equivalent of a nuclear meltdown. A subscriber to an e-mail discussion group posts a message that ticks off fellow members. Maybe it's a dumb mistake, like sending a request to unsubscribe from the mailing list to the list's entire membership instead of to its administrator. Maybe it's a violation of mailing-list etiquette, like posting an advertisement. Maybe it's a troll, a calculated attempt to start a fracas.

The chain reaction starts. A few list members decide to give the offender a dressing down—by e-mailing the entire list, of course, not just the miscreant. More people chime in to say "Me too!" or come to someone's defense.

As their mailboxes fill up, other list members get riled. They start firing off angry complaints and misdirected requests to unsubscribe from the list—prompting another round of irate rejoinders and futile pleas for peace.

The reaction becomes self-sustaining. Within hours, list members' mailboxes look something like this:

```
Subj: Quit replying to the entire list,
you idiots!

Subj: WOULD YOU ALL PLEASE CALM DOWN?

Subj: You're an idiot, idiot!!!

Subj: Get me off this list

Subj: unsubscribe

Subj: this is NOT the address to unsub-
scribe!
```

```
Subj: please make this stop
```

After hundreds of messages, much wasted time, and untold aggravation, the meltdown eventually burns itself out. You don't have to hang out on the Net long to witness one of these. They erupt with the regularity of Old Faithful—even on mailing lists populated by supposedly sophisticated Internet users. (High-tech types have high ego levels to match.)

How can you steer clear of these annoying, time-wasting flaps? First, mailing-list owners should make sure all users know list policies and the proper way to unsubscribe. (Include instructions for unsubscribing with every message, or send out a reminder regularly.) As for subscribers: When a meltdown begins, resist the temptation to post a complaint or a plea to the entire list. (The list owner, however, should feel free to post a message explaining the problem and requesting a cease-fire.) If the situation remains out of hand, users may want to sign off the list, or use options within their e-mail programs to block or filter out its messages, for a few days.

### Embarrassing E-Moment

In spring 2000, an executive at a Silicon Valley start-up called Everypath accidentally sent an internal report to hundreds of business journalists on the invitation list for the company's upcoming launch party. A few hours later, the company realized its mistake and sent out another message reading "We apologize for the accidental spam. . . . Please do not reply to that message or you will get hundreds of out-of-office replies and junk e-mails." Nevertheless, the supposedly e-savvy reporters started hitting "reply all," flooding one another's mailboxes with hundreds of messages like "I hate PR people" and counter-messages like "STOP ALL YOU MORONS." The Everypath exec who sent the original spam told the *New York Times*: "I feel like Monica Lewinsky, but I didn't have nearly as much fun as her."

## LIST SAFETY

When you first subscribe to an e-mail discussion list, especially one on which you may discuss details about yourself and your life with strangers (such as a health support group), it's best not to reveal too much about your identity. Depending on the nature of the list, you may not want to subscribe using your main personal or professional e-mail address. Create a new screen name or an account at a service like MSN Hotmail or Yahoo! Mail with a handle that doesn't give away your full name, location, or, sometimes, even your gender. (Dream up a memorable one using a nickname, hobby, favorite sports team, favorite fictional character—the possibilities are endless. You can even tailor it to the group you're joining: "Sporkdork," anyone?) This makes it difficult for scammers, creeps, or overly amorous fellow subscribers to connect the online you with the real-life you. It also protects your main mailbox from junk e-mail should a spammer get his hands on your mailing-list address.

Remember that nothing you post to an online discussion group is private—and that anything you say may live on in cyberspace forever. A Net-savvy snoop entering your name or e-mail address into a Web search engine might turn up messages you wrote—even, in some cases, messages you wrote years ago. Mailing lists sometimes archive their old messages on a Web site, and any subscriber can save or forward any message. Postings to Web message boards or Usenet newsgroup postings may stick around indefinitely.

It's a scary notion: Want your employer to turn up messages revealing your health problems or political beliefs? A new beau to turn up your old newsgroup musings on sex, drugs, and rock 'n' roll? Your hipster friends to discover your secret penchant for alt.fan.barry-manilow? Using a secondary e-mail address and a creative alias will make it more difficult for a nosy Netizen to pry into your online activities. But it's not impossible: If you have reason to be paranoid, avoid high-risk chatter.

Checking someone else out in this manner might be tempting, but it's an etiquette don't in most cases. Prying into an employee's or a co-worker's personal business is an improper invasion of privacy; snooping on a friend is sneaky. It might be acceptable, however, if you have a truly compelling reason to check up on someone, like an online romantic interest you plan to meet face-to-face.

Remember that on the Net, people aren't necessarily who they say they are. Someone subscribing to a list for single moms may not be female, single, or a parent. A person professing to be a medical expert might be a burger flipper. People have even been known to fabricate illnesses for the camaraderie they find in Net support groups.

Similarly, don't take any facts, news, or expert advice you hear on a Net discussion group as gospel. The Net teems with hoaxes, misinformation, and well-meaning but misguided advice. Someone suggests an herbal remedy for your ailment? Look for more information on a reputable medical Web site—and ask your doctor. Heard a shocking piece of news about a celebrity? Head to a reputable news site to check the facts—or turn to Chapter 9, "E-Mail Hoaxes," to learn how to identify the Net's most popular whoppers.

# 6

# *E-Mail Etiquette on the Job*

- *Is it appropriate to use e-mail to reprimand an employee? To tell my boss "I quit?" To forward chain letters to co-workers?*

- *How can I get my co-workers to quit e-mailing me chain letters?*

- *What should I do about my e-mail when I go on vacation?*

If you entered the working world in the last decade—or, in many industries, even earlier—you may have never known an office without e-mail. (But Gen-Xers can imagine the unwired office—we've seen it on Nick at Nite. Would a twenty-first-century *Mary Tyler Moore Show* have Mary e-mailing messages with subject lines in indignant capital letters: "MR. GRANT!"?) Others among us have watched our offices get dragged kicking and screaming into the Internet Age as old-timers clutched their Smith-Coronas.

But for most of us now, e-mail has become as natural a business tool as the phone. We don't put much thought into the technology behind it. We take its revolutionary benefits—being able to zap a document across the country in an instant, to send a message to hundreds of people with a few clicks, to correspond with people overseas without regard to cost or time zones—for granted. And we don't spend too much time pondering the choices we make dozens of times a day, like salutations or subject lines, and how they affect others.

Indeed, most of us don't exactly spend a lot of time mulling over e-mail etiquette at work—until a major faux pas or a spate of irritating minor ones brings the issue front and center. In almost every office's gossip lore, there's a legendary embarrassing e-mail moment: an executive who accidentally sent a steamy note to the wrong person, a staffer who got in hot water for forwarding an X-rated joke, the manager who hit the wrong button and spammed an expletive-laden rant about the CEO to the entire staff. And almost every office e-mailer can reel off a long list of pet peeves: the barely Net-literate boss who never puts a subject line in e-mail, the well-meaning co-worker who forwards the latest phony virus warning to the entire staff, the supervisor who uses e-mail as an excuse never to see supervisees face-to-face. Finally, there's the most ubiquitous of all complaints about e-mail at the office: "I get too much of it!"

Is e-mail the biggest boon to business since the doughnut, or have workers simply traded the old set of communications irritations and inconveniences for new ones? A few rules and courtesies—as well as smart, well-publicized corporate e-mail policies and a few cautionary tales about the consequences of bad or careless behavior—can go a long way toward making e-mail the best business tool it can be.

### Survey Says
*80 percent of employees say that for the majority of their business correspondence, e-mail has replaced snail mail, 72.5 percent say that e-mail has replaced faxing, and 45 percent say e-mail has replaced phone calls.*

*Source: Vault.com*

## What's In and What's Out in the Wired Office

|  | OUT | IN |
|---|---|---|
| Eyestrain | Blurry third-generation faxes | Multicolored fonts |
| Annoyance | Carbon paper | Co-workers who insist on sending you cc's of e-mails you couldn't care less about. |

|  | OUT | IN |
|---|---|---|
| Time-waster | Watercooler chat | Spending your lunch hour forwarding jokes to friends |
| Malady | Neck cramps from wedging the phone between your ear and shoulder | Carpal tunnel syndrome |
| Measurement | How humongous your office is | How teensy your e-mail-enabled cell phone is |
| Executive perk | "Take a memo, Miss Jones." | An assistant to sort through your incoming e-mail, chuck the dreck, and forward summaries of the important stuff to your wireless-modemed laptop |
| Humiliation | Blurting out something dumb to the boss after a three-martini lunch | Accidentally outing your affair with the boss by misaddressing a steamy e-mail to the "All employees" list |

## KHAKIS OR SUITS? THE OFFICE (AD)DRESS CODE

One key to proper office e-mail etiquette is learning your office's particular e-mail culture—both the official rules and the unspoken ones. Corporate e-mail culture varies greatly: At some offices, e-mail is the main form of communication, even between employees who sit a few yards apart. At others, employees may check their e-mail only sporadically. Some companies don't mind if employees manage their social lives from their work accounts; at others, it's a firing offense. Some CEOs welcome e-mail from low-level employees, some CEOs detest e-mail from low-level employees, and some CEOs don't know a computer from a coffeepot.

Learning the idiosyncracies of a company's e-mail culture is a bit like figuring out the fine points of a so-called casual dress code: Obviously, three-piece suits are out. Yes, the rules forbid shorts and tube tops. But are fishnet stockings too wild and crazy? Is there an unwritten understanding that managers don't wear jeans? The only way to find out is by watching and waiting (or quizzing an in-the-know colleague). Same deal with e-mail: When you move to a new job or even a new position within a company, observe the local e-mail culture—or ask a savvy co-worker for tips—before you become a power user. A few questions to investigate:

- Is the tone of e-mail between colleagues usually formal or freewheeling? Does the e-mail network pulse with brainstorming, gossip, and inter-cubicle socializing, or does it serve mostly to transmit stately memos?

- Are low-level employees welcome or expected to e-mail suggestions or questions to top executives, or does e-mail generally travel along a strict chain of command?

- Do staffers typically e-mail nearby colleagues, phone them, or walk to their desks for a face-to-face conversation? How do they typically communicate an urgent or sensitive message?

- Do all employees have access to e-mail? Do they receive and read messages immediately or check it only periodically?

- Are staff-wide announcements made via e-mail? Memo? Tacked to a bulletin board? Put on the company Web site?

- Do colleagues frequently send staff-wide e-mail messages for personal reasons, such as "I'm looking for an apartment" or "Anybody want to buy my tickets for tonight's basketball game?" or is there another area, online or off, set aside for such messages?

- Does the company have any written policies regarding e-mail and Net use? Is a certain amount of personal e-mail and Web surfing tolerated, or is there a zero-tolerance policy? Does any written policy (or perhaps tech staffer plied with a few drinks at happy hour) reveal whether supervisors or software programs are monitoring the content of employees' e-mail?

**Survey Says**

*Most online Americans now prefer e-mail to the phone for communicating with business associates and co-workers. For outside contacts, 50 percent say they prefer to use e-mail, versus 34 percent who pick the phone. A few more like to give co-workers a jingle: 48 percent prefer e-mail, 38 percent the phone.*

*Source: The America Online/Roper Starch*
*Worldwide Adult Cyberstudy 2000*

## GETTING DOWN TO BUSINESS

Whether you work at a Fortune 500 company, a mom-and-pop operation, or the kind of anything-goes start-up with more pool tables than conference tables, some e-mail etiquette rules are universal. Here are some tactics for staying on your co-workers' good side—and avoiding common slipups.

Get the right address. "Oops, I did it again!" could be the theme song in thousands of workplaces as anguished employees feel their hearts leap into their throats when they realize that their mash note, criticism of a colleague, salacious gossipgram, or worse is racing its way toward the wrong mailbox. It's always easy to enter an incorrect address or to hit "reply" when you meant to hit "forward" if you're distracted (you'll scoff until you do it yourself some late night). But it's particularly easy to slip up at work, where e-mail software often has you select addresses from a company-wide list of employees or automatically guesses at a recipient's name once you type the first few letters. Watch out for co-workers with easy-to-confuse names (like Allen and Allan, or Charles David and David Charles), colleagues with exact or near namesakes in far-flung divisions, and, most dangerous of all, e-mail addresses that represent mass-mailing lists, lest a slip of the finger zap your note intended for a colleague named Allan to "All staff" instead. Make a habit of double-checking the address before you hit "send" on any message.

A few more tips: Never guess at someone's address. If in doubt, call and ask, or confirm it by looking at a recent message he sent you. And be extra alert when you reply to any message sent to multiple people. If you want your reply to go only to the sender—and not to all your fellow addresses—make sure you hit "reply," not "reply all," and double-check the addresses that appear on your reply. (N.B.: If you subscribe to e-mail mailing lists that use special software to distribute messages, "reply" may route your message to an address that sends it to all the other list subscribers. For more on mailing lists, see Chapter 5, "Mass Mailing minus the Mess.")

---

## Net Peeve :(

When people use the global address list at work and don't pay attention exactly to whom they are sending a message (yes, there are multiple Smiths, Joneses, etc.) and send e-mails to the wrong individual.

---

### Embarrassing E-Moment

A misdirected e-mail can be mortifying for the sender, but it can also be emotionally wrenching for the recipient. In October 2000, Lauren Zalaznick, a top executive for the cable channel VH1, wrote an essay on the Web site Open Letters about accidentally getting an e-mail in which a producer with whom she frequently worked referred to her using a particularly foul four-letter word. She replied, sending the message back to him with no comment. The producer and his partner (to whom he had meant to send the e-mail) apologized profusely via e-mail and in person. But, wrote the executive, "there's something about seeing the words on the page—well, on the screen—that is so irretrievable and irrevocable. So easy to pore over, it's not like an overheard conversation. It's text, and text still has the power of being something you can't 'take back.'"

Don't write anything in e-mail you wouldn't want to see tacked to the office refrigerator. At work, once you've sent a message, you can never be sure who's going to see it. The recipient could forward it—on purpose or accidentally. Your e-mail could be monitored. Even deleted messages can be dredged up if a court case or internal investigation demands them (and it wouldn't have to be you getting investigated—what if one of your recipients is?). So keep your workplace e-mail messages free of complaints, gossip, asides about your personal life, discussion of particularly sensitive issues facing the company, and anything else you wouldn't want to announce to a room full of co-workers. Or to a judge. If this means some work can't be accomplished via e-mail, better safe than sorry—too many individuals and companies have learned this the hard way.

### Embarrassing E-Moment

Bryant Gumbel knows the perils of bad-mouthing colleagues via e-mail: In 1989, an e-mail the then *Today*-show co-host wrote to a producer was leaked to the media. In the message, Gumbel grumbled about various on- and off-camera staff. Among those slammed: Gene Shalit (his interviews "aren't very good," wrote Gumbel) and weatherman Willard Scott, whom Gumbel accused of holding the show "hostage to his assortment of whims, wishes, birthdays and bad taste."

Don't get addi-cc-ted to carbon copies. Misdirected e-mail can destroy a career, but recipients' biggest e-mail peeve is a surplus of properly directed messages. Unsolicited e-mail from outside the office is part of the problem, but many workers, particularly managers and executives, get buried in a barrage of unrequested cc's and bcc's from colleagues on messages they have little interest in or don't have to read. (Call them CYA—cover your, um, tail—copies.) Just because e-mail makes it easy to keep a supervisor or colleague "in the loop" doesn't mean he or she necessarily wants to be in it. Unless you've been requested to or it's standard practice in your workgroup, keep cc's of messages to a bare minimum. As for blind carbon copies, as a way to sneak a copy of a message to someone else without the main recipient knowing, they're usually a bad idea. (So many people are unfamiliar with how bcc's work that bcc recipients often don't realize their copy was supposed to be secret.)

> "I have come to believe that if anything will bring about the downfall of a company, or maybe even a country, it is blind copies of e-mails that should never have been sent in the first place."
>
> —Disney chairman and CEO Michael Eisner, to the May 2000 graduating class at USC

Stay tuned to tone. In e-mail, humor, sarcasm, and silliness are easy for readers to misinterpret. Out of context, a gag that would be a knee-slapper in person can make you sound sad, angry, or even a little deranged. A disclaimer like "<grin>" or "(just kidding!)" can help (emoticons are too frivolous for the office), but it's usually safer to avoid the situation. The temptation to crack a joke in e-mail to colleagues can be strong, especially when you've thought of the perfect line to liven up a boring memo. It's usually wise to resist it. Save the gag for your next face-to-face chat.

Likewise, a tone that's even mildly angry or critical can often come across as much more strident to readers. Keep office e-mail, even notes to colleagues you consider friends, bland and businesslike. Show your personality in person.

### Survey Says
*51 percent of workers think the tone of their e-mails is sometimes misunderstood.*

*Source: Vault.com*

Don't be a forwardin' fool. The e-mail flotsam you swap with your friends is up to you and them, but chain e-mail of any sort— be it dirty joke, clean joke, petition, political propaganda, advertisement, hoax, or "send this to ten friends so you won't have bad luck"—has no place in the office. Many companies wisely levy official bans on this sort of clutter. If you have friends in your office who dig it, forward items to their personal accounts—and check your own after hours.

**How can I get co-workers to stop sending me chain letters over e-mail? This conduct is unprofessional.**

You could warn them whatever misfortune the next chain letter says will befall those who don't forward it will be nothing compared to what you'll do to them if they do—but that wouldn't be professional, either. A better move: Without naming offenders' names, ask your supervisor or technology manager to send a note reminding all employees that chain letters are an office no-no. Many companies have written policies banning them. If yours doesn't, urge someone to write one.

"I" before "e," except after "c" . . . Poor spelling and grammar are bad manners in personal e-mail, but the "I'm too busy to be literate" attitude is even worse in business e-mail, where your reputation is always on the line. You don't have to consult Strunk & White's *Elements of Style* with every keystroke, but give every outgoing message a spell-check and a second reading. No one will condemn you for the occasional typo.

---

## Net Peeve :(

When someone e-mails a résumé for a job application and doesn't apply the same standards (uh, spell-checking) to his e-mail cover letter as he would to a regular cover letter. Even worse: forwarding a résumé with *no* letter.

---

**Survey Says**
*85 percent of Americans say it's "extremely" or "very"
important to use proper grammar and capitalization
in business e-mail.*

*Source: Nov. 2000 E-Etiquette National Survey, sponsored
by 1-800-FLOWERS.COM and Luntz Research*

Lose the funky formatting. The good news about office e-mail
systems: Any formatting you do—italics, boldfacing, multiple
fonts, colored text—isn't likely to be lost, as it sometimes is when
e-mail wends its way over the Net. The bad news about office e-
mail systems: Any formatting you do isn't likely to be lost. Getting
overly ornate in casual e-mails accomplishes nothing but making
them hard to read—and it makes you look more like a frivolous
ditz than a frustrated artist. Don't use italics or boldfacing to highlight more than the occasional word; never use more than two
fonts. And avoid colored text—that went out with those purple
pens you loved in junior high school. Adults use basic black.

## RED LIGHT, GREEN LIGHT: AT THE OFFICE

What messages are appropriate to send via e-mail at the office?
Even in the most e-mail-addicted of workplaces, some kinds of
messages can be rude, time-wasting, or downright dangerous.
Keep your corporate e-mail culture in mind, but these rules apply
across the board:

### Green Lights

- *Simple, direct questions, requests, to fellow staffers:* "Can you
  please proofread the following reports?" "When do you need
  them done?"

- *Information recipients will want to save.* "My brain is a sieve!"
  an old boss of mine liked to sigh, and the malady is mutual.
  If we e-mail something—the time and place of an upcoming

lunch, a list of story ideas—we can refer back to the e-mail after our short-term memory fails and long after any paper memo would be buried at archaeological-dig depths.

- *Information recipients may want to use verbatim in another document.* If you're making a suggestion about how to word a report—or writing a memo you know your recipient will want to bounce off his boss—e-mail is a no-brainer.

- *Official company-wide announcements no more than a few pages long.* A change in the travel policy? News about a new hire? A reminder about the holiday party? Save trees. Send these daily doses of bureaucracy via e-mail (assuming, of course, everyone at the office has access to e-mail). And make sure they go only to recipients who will find them relevant.

---

## Net Peeve  : (

When I read e-mails sent to my company's entire staff, I'm always finding out they're serving bagels on some other continent.

---

- *Major personal announcements.* Someone's a new mom or dad? Only a grinch would object to a co-worker's spreading the happy news to colleagues who know the new parent (assuming parental permission, of course). E-mail is also a good way for a close colleague (again, with permission) to spread the sad news of a death in a co-worker's family. In most larger offices, any life event less monumental (engagement, son's college graduation) doesn't warrant a company-wide e-mail.

### Yellow Lights

- *Thank-you notes.* An e-mail thank-you for a lunch meeting or job interview is usually acceptable, but in many situations a prompt snail-mail note will stand out more—and so might be the smarter move. For big-deal thanks, a card or gift is in order.

- *Important but lengthy memos.* "Below please find our new forty-page expense account policy." I'm all for preserving forests, but sometimes paper is the way to go. Long documents are hard to read on-screen—which will lead to printer gridlock when half the staff tries to make hard copies at the same time. Plus, photocopying is cheaper than using a printer. However, for a useless memo few employees are likely to read—the latest mission-statement rewrite, perhaps—e-mail may indeed be the ecologically correct choice.

- *Communications that might actually be more convenient in another medium.* A question requiring a yes, no, or short answer is fine; one requiring a complex answer or multiple rounds of mundane follow-ups and answers (like setting up a lunch meeting, which can take half a dozen or more messages by the time you hash out who, where, and when) might be easier to do over the phone or in person.

- *Praise.* An e-mail message to tell someone you work with "Thank you!" or "Great job!" has a nice official aura to it, and it's always good to be able to open up a nice note again and again. But be sure also to tell her in person. Everyone needs a little face-to-face validation sometimes.

- *Minor bureaucratic requests.*

**Is it okay to send e-mail to my boss to say I'll be out sick that day, or should I call?**

If you're sure your boss will check his or her e-mail first thing in the morning, you could give it a shot—best to ask first, though. But in most offices the phone will probably stay the gold standard for sick-day requests. Even the most trusting of supervisors secretly wants to hear just how hoarse, stuffed-up, and generally incapacitated (or suspiciously perky) you sound.

- *Company-wide personal requests.* Some office workers use e-mail like a bulletin board, mass-mailing entreaties seeking apartments, tennis partners, or takers for their extra tickets to tonight's game. Supervisors, particularly in larger companies, may frown on such use of the company's e-mail system—and officemates may resent the interruption no matter what the company's size. Check your company's written policy or ask a supervisor if you're not sure whether your message will be thought appropriate. If you're being bombarded by mass e-mailings, encourage your office to come up with a more Netiquette-friendly alternative: perhaps a Web message board or mailing list officemates can opt out of if they don't care to get such messages. Or maybe it's time to go back to the old-fashioned pushpin-and-paper bulletin board.

- *Union material:* Do labor unions have the right to contact workers by sending e-mail through a company's computer system? Several companies and unions have clashed over the question, though no court has yet issued a definitive ruling. Companies generally say computer networks and equipment are company property that they have the right to control. Unions, traditionally guaranteed access to certain workspaces, argue that networks are a place where employees gather—the modern equivalent of the watercooler.

  While it's likely a dispute could soon lead to a court ruling on the issue, for now it's a good idea for unions to steer clear of distributing newsletters or recruitment information to employees' work e-mail addresses. Such electronic campaigning could provoke a nasty legal battle—or even be seen as unwanted spam by some workers. Safer ways to e-campaign: a Web site employees can access from anywhere, or an e-mail newsletter they can sign up for from any address.

- *Invitations to corporate parties.* E-mail is fine for a party for fellow employees (as long as they all have e-mail and check it). If you're inviting employees of other companies, use caution: E-mail might be fine for a tech-industry shindig, but if the bash is more formal or very important to your company, even techies will be more impressed with (and less likely to forget about) snazzy printed invitations.

## Red Lights

- *Major job requests.* Even in workplaces where almost every-thing happens via e-mail, serious wheeling and dealing—like requests for raises or promotions and resignations—requires face-to-face meetings. An e-mail request isn't likely to be taken seriously, and it might even be seen as cowardly. Plus, the only way to play real hardball is in person. Why else would diplomats rack up so many frequent-flier miles?

**I want to quit my job by e-mail while I'm on vacation so I won't have to face my boss. Is this acceptable?**

Only if you're bucking for a new position as Senior VP of Wimping Out. This is one of those times that call for an eye-to-eye confrontation. Otherwise you won't get the appropriate dose of guilt (if your boss is a dear)—or glee (if not).

---

**Survey Says**
*82 percent of Americans call resigning from a job via e-mail inappropriate. 85 percent call requesting a raise or promotion via e-mail inappropriate.*

*Source: Nov. 2000 E-Etiquette National Survey, sponsored by 1-800-FLOWERS.COM and Luntz Research*

---

## Net Peeve :(

A staff member who didn't want to face me sent in his resignation via e-mail. I gladly accepted his resignation, but I was so angry I decided I wouldn't give him any of the good-bye perks I sometimes give staffers, like issuing him a good-bye bonus or letting him keep his laptop.

- *Forwarded funnies and chain e-mail of any sort.* Whether humorous tidbit, inspirational message, political propaganda, good-luck charm, dire warning, or heart-tugging plea, keep the Net flotsam and jetsam off the office e-mail system. These messages perpetuate hoaxes, waste company time, often violate company e-mail policies—and, most importantly, many recipients detest them. If you have office pals who enjoy this stuff, send it to their personal e-mail accounts on your own time.

- *Off-color jokes and racist or sexist comments.* Yet another reason to put a lid on "Psst! Pass it along" e-mail: The frequently raunchy or tasteless gags zapped around in e-mail chain letters can be ticking time bombs at the office. Somehow they aren't quite as uproarious when they pop up as evidence in a harassment suit or disciplinary hearing. (Sorry, up-and-coming Jay Lenos or Chris Rocks: original material doesn't win you any extra artistic license.) Off-the-cuff comments—like remarks about co-workers' appearance, ethnicity, or sexual habits—can have severe consequences too. Remember, even if you e-mail a message to recipients you deem "safe," there's no telling where it might wind up after you hit "send." And supervisors, worried about harassment lawsuits, may be monitoring office e-mail looking for just such infractions. (For more on corporate e-mail monitoring, see Chapter 12, "Spy Games.")

  So e-mail isn't the place to play comedian, curmudgeon, or beauty-pageant judge: Keep e-mail to co-workers as well as contacts outside the office squeaky clean. Remember, even as some types of raunchiness get ever more acceptable in pop culture, the workplace is a far different story. Remarks that would be fine in a cable-TV comedy special or even a prime-time network sitcom can bring a heap of trouble in corporate America.

  Of course, steering clear of potentially offensive e-mail isn't just a matter of keeping yourself out of trouble with lawsuit-paranoid Puritans. Even if you disagree with some of the excesses of today's prudish workplace climate, such messages violate good etiquette. Law or no law, belittling co-workers, trading laughs behind others' backs, and encouraging a culture where some people aren't respected is bad manners.

### Embarrassing E-Moment

In 1997, African-American employees at Citibank brought a racial-discrimination lawsuit charging white managers swapped racist joke e-mail ridiculing "Ebonics" with a list of definitions, such as "disappointment: My parole officer tel me if I miss disappointment they gonna send me back to da big house." The suit was later dismissed.

- *Flirting.* Avoid office romances? Heck, no—where do you think people find mates nowadays? But e-mail, always susceptible to prying eyes or slips of the "send" button, isn't the place to go hunting for a date or to get steamy with your squeeze. Save it for personal e-mail—or late-night rendezvous in the storage closet.

### Embarrassing E-Moment

"A co-worker of mine was e-mailing a female colleague about a story they were working on and also flirting by e-mail with the male colleague he was having an affair with. He accidentally outed their affair (which was not common knowledge at all) with a suggestive e-mail to the wrong colleague."

- *Requests for money.* No matter what your office e-mail culture, mass-mailed pleas to buy Girl Scout cookies, give to school fund-raisers, or contribute to charity athletic events are an etiquette no-no. Hitting up your co-workers for bucks puts them on the spot in an unfair way: Even if you're not their boss, they may feel obligated to ante up. If you absolutely must solicit at the office, keep it as quiet and nonconfrontational as possible: a notice on the bulletin board, an order form taped to your door.

- *Gossip.* Know who the boss is sleeping with? Got the poop on why the receptionist was fired? For heaven's sake, don't spread the news via e-mail. Once you've hit "send" on your scandalgram, you lose control of it: It could be forwarded, accidentally or on purpose, into the hands of just about anyone, from the rumor's subject to your boss to the *National Enquirer.* And who can resist spreading gossip? Save your office gossip for in-person whispers—or your memoirs.

---

### Embarrassing E-Moment

In November 2000, the CIA fired four employees, suspended several others, and revoked the security clearances of nine private contractors for exchanging "inappropriate" e-mail in computer chat rooms they hid from higher-ups at the agency, *The Washington Post* reported. A former CIA analyst who had been part of the chats told the *Post* that fellow participants were mostly tech-savvy staffers who enjoyed bonding covertly: "The odds are pretty good," he said, "that what this was, at worst, was bitching about management."

---

- *Discussions of anything illegal or unethical.* Don't leave a paper trail; do your plotting in person.

## E-MAILING UP, DOWN, AND ALL AROUND

E-mailing clients or contacts outside the office? E-mailing the boss? You are the boss? Here are some special e-mail etiquette considerations.

When you're e-mailing your supervisor (or someone farther up the ladder):

- Don't use a jokey or too-casual tone just because the person isn't in front of you. And even if you're ultra-informal with your supervisor in person, keep e-mail crisp and businesslike: You never know when your boss might want to forward something on to *her* boss.

- Never e-mail angry. Cool down, then do any complaining in person.

- Don't e-mail over your supervisor's head. Yes, in many companies, e-mail has made top executives much more accessible to employees—a change that can be great for business. But in most situations you shouldn't cut your immediate manager out of the loop. Let him know about any idea or question you plan to bounce off the big shots; they should send him a copy of messages they send you.

- Keep the cc's to a minimum. Sometimes it's necessary to zap your boss a copy of a message you're sending to a co-worker or client—but not always. Be selective—unless your boss is a zealous micromanager, he doesn't need his mailbox cluttered with copies of every note you send.

- Find out how your manager prefers to hear ideas, brainstorms, or questions: e-mailed or in person? Succinct or detailed? As soon as you dream them up or fully polished?

**Survey Says**
*70 percent of workers believe that e-mail has improved communication with their bosses.*

*Source: Vault.com*

## IMHO (In My Humble Opinion): Pluribus or Unum?

Net Peeve from a tech-company executive:

"People who send an e-mail for every thought they have, rather than saving up three or four thoughts and putting them into one e-mail."

Net Peeve from another high-tech honcho:

"Something about e-mail lends itself to one idea at a time. I get e-mail with four or five different thoughts, and I don't know what to do."

More extensive research confirmed a deep divide on this issue. When underlings have several unrelated ideas or comments, about half of managerial Netizens prefer receiving separate messages. The other half like getting one long one. And each camp's approach apparently bugs the heck out of the other camp.

Clearly, it's time for e-mail etiquette to take a side—but which? While separate e-mails make it easier for recipients to keep track of each topic and any ensuing back-and-forth conversation, it's annoying to get several messages in quick succession from the same person. One longer e-mail reduces mailbox clutter, but makes it more likely the recipient will overlook some of its contents, like the brilliant idea after the "by the way" 500 words in.

The polite solution? Well, given the great divide, it's wise to find out whether your boss likes to chew over ideas in hors d'oeuvre–like nibbles or one big Dagwood sandwich. But in general, if your suggestions are urgent, fire away. If they're not, save 'em up until an appropriate moment, then make sure it's clear that your message contains a grab-bag of goodies so none is overlooked. Try using a subject line like "three questions" or using bullets to highlight different points.

And to all you peeved managers: Chill out. Having a staff that thinks *too much*—and communicates freely—isn't the working world's worst nightmare.

---

### Net Peeve  : (

One of my employees sent me a long report and put a question for me at the very end. I figured the message was just the report and saved it to read later. Then the employee e-mails me asking "Didn't you get my question?"

---

## E-MAILING SUPERVISEES

When it comes to their bosses, workers' biggest Netiquette beefs stem from one overarching problem: E-mail encourages some managers to hide behind their monitors, dispensing criticism, praise, and marching orders while rarely seeing colleagues face-to-face. No matter how wired you are, managing by walking around is a crucial key to good leadership.

- Don't use e-mail for reprimands or criticism. In the terse, emotionless context of e-mail, criticism can often read as harsher than intended. Employees also detest e-mail criticism as unfair and even cowardly: They deserve a chance to offer up a defense or discuss details of a touchy situation face-to-face.

- Everyday praise is fine via e-mail (I, for one, never tire of opening a "nice job"-o-gram again and again). But while an e-mail thank-you feeds the mind, an in-person thank-you feeds the soul—and public recognition feeds the not-to-be-neglected ego. (A box of chocolates, meanwhile, feeds the tummy, which, for many of us, is the real key to winning our undying loyalty.) For feats truly above and beyond the call of duty, a combination package is the ticket.

- While e-mail is a useful way to mete out some tasks, complex assignments are best explained in person or on the phone.

---

## Net Peeve : (

If you're my boss and you're going to tell me to do something unpleasant, better do it to my face.

---

**Survey Says**
*81 percent of Americans say reprimanding an employee via e-mail is "inappropriate" or "downright rude."*

*Source: Nov. 2000 E-Etiquette National Survey,*
*sponsored by 1-800-FLOWERS.COM and Luntz Research*

## E-MAILING OUTSIDE THE OFFICE

In most jobs, you'll wind up e-mailing not only colleagues but also customers, clients, or contacts outside the company. A good command of e-mail etiquette is crucial in these situations, when a faux pas can affect not just your reputation but also your company's. Pay close attention to basic rules like good spelling and proper mass-mailing techniques. A few more tips:

- Find out new contacts' preferred method of communication. E-mail isn't everyone's first choice; some prefer the phone or even snail mail. Some people have multiple e-mail addresses—make sure you have the right one.

- Keep the tone of the message formal the first time you e-mail outside contacts. Address them by their last names and titles— "Ms. Smith," "Dr. Jones"—even if you're in an industry where CEOs go by "Yo, dude." (You can switch to a first-name basis later—follow the contact's lead. In some situations and lines of work, of course, it's last-name-basis forever.)

- In a first e-mail to a contact, introduce yourself in the first few lines of the message's text; sign off with your full name and complete contact information, including your phone number, your company's name, and your job title.

- Use plain text—e-mail programs different from yours may have difficulty with any exotic character or formatting.

- Don't send attachments until you check with the contact about what size and type of documents he can (or wants to) accept.

- Be aware of any legal or ethical e-mail guidelines specific to your profession. For example, communications between stockbrokers and clients are heavily regulated (and monitored) to avoid fraud or insider trading. The American Medical Association recently passed a set of e-mail ethical guidelines for doctors to help safeguard patients' privacy, many of which are good ideas across the board. Among the AMA policy's provisions:

  1. Never send group e-mails where other recipients' names are listed.

  2. Let patients know exactly who has access to e-mail messages they send and receive.

3. Use password-protected screen savers at the office, at the hospital, and at home.

4. Don't share patients' e-mail addresses with marketers.

5. Acknowledge messages promptly and set a reasonable turnaround time.

---

### Net Peeve : (

People who call me up at work and tell me that there must be something wrong with my server because they keep sending me an e-mail and it keeps bouncing back, when the real problem lies in the fact that they are spelling my name incorrectly.

---

## GETTING TOO PERSONAL

"Don't e-mail me at work," some of us have to warn friends and family. Meanwhile, others spend hours working the wires—setting up weekend plans, arranging eBay purchases, gossiping with buddies—ready to click over to a spreadsheet at any moment should the boss look over our shoulder.

Employers' attitudes toward employees' sending personal e-mail on company time and company computer equipment vary widely. Some ban it—and use monitoring software to crack down on violators. Some belong to the "anything goes as long as you get your work done" school. So proceed with caution. Find out your company's official policy, and ask co-workers for the unofficial skinny about what is and isn't tolerated (keeping in mind that a toothless official policy could suddenly turn into Jaws). A few tips for e-mailers who dare to mix business with pleasure:

• Use a personal e-mail account separate from your work account, then check your account via the Web. This won't necessarily make your e-mail snoop-proof—a sophisticated office surveillance system can still record your keystrokes or take pictures of your screen—but it will help you keep your business and social life separate. Also, if you change jobs you don't want all your friends to have to learn a new e-mail address.

- Don't count on privacy. Sending e-mail about any super-sensitive topics—like chats with a recruiter or your doctor—on a work computer, whether you're using a personal address or not, is playing with fire. Wait until you get home.

- Be careful when e-mailing someone else at the office, even if you're e-mailing from home. Incoming e-mail isn't private, either. And if someone asks you not to send him any personal e-mail at work, honor the request. Many offices are much stricter than others about personal e-mail on the job.

### Embarrassing E-Moment

"I used to work with this one guy who was a real schmoozer. He spent a lot of time at bars meeting women. During one of his weekend forays he struck up a conversation with a woman and wound up giving her his business card, obviously hoping to connect with her in the future. Less than a week later she sent him an e-mail using the work e-mail address on the front of the card. This would all be fine if he worked for a company that had reasonably private e-mail for its employees. However, the standard protocol for almost all e-mail (very high management were exempted) at my company was to have all e-mail automatically printed out and delivered on paper to the intended recipient. Further complicating matters, the employee who tended the printer was the biggest gossip in the company. When the e-mail arrived asking my co-worker out (it was not as bad as it could have been), the story got circulated around the entire office. Probably fifty people knew about this e-mail before its intended recipient did."

"I've had the humiliating experience of my personal e-mails being printed for the world to read. [So] until all of the investigations are over and there's no possibility of anything personal being subpoenaed, I try to curtail my e-mail use to strictly business."

—Monica Lewinsky, to *Yahoo! Internet Life* magazine, February 2001

### Survey Says
*Vault.com asked workers how many non-work-related e-mails they send during a typical workday.*

*None: 18 percent*

*1-5: 56 percent*

*6-10: 13 percent*

*11-20: 6 percent*

*21+: 7 percent*

*The site also asked employers how many personal e-mails employees should be allowed to send during the workday:*

*None: 12 percent*

*1-5: 54 percent*

*6-10: 18 percent*

*11-20: 6 percent*

*21+: 11 percent*

*Source: Vault.com*

## INTERNATIONAL MAIL

International business etiquette is tricky business. With e-mail, at least you don't have to worry about table manners or handshake habits, but there are still quite a few special considerations to keep in mind:

- Address people by their titles and surnames, not their first names, and keep the tone of your message formal. Many countries' business culture (especially in written communications) is more formal than that of the anything-goes U.S. Need help with foreign titles? A reference like *Merriam Webster's Guide to International Business Communications* will help you sort out your Monsieurs, Madames, Herrs, and Fraus.

- Avoid humor or sarcasm, which usually don't translate well.

- Give metric equivalents of English measurements.

- Be careful with calendar dates: In most of Europe, 2/6/02 means June 2, 2002, not February 6. And the Japanese sometimes use a year/month/day format. To be safe, write out the name of the month: 6 February 2002 or February 6, 2002.

- If you're giving monetary figures, be sure to say what currency.

- Give country codes for phone numbers, U.S. residents can give their digits as +1 (555) 555-5555.

- Steer clear of brand names. Use generic terms instead: "photocopy," not "Xerox."

- Be specific with geographical locations: "I'm flying back to Boston on Tuesday," not "I'm flying back to the east coast on Tuesday."

- Watch out for time-zone confusion: When you write "I'll call you at 5 P.M.," make sure you specify *whose* 5 P.M.

---

## Net Peeve :(

I'm a member of several e-mail mailing lists for my industry that have an international membership. Most of the conversation is in

English, but every once in a while someone posts a report or newspaper article in Danish, and all the people who know Danish go on to discuss it, leaving the rest of us out.

---

**Survey Says**
*E-Mail around the World*

*Percentages of residents of various countries who had Internet access:*

*Sweden: 74 percent*

*United States: 66 percent*

*Canada: 60 percent*

*Australia: 60 percent*

*Argentina: 35 percent*

*Great Britain: 35 percent*

*Brazil: 32 percent*

*Japan: 27 percent*

                    *Source: 2000 American Express Global Internet Survey*

## GETTING OUT OF TOWN . . . POLITELY

It gets worst around August, or maybe December. You're doing some routine mass e-mailing—a note briefing your company's employees to some new rule or regulation, perhaps—when your e-mail programs' new-message alert starts jingling merrily. Recipients dying to debate your communiqué's fine print? No such luck. Rather, your in-box is filling up with messages reading something like "Joe Blow is out of the office"—the automated "gone fishin'" e-mail replies your absent colleagues turned on when they blew town for the beach house or ski slopes. It's enough that they scrambled for the exits and left you covering the duties of three vacationers, but do they have to rub it in?

To be sure, out-of-office notices probably come in handy far more often than they annoy. When you're e-mailing an urgent question or document to someone outside your company, or somewhere distant within a large office, it can be a lifesaver to find out he or she is temporarily incommunicado. Not knowing whether a recipient has read your message is a major e-mail drawback: If you telephoned while a target was out of the office, at least you'd stand a chance of being alerted by her voice mail (if she remembered to change the outgoing message) or by the assistant who picks up the phone (if his line about the boss being "on a plane and completely unreachable" is nonfiction).

Still, most e-mail programs' out-of-office-alert features need a lot of fine-tuning to become fully politeness-compliant. In an ideal world, your program would notify the people who need to know you're out of the office, and not bug the people who don't need to know. Some programs make it easy for you to specify certain people (like senders of newsletters or other non-urgent mass mailings) who shouldn't receive the automated replies, or set up different replies for different senders (you could supply your pager number to co-workers, perhaps, but not to outside contacts). Other programs don't include the out-of-office feature, but if you're a whiz with filters—the feature in some e-mail programs that lets you set up rules to sort e-mail—you can create your own system of automatic replies.

What's the polite thing to do? Start by following your co-workers' lead (or any company policy): If they use out-of-office notifiers, you're probably expected to too. Then investigate your e-mail program's out-of-office reply system for any features that might make life easier for you and your correspondents, such as excluding some senders. If you subscribe to any e-mail discussion groups, it's a good idea to put them on hold (most lists offer this option; check your list's specific instructions) so fellow members or the humans or computers that run the list aren't bombarded by your out-of-office messages.

---

## Net Peeve :(

Getting automatic "I'm on vacation" repliers, especially if you're on an e-mail mailing list.

---

## WHAT ABOUT PERSONAL E-MAIL?

**I won't be checking my e-mail when I go on vacation. Should I do something to tell people who write me?**

Some e-mail programs let you send automatic "gone fishin'" messages to anyone who writes while you're away. But broadcasting your absence isn't especially prudent—and some correspondents might find the robotic responses annoying. A better plan: Warn frequent e-mail pals before you leave (go ahead, make 'em jealous); others can hold their horses till you're back.

> **Survey Says**
> *37 percent of online Americans check their e-mail when traveling for business. 32 percent check in while on vacation.*
>
> Source: *The America Online/Roper Starch Worldwide Adult Cyberstudy 2000*

The downside of vacations, of course, is that you have to come back—often to an in-box overflowing with e-mail. One good strategy is always to read and answer the most recent messages first. That way at least you're being prompt about returning some of them—and you won't fly into a panic about an outdated message only to find a more recent one reading "Crisis Averted!"

# 7

# E-Mail Etiquette with Friends and Family

- *Is it proper to send a thank-you note via e-mail? A holiday card? Party invitations? Wedding invitations?*

- *How should I handle an Internet fight with a friend?*

- *What's the polite way to get a relative to quit his bad e-mail etiquette habits?*

From the "Internet Manners" mailbox:

Dear Miss Wise-Beyond-Her-Years e-mail manners expert,

You may dismiss this as old-fashioned, but I have an e-mail peeve. I've gotten over the formality of "Dear so-and-so" and adopted a more casual Internet style (such as "Hi Alice"), but their notes to me rarely include a salutation or a closing. I understand the theory that this is supposed to be a minimal-effort type of communication, and that I can recognize the author by the e-mail address that accompanies each correspondence. Nevertheless, I feel a teensy twinge of discomfort when I read mail from my daughters that jumps

right into the news without even a per-
functory greeting ("Ma" or "Mama" would
suffice). Am I just a hopeless old fuddy-
duddy, or do I have a legitimate peeve?

Most respectfully and quite sincerely (and,
in your case, lovingly),

Mama

P.S. Does this get me into your book? Huh?
Huh?


Dear Ma,

Yes. For an answer to your question, see
p. 133.

Love,
Sam


Start a national advice column, print an address to send questions to, and, soon enough, your friends and relatives will realize
they've gained an official forum to lodge complaints about your
conduct. I opened the "Internet Manners" e-mailbox one day to
find a thinly disguised e-nudge from my sister, grousing about
how people—meaning me—should change the subject lines of
their e-mail messages more often. A longtime friend of mine
wrote: "Is there etiquette for dropping pronouns in e-mails? Often
people say things like 'Sold soul to devil today. Got whole doughnut in return. Realize now should have at least asked for glazed.'
[Yes, she's a *Simpsons* fanatic.] You wouldn't write that to someone you wanted to impress, unless you wanted to be offhand and
cute." I knew the culprit she had in mind: me. I used to dash off
many such diary-style messages, thinking they were, well, offhand
and cute, but in a *good* way. Not anymore.

For many of us, e-mail has been a tremendous boon to our

relationships with friends and family members. By making communication so convenient, e-mail has encouraged us to both deepen and broaden our social ties. I think of the college classmates whom, several years after graduation, I e-mail a few times a week and still consider among my best friends, even though I rarely phone them and see the furthest-flung ones once a year at best. I think of friends who have made new connections with their parents or siblings, exchanging e-mail about topics—from personal relationships to favorite novels—they had once been too reticent or rushed to explore. I think of wired grannies who swap jokes with their grandchildren, of new parents who zap pictures of Junior to friends around the world before the li'l nipper is an hour old, of people who happened across a Web site where they could search for others' e-mail addresses, said "What the heck?", and wound up renewing friendships with high-school buddies, long-lost pals, or long-ago sweethearts.

But when it comes to e-mail in relationships, it's easy to confuse quality with quantity. Forwarding jokes and mass-mailing tidbits of personal news might make you feel more connected to friends and family, but it doesn't exactly qualify as meaningful communication. E-mail is also fertile territory for misunderstandings and arguments—and even seemingly minor e-etiquette infractions can, over time, take a toll on friendships.

So e-mail etiquette with friends and family spans a range of issues, from respecting others' feelings, time, and privacy to understanding how to nurture a real friendship amid all the e-frivolity. Minding your e-manners also means understanding the social circumstances when e-mail is appropriate and when another mode of communication would be more considerate or more effective.

### Survey Says

*44 percent of wired Americans say they're more in touch with their siblings because they are online. 23 percent say they're more in touch with their parents, 12 percent with their grandparents.*

*Source: The America Online/Roper Starch Worldwide Adult Cyberstudy 2000*

## WHEN E-MAIL IS APPROPRIATE—AND WHEN IT'S A NO-NO

E-mail may be convenient, but it's not appropriate in every situation. Sometimes traditional etiquette calls for handwritten notes, and e-mail—even in this casual-Friday society—is simply too informal. Sometimes you want to convey something delicate or emotionally loaded, and e-mail can't take the place of a telephone call or face-to-face conversation. In some situations, e-mail is inappropriate because it's *less* convenient.

Different families and groups of friends, of course, have different e-mail cultures—and therefore will have different standards about the situations in which e-mail is appropriate. At many colleges and techie enclaves like Silicon Valley, *everything* happens over e-mail. E-mailing someone to ask for a date? Sure. E-mail wedding invitations? Few eyes would blink in Palo Alto, but just don't try it on Park Avenue.

### To E or Not to E? Questions to Ask in Any Situation

- Does this message have too much emotional nuance for e-mail? For those not averse to exclamation points, e-mail can convey basic happiness or excitement ("Congratulations!!!"). But trying to communicate any more complex emotion—sadness, sympathy, anger, apology, sarcasm—can be difficult. Consider a phone call or face-to-face conversation instead. And e-mail is definitely not the medium for criticism, however constructive. It's likely to get taken the wrong way, and you won't be there to smooth over the problem.

- Will sending this via e-mail make the recipient's life easier or more difficult? If you're sending a message to ask a question or arrange something, like a visit, will it be easy for your friend to craft a short, simple response? Or is it the sort of complicated conversation that would be easier to handle by phone or in person?

- Does the recipient check his e-mail often enough to get the message in time? There's little use zapping a "Wanna come to a movie tonight?" note to someone who checks her e-mail just a few times a week—and she may feel hurt when she discovers the message too late.

- Before sending an invitation via e-mail, think: Is this a once (or a few times) in a lifetime event, like a wedding, a new baby, or a college graduation? Even if you're not a traditionalist, you and your recipients might want that engraved invitation or handwritten thank-you note as a keepsake. A printout just wouldn't be the same.

- Would it spell trouble if someone other than the intended recipient saw this message? While work e-mail may be monitored by employers, it's illegal for anyone to intercept personal e-mail (assuming you're not using your work address for personal mail, an unwise idea). That doesn't mean your message is guaranteed privacy. Someone who shares your or your recipient's computer could see it, accidentally or on purpose. A blunder could send your message to the wrong address, or the recipient could forward it. A legal proceeding could force you, your recipient, or your Internet service providers to turn over messages, unearthing even deleted e-mail. Weigh the risks carefully before you use e-mail in particularly sensitive situations. You might want to switch to the phone—or, better yet, take a cue from *Sex and the City* and dish over brunch.

**Survey Says**
*Three-quarters of online Americans expect more people to know their e-mail address than their phone number in the future.*

*Source: The America Online/Roper Starch*
*Worldwide Adult Cyberstudy 2000*

## RED LIGHT, GREEN LIGHT: SOCIAL E-MAIL

Green light: E-mail is perfectly polite.

Yellow light: E-mail may or may not be appropriate.

Red light: E-mail is not appropriate.

## Thank-You Notes

*Thank-yous to close friends and for small favors: green light.*
Thanking a pal for the birthday gag gift, a party invitation, or a
contribution to the school bake sale are all fine via e-mail. Since
most of us wouldn't ordinarily write a thank-you in such situations, e-mail ought to be a pleasant surprise.

*Thank-yous for not-so-small gifts or not-so-close friends: yellow
light.* Your co-worker let you use his beach house for the weekend? Your boyfriend's mother knit you a sweater for Christmas? It's
probably time for a handwritten thank-you note.

*Thank-yous to relatives: yellow light.* It all depends on how formal—and how wired—your family is. When in doubt, especially
with older relatives more likely to be traditionalists, go for the
handwritten note.

**Can I use e-mail to send thank-you notes for my holiday loot?**

Nice try, lazybones. You think a few electrons can repay
Grandma for battling the shopping-mall hordes (never mind those
Amazon.com boxes in her trash)? Pick up a pen—retro is trendy!
E-mail is okay for informal notes to pals and in geek enclaves like
Silicon Valley, where folks e-mail wedding invitations (!). But
when in doubt, write it out.

*Thank-yous for wedding gifts: red light.*

**Is it acceptable to e-mail thank-you notes for wedding presents?**

Prepare for finger cramps: Brides might wear bikinis these
days, but handwriting thank-yous is one tradition that still has
teeth. And hey, all you doctors and cyberbabies who had computer mice instead of rattles in your cribs: That means legible
handwriting.

## Invitations

*Not-exceedingly-formal parties: green light.* This goes for your dinner parties, cocktail parties or brunches, adults' birthday parties,
Halloween parties, keggers, pajama parties, Tupperware parties,

raves—as long as you know all your prospective guests have e-mail and check it regularly, e-mail is a convenient way to handle invitations. You can even include handy links to Web sites with driving directions and maps. (Some great party-invitation Web sites, like Evite.com and invites.yahoo.com, let you send e-mail invites, track RSVPs, and provide details and directions on the Web.)

If only some of your invitees have e-mail, however, don't send printed invitations to some and not to others. If only a few don't have e-mail, give them a phone call—or send printed invites to everyone, so your unwired guests don't feel like second-class citizens.

*Formal parties: red light.* If you're hosting a benefit bash for 300 in your Fifth Avenue penthouse, throw a stationer some business.

*Kids' birthday parties: red light.* Birthday bashes are far from formal, but kids get a kick (and a lesson in social correspondence) out of sending and receiving invitations. Plus, a mailed invitation is less likely to be overlooked by a harried mom or dad.

*Wedding invitations: red light.* Reports trickle in of a small but growing number of couples—mostly Silicon Valley dot-com types—sending their wedding invitations via e-mail. Etiquette isn't ready to say "I do" to this trend. If your nuptials are anything more formal than a quick sprint to city hall, spring for paper-and-ink invitations.

Weddings, more than any other event, are all about tradition: "I do"s, rings, taste-impaired bridesmaids' dresses. (Even "nontraditional" barefoot-on-the-beach or skydiving weddings are lousy with tradition—if you think of yourself as truly revolutionary, why not just shack up and skip the vows?)

Wedding traditions, of course, now come à la carte—most couples feel free to pick and choose which items from the menu to keep and which to dump (like that "love, honor, and *obey*" business). But ditching paper invitations? They offend no one. (Well, maybe environmentalists, but there's always recycled paper.) They're not nearly as expensive as other wedding luxuries. They provide a lovely keepsake for guests. They set the dress code—and help suggest the entire tone—for the event. (Send invitations via e-mail and beware of guests showing up meeting-ready in khakis and holstered Palm Pilots.)

Another problem with e-invitations is that every guest should get the same type of invitation. Sending beautiful paper invitations to your relatives and e-vites to your friends is an unacceptable double standard.

So if you're trying to make a statement—"How groovy and high-tech we are!"—make it some other time. You could always register for wedding gifts on the Web. (Just don't send your thank-you notes by e-mail.) Heck, write something into your vows about staying on each other's Buddy Lists until death do you part.

Or here's an option for true technophiles: Send e-invitations in addition to paper ones. Evite.com or many wedding-planning Web sites will help you create bulletins that link guests to helpful information like maps—or remind laggards to RSVP.

## Embarrassing E-Moment

"I went to a wedding where the bride and groom had sent out computer invitations. They hadn't been very clear about what to wear, and it seems like half the guests had taken the e-vites as an excuse to dress very casually. (Or maybe they were just tech people.) Anyway, the groom was in white tie and tails."

### Survey Says
*Evite.com estimates that 5 percent of the 4 million greetings sent through the site are wedding invitations.*

*Baby showers: yellow light.* These invitations are usually printed and snail-mailed by the host, but if the mom-to-be's circle of friends is highly wired, a baby step away from tradition ought to be just fine.

*Bar and bat mitzvahs: red light.* For a big blast, go with printed invitations (also less likely to get lost by the celebrant's pals). If you're inviting only family and a few friends, the phone is more personal.

*Baptisms and confirmations: red light.* These rites are usually small family affairs, so the phone works best.

*Graduations: yellow light.* For the event itself, the high school or college usually provides painfully rationed tickets for you to mail or give to invitees. Some people also send graduation announcements to those they can't squeeze into the ceremony; since these are strictly a formality, stay formal and send them by mail. If you're hosting a reception afterward, how formal to make the invitations—snail mail, e-mail or phone—is up to you and your family's general level of formality.

### Other Special Occasions

*Birth announcements: yellow light.*

**My husband and I just found out we're having a baby. I've kept up with many of my old college friends solely via e-mail. Can I send them e-mail announcements of the upcoming birth?**

If you're planning to mail out paper announcements, as is traditional, to lower-tech friends and relations, better print enough for all—you wouldn't want anyone feeling like a second-class citizen. But you can send an informal e-mail news flash after Junior's arrival if you feel up to it. (If you like cutesy cartoons of storks, sites such as greetings.yahoo.com offer e-mailable announcement cards.) Really goo-goo gaga for the Net? Attach a digital photo of the new baby.

*Sympathy notes after a death: red light.* Of all occasions, this is the one where the personal, handwritten touch means the most to the recipient. It's not as important to send such a note immediately as it is to take the time to craft a meaningful one.

---

### Net Peeve  : (

When relatives e-mail you to tell you that someone in the family has died.

---

*Death announcements: Red light.* E-mail is not an appropriate way to notify family members or close friends that someone has died. The emotionless nature of e-mail means the news will arrive with an extra shock—or, to some recipients, a note of callousness. And it's far better to hear this sort of news from a familiar voice, someone you can talk to for at least a few moments—not in the isolation of e-mail.

E-mail can be appropriate, however, in notifying the larger community of a death—the deceased person's colleagues, for example. A family member should ask someone the dead person was close to to spread sad news and, if appropriate, information about funeral arrangements.

**Someone recently e-mailed me the news that a member of my family had died. I felt it was a cold, rude way to inform anyone of this kind of news. What are your thoughts?**

You're absolutely right. Of all the situations in which e-mail is inappropriate, this one may take the cake.

A subsequent message from the "Internet Manners" mailbag:

I have to disagree with your response. My mother passed away on August 8 of this year after a six-month battle with cancer. I used my e-mail to inform a lot of people quickly that this had happened. They all knew she was terminally ill, but many of the people I e-mailed I would not have gotten a chance to call until after the funeral. I got many positive comments from people that received my e-mail who were glad they were able to hear the news right away and make arrangements to attend the funeral. I am an only child and at this devastating time, there were a lot of other things to arrange without having to worry about calling dozens of people.

The writer is right: She shouldn't have had to worry about calling dozens of people. One way to avoid that painful situation would be to ask a few close friends to make the calls for her—or to enlist the first people who replied "I'm so sorry. What can I do to help?"

> ### Survey Says
> *78 percent of Americans say they think sending a card for a special occasion via e-mail is just fine. 76 percent approve of sending party invitations via e-mail, and 74 percent gave their blessing to e-mail thank-you notes. But 63 percent feel that sending condolences via e-mail is inappropriate.*
>
> *Source: Nov. 2000 E-Etiquette National Survey, sponsored by 1-800-FLOWERS.COM and Luntz Research*

## IMHO (In My Humble Opinion): E-Greetings: When You Care Enough to Send the Very Least

What accounts for the massive popularity of e-mail greeting cards? It sure can't be the abundance of witty, artful designs. I've been to the sites. Online greetings are all about the three T's: treacly, tacky, and tasteless. And the graphics? Most of 'em make your local Hallmark store look like the Rembrandt room in the Metropolitan Museum of Art.

Okay, I should lighten up a little. If you look hard, there are acceptable e-cards out there. (Avoid any sporting original poetry, however, if you value the contents of your stomach.) And some of the tasteless-on-purpose offerings could indeed give you a giggle if they caught you in the right mood. Of course, most e-cards share one incredibly compelling characteristic: They're free.

But are they proper etiquette? It depends. When sent for no special occasion—or for the silly holidays like International Flirting Week and Love Your Pet Day some sites like to tout—e-cards can brighten a recipient's day and give a sender an easy way to say "I'm thinking of you." (An effort- and expenditure-free way to show affection—hmm, no wonder a reported 40 percent of e-cards, a far higher percentage than for real-world cards, are sent by men.) But on occasions when you would normally give a real card or gift, e-cards don't cut the mustard. Contrary to cliché, when it comes to cards and gifts, it's not the thought that counts—it's the time. Schlepping to the drugstore, picking out a card, slapping a stamp on it, and mailing it are a grand pain in the rear—but it all proves you're willing to go out of your way to show you're thinking of someone. Even if you took hours to scour Web sites for the perfect e-card and craft a message, the recipient probably perceives it as a minimal-effort gesture. And a scribbled signature written in your own hand, with your own pen, conveys more of a personal connection than electrons ever could.

So here are some bottom-line e-card do's and don'ts:

DO: Send e-cards for fun—to spice up regular e-mail or to give someone a smile on no special occasion.

DON'T: Use e-cards on occasions when you would normally do something more personal, like send a real card or gift, or make a phone call or a visit. They're an inferior substitute. But if you wouldn't normally send someone a birthday card, or don't usually send out Christmas cards, electronic versions might be a nice gesture.

DON'T: Use e-cards to express sympathy. When someone has lost a family member, it's the personal touch that lends comfort.

DON'T: Send an e-card on a high-pressure romantic occasion, like Valentine's Day or an anniversary. It'll say, "Honey, I forgot about it until today."

DON'T: Use e-cards in professional situations, like sending a thank-you note to a job interviewer. You'll come off as frivolous, and most e-card designs don't exactly project a professional image. Send a regular e-mail, or a letter or gift for more formal occasions. As for sending friendly e-cards to co-workers, it depends on your office culture. Steer clear of raunchier e-cards, which may run afoul of company rules.

DO: Be careful when sending an e-card to someone at work—or anytime you open one in public. You don't want an audience when you click open the card to see a photo of antler-bashing antelopes with a caption reading "Feeling kinda horny?"—or to hear an audio track of Marvin Gaye's "Let's Get It On."

## *Where to Find E-Greetings: Popular Sites*

AmericanGreetings.com

BlueMountain.com

Egreetings.com

Yahoo! Greetings: greetings.yahoo.com

> **Survey Says**
> *32 percent of Internet users sent e-greeting cards for the winter holidays in 2000, while only 24 percent actually bought gifts online.*
>
> *Source: Pew Internet and American Life Project survey*

**Many** of my friends want me to send them postcards when I go abroad this summer. How about if I just send each of them an e-mail from the road?

Remember, an e-mail message sent from that groovy cybercafé in Izmir looks just like one sent from your living room back home. Send all the e-mail you want to update your friends, but don't be a peseta-pincher. Spring for one postcard per pal.

## E-MAIL E-XASPERATION

Knowing when e-mail is apropos—and when to just say no—is one aspect of proper e-mail etiquette with friends and family. But as every Netizen knows, and the pleas and peeves that pile up in my "Internet Manners" mailbox illustrate vividly, e-mail relationships can lead to a staggering array of sticky situations. E-mailers confront issues ranging from handling e-mail spats to dealing with incorrigible Netiquette offenders who happen to share your genetic material. Here's a look at some of personal e-mail's prime pitfalls—and proper ways to patch up problems.

## Generation Gaps

Eight-year-olds e-mail eighty-year-olds, parents e-mail their children, Net newbies e-mail wired-since-birth Webheads—as entire families forge paths onto the Net, their members often have to learn to bridge generation gaps in their approaches to e-mail. There are differences in style: Terse, abbreviation-riddled messages can raise eyebrows among those who think of e-mail as a formal letter. There are differences in habits: Twentysomething techies might be wired around the clock while their parents check their e-mail once a week. And there are differences in interests: A grade-schooler's forwarded knock-knock jokes are likely to please only the most indulgent grandparent.

The proper way to handle generation gaps? Learn to live with them. Tolerate stylistic differences. Respect differences in e-mail habits—don't send infrequent e-mailers urgent messages then complain that they don't check their e-mail often enough. And remember that family members aren't necessarily interested in topics just because you're interested in them.

Some families go so far as to create e-mail mailing lists for members so any message sent to the list reaches every other subscriber. If you do this, be sure to establish a set of ground rules—whether to allow forwarded jokes, for example—and pick one particularly patient person to arbitrate any problems.

**When I begin an e-mail with a greeting such as "Dear Daughter" and conclude it with a closing like "Love, Dad," isn't it good manners for my children to respond using a greeting? They just launch into a message and frequently sign it "me." They tell me I don't understand computer protocol.**

You're not in cahoots with my mom, are you? She zings me with the same gripe. It's a generation-gap thing: You probably think of e-mail as akin to a letter, while your kids see it as a speedy, informal way to stay in touch. Both styles are perfectly polite—so don't try to persuade each other to change. Just move on to the next argument.

## Net Peeve : (

I Internet-enabled my father, and it's been a blessing and a curse.
Most of the e-mails he sends me are forwards from a mailing list
for seniors—stuff I really don't care about.

## Net Peeve : (

At least twice a month my mother forwards me lists with vary-
ing titles on the theme of Top Ten Ways to Improve Your Life.
The latest was Top Ten Ways to Fight Perfectionism. Funny, for
the first time in my life, at age thirty-three, my mother is calling
me a perfectionist. I don't know where she gets this stuff.

**Survey Says**
*71 percent of online Americans prefer the phone over
e-mail or snail mail for communicating with family
members. 57 percent prefer to phone friends—but
among people who have been online for more than
three years, the majority prefer e-mail.*

*Source: The America Online/Roper Starch
Worldwide Adult Cyberstudy 2000*

*Let's Get Personal*

## Net Peeve : (

Last week I spent a good twenty minutes or so writing a nice,
personal e-mail to a friend. I got a reply today, but not only did

it not answer any of my questions, it was a generic "here's what I'm doing in my life now" e-mail sent to about ten different people. If I'm going to spend time writing something nice and personal, I expect something personal to be written to me, not to everyone and their mother.

---

Remember those letters people used to send out at Christmas, updating friends and relatives—if recipients could make out the smudgy mimeograph—on the past year's family highlights, from Hawaiian vacations to Little League triumphs? Well, now that mass mailing is as simple as a few mouse clicks, such missives aren't just for Christmas anymore—and not everyone is merry about it. Mass e-mailings to family and friends have their perfectly polite uses, such as spreading urgent news ("It's a girl!") and passing along interesting tidbits, assuming that recipients find them as fascinating as you do. Problems arise, however, when an e-mail relationship deteriorates into only such impersonal messages—or when personal notes are met with impersonal replies.

Family and friends expect, and deserve, to receive the occasional message written just for them. Adding a personal touch to e-mail doesn't have to be a burden: A short note above a forwarded joke can make all the difference to a recipient. Or instead of mass-mailing a "here's what's up in my life" letter to several people, you can recycle a few passages—the account of your trip to the Paul Simon concert, the update on your wedding plans— while tailoring other sections to the recipient. One hard-and-fast etiquette rule: A personal note deserves a personal reply.

**My niece sends e-mails about her job, classes, boyfriend, etc., to about eleven friends and relatives at a time. Are we expected to reply if she hasn't e-mailed us personally?**

You're not obligated to respond every time to a mass-mailed Me Newsletter. But do reply occasionally—unless you want your subscription canceled.

**Survey Says**

*41 percent of online Americans say getting on the Net has allowed them to find or reconnect with people they had lost touch with—people they had not been in contact with for an average of twelve years.*

Source: *The America Online/Roper Starch*
*Worldwide Adult Cyberstudy 2000*

## Can I Get a Little Privacy Here?

"Whatcha reading?" "Who are you mailing?" "What's so funny?" It's those kinds of questions that make many of us shudder at the thought of checking our e-mail with other people in the room. Most of us feel our e-mail is, or at least should be, as private as a diary. Yet some e-mailers blithely forward the most personal of messages ("So, do you think this means he really likes me?") and even share account passwords with friends.

Respecting privacy is an important part of e-mail etiquette. Even if you don't mind sharing a message with others, the person who sent it to you has a right to expect privacy too. E-mailers should never reveal their account passwords—and shouldn't share an e-mail account with anyone else. (It's not even a good idea to share an address with a spouse.) Snooping around in someone else's e-mail or pestering him or her for access to it are also no-nos—as is showing or forwarding an e-mail message to anyone else without the sender's permission.

**My best friend reads my e-mail all the time. It bothers him if he is not allowed to read it. Wouldn't you classify it as a diary? How can I ask him to stop without hurting his feelings?**

Some unkind phrases come to mind—like "Butt out!" You should use more polite language, but be firm. His nosiness is an unacceptable intrusion on your privacy and on the privacy of the people who e-mail you. (Which makes it, in a way, even worse than diary-snooping.) And never share your password—if you already did, change it.

Some companies automatically attach messages to the bottom of employees' e-mail saying the e-mail is "private" or "confidential." What if it's just a personal note? Can I get in trouble if I pass it on?

These legalese postscripts look pretty silly following a forwarded joke or news about a pal's new baby. Feel free to use your common sense: If the e-mail obviously isn't business-related, don't worry about letting your friends in on it. By the way, such postscripts don't carry much legal weight—a real confidentiality agreement would require you to swear secrecy in advance. But be careful anyway.

Is it really rude to shoo other people out of the room when I check my e-mail? I like privacy.

Not only do you ignore your guests (or roommates or siblings) in favor of virtual socializing, you want to give them the boot, to boot? Yes, that's rude. If you absolutely can't live without a quick e-mail fix, try buying a privacy screen (anyone sneaking a sidelong peek won't see anything). Or just ask bystanders not to look—and don't tempt them by giggling or groaning.

Is it rude to ask if I can check my e-mail on the computers of people I'm visiting?

Go ahead, but don't get mad if they say no. Like owners of stick-shift cars, some tech-heads don't want to risk allowing others into the driver's seat. If you get an okay, leave everything the way you found it, and no snooping.

> **Survey Says**
> *25 percent of Internet users say they have felt ignored because another household member spends too much time online. 37 percent have felt ignored because another household member watches too much TV.*
>
> *Source: The UCLA Internet Report: "Surveying the Digital Future" UCLA Center for Communication Policy*

### Them's Fightin' Words

Ever get ticked off at a friend, send her a crabby e-mail, then wake up the next morning wishing you could crawl into your computer, get beamed across cyberspace, and take the message back? E-mail is a particularly fertile medium for sprouting spats. It's easy to misunderstand the meaning or tone of an e-mail message: Sarcasm can be mistaken for anger, a brief message can be taken as brusque. And when you really are angry at someone, e-mail can escalate the fight—it can be tempting to tell someone things via e-mail you would never say to her face.

One key to keeping the peace: Never send an e-mail message when you're angry. If you're tempted to tee off on someone, wait twelve hours—you'll likely cool down by then. Or type up the nastygram you feel like sending, then delete it. It's also important to avoid misunderstandings: When you read messages over before you send them, keep an eye out for any ambiguities. And don't be afraid to use an emoticon or parenthetical aside like "<grin>" or "(just kidding)" to avoid rubbing a reader the wrong way.

If you do get tangled in an e-mail squabble with a friend or relative, it's usually best to untangle it on the phone or in person. For the same reasons e-mail is prone to sparking arguments, it's a poor way to solve them. A proper apology requires more emotional nuance than e-mail can handle.

**How do you handle an Internet fight with a friend or loved one? Sometimes when I'm chatting arguments arise, but I don't see people I talk to online as often as other friends.**

It's easy to get snippy when conversing in rapid-fire snippets. Simmer down, then craft an e-mail extending the olive branch and apologizing for any harmful words. If the tiff got really nasty, phone.

**I got into an argument with a friend over something minor. He wrote me an e-mail telling me all the things he couldn't stand about me. I replied and told him all the things I couldn't stand about him. We started seeing each other again and never mentioned the e-mail**

exchange. Then we argued again and he wrote me another nasty e-mail. Since then, we've spoken only about superficial matters. I miss our friendship and would like to put all the bad stuff behind us. Should I send him an e-mail?

This "friend" turns into a venom-spewing Mr. Hyde when the chips are down and hides behind his keyboard to do it—and you want him back in your life? E-mail isn't some parallel universe you can wall off from the real world. Nor is it a good medium for settling spats. To have any chance at a healthy friendship, you two need to have a face-to-face talk—and do some face-to-face apologizing.

**Survey Says**

*If you were stranded on a desert island, would you rather have a telephone, a television, or a computer connected to the Internet? 69 percent of online Americans picked the computer.*

*Source: The America Online/Roper Starch*
*Worldwide Adult Cyberstudy 2000*

## Rudeness Shouldn't Beget Rudeness

A pal e-mails you chain letters when you've asked her to stop. Your mom forgets to enter subject lines for her messages. Your aunt insists on typing e-mail messages in all capital letters. You want to set them straight, but you don't want to hurt their feelings. What should you do when others violate e-mail etiquette rules?

One polite solution—and sometimes the best one—is simply to ignore the problem. After all, pointing out others' etiquette mistakes is often poor etiquette in itself. It's certainly bad manners to call attention to others' faux pas just so you can feel superior to them, and doing so using a snobby or indignant tone is extremely rude—not to mention a good way to spark a nasty war of words.

However, when others' e-mail etiquette mistakes truly inconvenience you—or when they could pose a risk for the sender or other addressees—you may legitimately attempt to set the offenders straight. Spell out the problem gently but clearly, via e-mail or in person. Explain why it poses an inconvenience or risk. Don't let the tone of your message suggest that you attribute their mistake to stupidity or spite. Say "please" and "thank you"—and say something nice to cushion the request: "I love hearing from you, but I'm afraid I have little interest in these political messages you forward to me. Please leave me off your list."

**How can I politely request a friend use spell-check when e-mailing me? His e-mails have so many errors they can be hard to read.**

While sending error-riddled e-mail is stinky etiquette, offenders can get huffy about complaints that smack of superiority. Don't impugn his manners or education, just explain: "I know you're busy, but spell-check makes e-mail easier to read."

What to do if an offender proves incorrigible—even after you've asked him to change his habits? Now there's a sticky e-mail etiquette situation. You have three basic choices: If the friendship means more to you than the flaw, you can ignore the problem. If you're not so sure anymore, you can stop exchanging e-mail with the friend. (You don't have to end the friendship, just rewind it to the pre-Internet era of phones, letters, and after-work drinks.) Or in some cases you can find a solution in technology: Use your e-mail program's filters to block out unwanted types of messages, for example, or get a personal e-mail account so chain letters don't waste your time at work.

---

### Net Peeve :(

People who get pissy and rude when you break their own personal e-mail etiquette rules.

---

**A friend forwards e-mail to me all the time. Sure, I'm concerned about the well-being of women in Afghanistan and of course I'd**

love to get a check for $4,000, but I don't appreciate these modern chain letters. I've let my friend know how I feel about this on numerous occasions, and her refusal to stop is starting to affect our friendship. I don't think she respects me enough to pay attention. Should I go so far as to cut off all contact with her?

Issue one last plea—a face-to-face ultimatum might stand the best chance of penetrating her thick skull. (Perhaps she simply forgot to delete your address from a group mailing list.) If she persists, try returning every unwanted tidbit to her with a cease-and-desist note. Or set up your e-mail program to block her messages. Whether to preserve your real-world relationship is up to you— some people just shouldn't be allowed near a computer keyboard.

## IMHO (In My Humble Opinion): Why Spelling Counts

A while ago I found myself browsing the personals ads on a Web singles site. (One of the great things about my job is that this kind of activity qualifies as research.) As I read postings from guy after guy waxing poetic about his favorite movies, his predilection for Mozart or mountain biking, and his ardor for long walks on the beach and/or rain (either better than long walks on the golf course, I guess), I noticed that every one had something in common: atrocious spelling. And god-awful grammar, too. No matter how appealing the online singletons sounded otherwise, a certain part of my brain couldn't envision spending the rest of my life with someone who didn't have a grip on the difference between "its" and "it's."

Of course, being a writer and proud second-place finisher in my fourth-grade spelling bee, I'm more sensitive to language than many people. (And, some would hasten to point out, still single.) But I'm not alone in believing that good e-mail etiquette requires proper spelling and grammar.

A sizable faction of e-mailers disagrees. The point of e-mail is to communicate as quickly and efficiently as possible, say these people. Who cares if an e-mail is riddled with mistakes, as long as it gets the idea across? They don't have time to make their e-mails pretty, they complain. "I'm too busy to capitalize!" whines one friend who likes to send her typo-filled messages e. e. cummings–style.

There are two problems with this approach. One is that whether you like it or not, recipients judge you by your language. With e-mail, you can't tell what someone looks like or hear his voice. But you can examine his words, so even a few errors can dramatically affect a user's credibility. Spelling and grammatical sloppiness may make you seem uneducated, lazy, or both—and lead recipients to take you less seriously.

The other problem: Even when you're e-mailing people who know you well, sloppy spelling and grammar make messages hard to read—and that's rude. These rules weren't invented to torment schoolkids. They're in place to keep writing clear. Every second it takes your co-workers or friends to stumble over a garbled word or search for the beginning of an uncapitalized run-on sentence is a second you should have used to clean up the message in the first place.

Don't worry: Your e-mail doesn't have to be perfect. No one will (or no one *should,* anyway) fault you for the occasional honest typo. You don't have to live in fear of dangling participles or even use "whom" with 100 percent accuracy. Just make an effort to be considerate of recipients: Read your messages over before you send them. Use your e-mail program's spell-checker if you're an incorrigibly bad speller. Learn where apostrophes and commas go. Readers will thank you.

As for me, I'll continue to hold out for Mr. Right—not Mr. Rite. But if you find out that Russell Crowe can't spell, please don't tell me.

### Survey Says
*49 percent of Americans say it's "extremely" or "very" important to use proper grammar and capitalization in personal e-mail.*

*Source: Nov. 2000 E-Etiquette National Survey, sponsored by 1-800-FLOWERS.COM and Luntz Research*

# 8

# E-Mail Etiquette with Dates and Mates

- *Is it okay to ask for a first date via e-mail? To break up via e-mail?*

- *What's the proper way to take an online relationship into real life?*

- *Is cybersex really cheating?*

---

**Embarrassing E-Moment**

"I went to send my fiancé an e-mail saying 'Thanks for the quickie.' Except I hit the wrong address and sent it to my mother instead."

---

A few years ago, I wrote a story for *People* about married couples who had met on the Net. Some of the people we interviewed had gone online looking for love and found it in the expected places, like online personals sites and singles chat rooms. But the most intriguing pairs were the ones who had gone online without intending to meet a mate. One couple, a conservative foreign-policy analyst and a Democratic district attorney, fell in love on an e-mail mailing list dedicated to discussing the O. J. Simpson trial. Another met in a chat room devoted to their shared passion: pet potbellied pigs. He had three, she had one. After they wed, they opened an animal sanctuary to care for hundreds of abandoned pet porkers.

Those who look for—or luck into—love on the Net face a series of tricky situations when they try to move an online romance into the real world. Who should make the first phone call? How do you let someone down easy if the in-person chemistry fizzles? Good manners have to balance with proper prudence, and real-world dating etiquette doesn't always apply.

But you don't have to meet online for e-mail to play a big role in your relationship. Today, e-mail serves as a low-pressure incubator for many romances: At meeting spots like bars or parties, prospects often leave with an e-mail address, not a phone number, and couples often exchange dozens of e-mail messages before even venturing out on an official first date. Steadies and spouses put e-mail to work too, spicing up the workday (or any day) with notes that say "thinking of you," or something more steamy. Just beware of sorry-wrong-address snafus.

## MAKING A LOVE CONNECTION

For those who feel more like shy Cyranos than suave Valentinos when it comes to pitching woo, the Net might seem like the niftiest invention since the sonnet. There's nothing impolite about turning to e-mail in the awkward initial stages of a relationship. Many people feel less vulnerable giving out an e-mail address instead of a phone number. Some are grateful to have a guaranteed-stammer-free medium to carry out those first few nerve-jangling "Would you like to go out sometime?" conversations. Others like to let a romance sparked offline build over the Net. Exploring a potential partner's personality and interests before deciding whether to take the relationship to the next level.

### Can I ask for a first date via e-mail?

A casual "Met you last night, wanna have dinner?" note is a fine way for the tongue-tied to break the ice, though it doesn't exactly signal a hunk of burnin' love, so hope your fun e-Valentine digs shy types. One tip: spell-check.

A few etiquette tips for using the Net to nurture a real-world relationship:

- Don't leave someone hanging. If you've lost interest in some-one—or were never really interested in the first place—don't just let his or her e-mails go unanswered. Don't string him or her along, either. Make your position clear: "I'm flattered, but sorry, I'm not interested." "No thanks." "I'm seeing someone else."

- Take it slow. Once an e-mail exchange gets steamy, it's hard to dial back on the intimacy. If you're building a real-world relationship at the same time, getting carried away while cyber-flirting could lead to some face-to-face awkwardness.

- Remember that e-mail can sometimes be about as private as a postcard. E-mailing someone at work or from your own work account can be asking for trouble. And before you confess any deep, dark secrets, remember that your crush could forward or show any message to someone else—like a whole focus group of friends.

- Take the time you need to get to know someone, but don't let the relationship get stuck in e-mail purgatory. Those who turn to e-mail because of timidity can sometimes have problems working up the nerve to make a move offline, especially if both partners are shy types. But when the time is right, it's important to proceed to phone calls and real-world get-togethers, lest you miss the moment and never shift gears out of cyber-friendship.

### Is it appropriate to use e-mail to ask for a second or third date?

Better pick up the phone. Shyness is cute only for so long—after a while, your date may wonder why you're avoiding the phone. (Social phobia, or a spouse listening in on the extension?) Plus, there's that syndrome where it takes you eighteen e-mail messages to plan a dinner and movie ("What do you want to see?" "I don't know, what do you want to see?") that could have been accomplished in one two-minute phone call.

**Can I break up with my long-distance honey via e-mail?**

Dear John letters have an illustrious history, but don't use the Net to reach out and dump somebody. For one thing, your message might not end with your ex. Through the magic of forwarding, heartless e-kissoffs can morph into cyber–chain letters. Next thing you know, half the planet could be abuzz about what a skunk you are.

---

### Embarrassing E-Moment

"No e-mail is private"—or "Men are pigs?" The moral of a chain e-mail message forwarded around the world by outraged women depends on your point of view. The message's introduction claimed that a man and woman had met while out dancing. She had given him her e-mail address, and after he contacted her, she e-mailed him back with a few get-to-know-you questions, like "What's your last name?"

The man, according to the message, responded with an e-mail tirade: "You seem like a nice person," he wrote, "and I don't mean this as badly as it might sound, but I don't have time for twenty questions by email. I met five girls Saturday night, have already booked a first coffee with three of them, and meet more every time I go dancing. . . . Now, maybe you'll find someone who's so taken by a single dance with you that he's willing to negotiate by email for a chance to trek to your suburban hideout to plead his case. But you might not. And if such a person does exist, and you do happen to cross paths with him—what do you imagine a guy that desperate would have to offer?"

Recipients forwarded it along, adding angry comments like "He's sick," and "This guy should be shot." Was the message for real? A *Washington Post* reporter who investigated was unable to track down anyone who would admit to being the cad in question (the e-mail included his name). A man who shared the purported culprit's name told the *Post* he had received "hundreds" of harassing phone calls at his home. He had put a new message on his answering machine: "I buy my coffee at Safeway, I only dance in my kitchen, and I don't even have an e-mail address. But if you would still like to leave a message for me—or my wife, Deborah—please do so after the tone."

## MATCHMAKER, MATCHMAKER, MAKE ME A MATCH

### Survey Says
*24 percent of singles say they know someone who has found a romantic interest on the Net, while 5 percent of singles have tried to find romance online themselves.*

*Source: Bruskin/Goldring Research survey for FriendFinder.com*

A few years ago, telling friends that you met a significant other online would almost certainly bring you raised eyebrows—and probably some worried looks, too. Today, many people would barely bat an eyelash. Personal-ads Web sites like Love@AOL and Match.com boast hundreds of thousands of registered users and more marriages than the Moonies: Match.com claims more than 1,000 confirmed "I do"s. Online singles sites have distinct advantages over traditional newspaper and magazine personals. First, those who place online personals have room for far more detailed descriptions of themselves and the partners they're looking for, which make such postings more effective—not to mention less creepy—than those terse "SWM-seeks-SWF-for-cuddling" print ads. Online personals draw a larger audience, meaning a bigger dating pool. And e-mail provides a low-pressure, privacy-protecting means to get to know a potential partner better.

Still, using an online personal site—or pursuing a romance with any stranger you meet on the Net—is undoubtedly risky. You can't be sure whether someone is telling the truth about anything from his weight to his marital status. You don't get the important social cues you usually observe when meeting someone in person: the tone of his voice, how he dresses, how he treats others. Moreover, a person's online behavior may not necessarily reflect his real-world personality—and even if it does, online chemistry doesn't always translate to offline chemistry. So when it comes to looking for love online, one of the central etiquette principles is safety—both physical safety and emotional safety. Some rules of the road:

- Use an established personals site that provides you with an anonymous e-mail mailbox—one separate from your regular e-mail account—for receiving responses or contacting some-one.

- For the best chance of success with an ad, be specific in describing yourself and your desires. Steer clear of generic sentiments like "I love movies"—try naming your five favorite flicks (and your least favorites!). Listing particularly far-out interests, views, or accomplishments (your marathon time or 102 tattoos, perhaps) will help your ad make an impression. It's okay to be specific about requirements in a mate, but not if they come across as crass—saying you're seeking someone with a "nice butt" can be a big turnoff.

- Honesty is the best policy. It can be tempting to trim away a few years or pounds, but if you're seeking a real-life romance, you're going to have to come clean eventually, and being caught in a fib, no matter how small, can torpedo a budding relationship. (Who knows what else you might be lying about?) If you want to pretend to be someone else, there are plenty of places on the Net where living out fantasy lives is encouraged.

- Etiquette doesn't require that you respond to every initial inquiry—on larger sites, someone posting an appealing ad can get hundreds—but once you've exchanged e-mail with peo-ple, it's polite to let them know if you're no longer interested. You needn't—and shouldn't—give a specific reason, just send a short "no thanks" note so they know where they stand.

- Don't give out personal information that could be used to track down your real-life identity, like your last name, address, neighborhood, employer, or phone number, until you feel comfortable (and certainly not in the ad itself!).

- Wait for someone to respond before writing again, and give people several days to respond. Some people don't check their e-mail that often, and others need time to work up the nerve.

- Take it slow. Don't get too flirtatious, intimate, or confessional too soon—it's hard to go back to a lower level of intimacy.

- Save all your correspondence. Read over old messages occasionally, keeping an eye out for danger signs like inconsistencies in the way someone describes himself or a tendency to dodge certain questions.

- Trade photos with someone when the time is right. Most personals sites today let users post photos right in the ads. While this isn't a requirement, it increases response rates significantly. It's usually a good idea to include your own photo when responding to a photo personal. Otherwise, you should swap photos with someone at a mutually comfortable juncture in the e-mail relationship. Send a recent photo, not one from 1985. If possible, send a few candid shots, and ask for a few in return. You'll get a better idea of what the person looks like in various situations—and a whole photo album is harder to fake than just one picture.

- If everything's going well, talk on the phone several times before considering an in-person meeting. It's become something of a Net tradition for a man to give a woman his phone number first (*Fatal Attraction* notwithstanding, men are more likely to harass or stalk women than vice versa), but don't forget to block caller ID. Or use a cell phone or a public phone.

- If you decide to rendezvous in person, arrange for a brief meeting in a public place; a coffeehouse is perfect. (If you click, you can always decide then to extend the date to dinner or a movie, but keep to public places.) Take a friend and let another person know where both of you are going and when you'll be back. If you must travel to meet someone, make all your own arrangements. Get your own hotel room and rental car.

- Remember that having chemistry online doesn't necessarily mean you'll have chemistry offline. If things don't click, they don't click. Give the situation a little time to sink in—no one ever exactly matches our advance expectations—but if things are fizzling, don't pretend they're sizzling.

- If something goes wrong or you fear for your safety, don't be afraid to walk out (duck out the back door during a bathroom break if necessary). Better to be embarrassed than to be in danger. If you've been attacked or threatened, call the cops.

- Even if you hit it off and continue the relationship, stay aware of warning signs. Does the person call you only from work, hide elements of his personal life, or avoid introducing you to any of his friends? Some Web sites offer to do background checks on prospective dates or mates, although these services are both overkill and prone to omissions—remember *Who Wants to Marry a Millionaire?* groom Rick Rockwell, whose ex-girlfriend turned out to have filed a restraining order against him? If you are suspicious enough about someone to consider ordering a background check, trust your instincts.

  One do-it-yourself detective technique worth trying: Enter someone's name into a comprehensive Web search engine like Google.com. You could turn up everything from newspaper articles about the person to his résumé to his disturbing defense of Jar Jar Binks on a *Star Wars* message board.

## Looking for Love: Some Popular Online Personals Sites

FriendFinder.com

Love@AOL: love.com

Match.com

Matchmaker.com

Yahoo! Personals: personals.yahoo.com

Smaller specialty sites such as www.christiansingles.com or Blacksingles.com can also appeal to some users. But make sure any personals site you use takes steps to protect users' privacy.


**I met someone on a singles site. He sent me his photo, and I'm no longer interested. What do I do?**

First, feel guilty for being so shallow. Then, snap out of it—your e-suitor might have a way with words, but if there's no physical chemistry, it's best to call it off before anyone gets hurt. Break it to Mr. Great Personality gently but directly. Try a simple "It's been fun, but you're just not my type."


**My boyfriend and I met through a Web personals site, and we're kind of embarrassed about it. What should we do when people ask how we got together?**

You're under no obligation to tell the whole truth. (Otherwise lots of Valentines would be in trouble: Is "We ogled each other at a bar" or "We made out at a frat party" any less embarrassing?) While you needn't be so bashful—hip pals are more likely to respond "Cool! What site?" than "Ew, creepy"—you have the right to discourage prying. Try replying "Oh, through friends," in a tone that implies details are not forthcoming. Then let some insufferable couple who met in the cutest way possible commandeer the conversation.


**Is it normal to like a guy I met on the Net and have never met in person? And is it rude to talk about him all the time?**

Normal? Heck, cyber-romance is practically a national pastime. (Just don't throw caution to the wind—as your friends probably never tire of warning you, the typist of your dreams may not be all that he seems.) But while your pen pal need not remain a secret love, yammering on and on about someone your friends don't know—or any absent significant other, for that matter—is highly impolite. Keep the mooning to a minimum, or you may wind up having only virtual pals.

> **Survey Says**
> *More than 25 percent of Internet users say they have online friends they have never met in person. Twelve percent say they have befriended someone online whom they subsequently met in person.*
>
> Source: *The UCLA Internet Report: "Surveying the Digital Future" UCLA Center for Communication Policy*

## CYBERSTALKING

Cyberstalking is the dark side of online romance. While online stalkers may pick victims at random or target people who have angered them, often stalking is a reaction to a rejected advance. What exactly is cyberstalking? It can involve sending someone harassing, disturbing, or threatening e-mail or chat messages. Or it can involve using the Net to harass someone, for example, by spreading false rumors about someone online, hacking into someone's e-mail account, or posting someone's phone number with a "for a good time, call . . ." note in a sex chat room.

Should such a frightening situation happen to you, don't reply to harassing or threatening messages. Often a cyberstalker is just trying to provoke a reaction. Instead, save the messages and report them to the offender's Internet service provider: Forward them to "abuse@" the domain in the sender's e-mail address with details about the situation. (America Online members can also report abuse at keyword: Notify AOL.) Set up your e-mail or instant-message program to block future messages from the sender. If you met the person on an online dating site, you should also report the problem to the site, which can cancel the offender's account or help track him down.

If you're lucky, the above steps will thwart the stalker. But if the offender progresses to offline stalking like phone calls or letters, takes an online action that threatens your offline safety, or threatens to hurt you in real life, contact your local police. Many states have enacted anti-stalking laws, and law-enforcement authorities can work with Internet services to track down an offender's identity. Cyberangels (www.cyberangels.org) also provides volunteer assistance for victims of cyberstalking.

While cyberstalking goes well beyond bad etiquette, it's important not to get carried away when pursuing an online romance. Don't send flirtatious or sexual messages to anyone unless expressly invited, or continue e-mailing anyone who doesn't respond or tells you to stop. Don't e-mail when you're angry. Don't use an anonymous e-mail account to e-mail anyone without identifying yourself, even as a joke. And remember that "No" means "No."

## Embarrassing E-Moment

In October 2000, two candidates for district attorney in Bernalillo County, New Mexico, feuded over an e-mail love note one candidate sent to his opponent. Republican L. Skip Vernon claimed he accidentally addressed the message to his Democratic rival, Kari Brandenburg, instead of his wife. Disagreeing, Brandenburg's backers denounced the message as "inappropriate" and "sexual harassment." According to the *Albuquerque Journal,* Vernon's e-mail began, "All these songs on 99.5 seem to apply to us today. Of course most are about unrequited love." It continued: "Even if we could be together we probably wouldn't get along but I would keep you entertained and thinking. I think you would always need the variety of frequently differing others. Too bad. Might have been a fairy tale." It concluded: "Feeling guilty that I'm bothering or offending. No intent. Good bye." After much mudslinging—with Vernon and Brandenburg each accusing the other of assorted dirty tricks and cover-ups—Brandenburg handily won the election.

**Whenever I talk to guys online, all they seem to think about is sex. What can I do to stop them?**

Besides unplug your computer? Good luck. Stick to chat rooms about specific topics such as hobbies, which are less likely to be pickup scenes. (Not an adult? Get thee to a policed kids' chat room!) If a private chatter gets frisky, politely but firmly inform him you're not interested in cybersex and leave if he persists. Or go incognito: Switch to a male-sounding handle.

---

### Embarrassing E-Moment

A come-on e-mail supposedly sent by a college freshman to a female classmate turned into a cyber–chain letter when the targeted woman did more than groan at the cliché-loving Casanova's tired lines—she decided to forward them to all her friends. Of course, the guy may have deserved it: "Hey what's up dreamuffin," the forwarded message began, launching into a succession of grammatically challenged pickup lines: "I know that I am not that good in math but I know the equation of love. It equals you plus me. You complete me. You had me at hello the first time me and you met. Are you tired girl cause you have been running through my head all day." And more in the same vein. The woman's note on the forwarded message: "Hey guys . . . don't send gals e-mails like this or else serious retribution will incur, just like this guy will soon experience!!! bwahaha!!!"

---

## E-MAIL IN LOVE AND MARRIAGE

What's the place of e-mail in an established romantic relationship? For the most part, e-mail can be anything the two of you want it to be: a way to say "You're on my mind" during those long workdays apart, a means to take care of the mundane details of life ("I'll go to the grocery store; you pick up the kids from practice . . ."), even a window back to your wild and crazy days of cyberflirting. What isn't the place of e-mail in romance? It's not a medium suited to carrying out the serious emotional business of a relationship, from apologies to "state of the union" talks. And send a Valentine's or anniversary e-card at your peril—there's no clearer way to say "Honey, I forgot."

Sentiments that should not be expressed via e-mail:

- "We need to talk about us."

- "Happy Valentine's Day!"

- "Will you marry me?"

- "Happy anniversary!"

- "I'm pregnant."

- "It's over."

- "I want a divorce."

Even when there's nothing to hide about a relationship, e-mail privacy should be a concern. Remember, any message you send or receive at work could be monitored by your employer, so steer clear of any sensitive personal discussions. Remember that even messages you delete can be retrieved. And don't forget to triple-check those e-mail addresses!

---

### Embarrassing E-Moment

"I'm in college, and last Christmas vacation I got a call from the guy I was dating a couple weeks into the break asking me why I didn't reply to any of his love e-mails. When I told him I hadn't received any, he asked me what my e-mail address was. He had sent them all to someone else by mistake."

---

**Should couples read each other's e-mail?**

Even if your squeeze says it's okay, no good can come of snooping through what might include top-secret business tidbits, soul-baring chats, or the shipping confirmation for your next birth-day present. To avoid temptation, even spouses should keep their passwords secret. If you share an e-mail account, one of you use a free service like Hotmail.com. Look at it this way: You don't share a diary.

**I stumbled across some intimate e-mail sent to my significant other. I believe exchanging sexy e-mail is a form of cheating. What do you think?**

As any world leader would tell you, it depends on your defi-nition of "cheating." But while a strictly cyber affair obviously isn't as bad as the real thing, it's bad enough, even if it was "just for fun"—a frequently deployed excuse that only raises disturbing questions. And don't get roped into an argument with your s.o. about whether e-dallying really is cheating. If Snookums got steamy with someone else and has the gall to debate the techni-calities, maybe it's time for both of you to cut your losses and head to the singles chat room.

### Embarrassing E-Moment

Going down in history: Move over, Monica and Bill. Britain had the tale of Claire and Brad the Cad. After an apparent intimate encounter with a lawyer named Bradley, a young London woman named Claire e-mailed him a note compli-menting him on his performance in the sack. (Seems she enjoyed his, er, flavor.) Bradley couldn't resist forwarding her e-mail to several male friends, adding the comment, "Now that's a nice compliment from a lass, isn't it?" One of the friends forwarded it on to more people, writing, "I feel honor bound to circulate this." The message spread swiftly around the world, as readers tacked on comments like "What a top lass! Let's start a campaign to find her."

And soon enough, she was found. London papers quickly

tracked down the two click-and-tellers, running their names and photos, and dubbed the unchivalrous Bradley "Brad the Cad." One paper even interviewed Claire's parents. Brad the Cad's law firm announced that he and his co-workers were disciplined for violating the company's e-mail policy.

# 9

## E-Mail Hoaxes: There's a Sucker Logging On Every Minute

- *How can I recognize e-mail hoaxes?*

- *What's the polite thing to do if a friend sends me a message I know is a hoax?*

- *Why passing along an Internet petition is bad manners*

The $250 Cookie Recipe

Okay, everyone . . . a true story of justice in the good old U.S. of A. Thought y'all might enjoy this; if nothing else, it shows internet justice, if it can be called that.

My daughter & I had just finished a salad at Neiman-Marcus Cafe in Dallas & decided to have a small dessert. Because our family are such cookie lovers, we decided to try the "Neiman-Marcus Cookie." It was so excellent that I asked if they would give me the recipe and they said with a small frown, "I'm afraid not." Well, I said, would you let me buy the recipe? With a cute smile, she said, "Yes." I asked how much, and she responded, "Two fifty." I said with approval, just add it to my tab.

Thirty days later, I received my VISA statement from Neiman-Marcus and it was $285.00. I looked again and I remembered I had only spent $9.95 for two salads and about $20.00 for a scarf. As I glanced at the bottom of the statement, it said, "Cookie Recipe—$250.00." Boy, was I upset!! I called Neiman's Accounting Dept. and told them the waitress said it was "two fifty," and I did not realize she meant $250.00 for a cookie recipe. I asked them to take back the recipe and reduce my bill and they said they were sorry, but because all the recipes were this expensive so not just everyone could duplicate any of our bakery recipes . . . the bill would stand.

I waited, thinking of how I could get even or even try and get any of my money back. I just said, "Okay, you folks got my $250.00 and now I'm going to have $250.00 worth of fun." I told her that I was going to see to it that every cookie lover will have a $250.00 cookie recipe from Neiman-Marcus for nothing. She replied, "I wish you wouldn't do this." I said, "I'm sorry but this is the only way I feel I could get even," and I will.

So, here it is, and please pass it on to someone else or run a few copies . . . I paid for it; now you can have it for free.

(Recipe may be halved.):

2 cups butter
2 tsp. soda
5 cups blended oatmeal**
2 cups brown sugar
1 8 oz. Hershey Bar (grated)
2 tsp. baking powder
2 tsp. vanilla
4 cups flour
2 cups sugar
24 oz. chocolate chips
1 tsp. salt
4 eggs
3 cups chopped nuts (your choice)

**measure oatmeal and blend in a blender to a fine powder.

Cream the butter and both sugars. Add eggs and vanilla; mix together with flour, oatmeal, salt, baking powder, and soda. Add chocolate chips, Hershey Bar and nuts. Roll into balls and place two inches apart on a cookie sheet. Bake for 10 minutes at 375 degrees. Makes 112 cookies.

Have fun!!! This is not a joke—this is a true story. That's it. Please, pass it along to everyone you know, single people, mailing lists, etc. . . . Ride free, citizen!

This just in in your in-box: Nike is giving away free sneakers! Congress wants to bump off Big Bird! Bananas carry flesh-eating bacteria! You can help save a sick little girl just by forwarding this e-mail!

By now you probably know not to get excited about messages like these, just a few of the myriad hoaxes that infest the world's e-mail in-boxes, indestructible as cockroaches. Many of these urban legends predate the advent of the Net—I wouldn't be surprised if the Top Secret Neiman-Marcus Cookie Recipe hoax (yes, that's a tall tale, although the recipe reportedly turns out fairly respectable cookies) goes back to biblical times. (King Saul's Top Secret Matzoh Recipe, anyone?) But the Net, where "official"-looking documents can easily be created and forwarded around the world in a jiffy, has proven to be the best thing to happen to the urban legend since the invention of the summer-camp campfire. And on the Net—*pace* P. T. Barnum—there's a sucker logging on every minute.

Sure, hoaxes are fun to read about, and you've gotta admire the diabolical brilliance of some of them. But forwarding a hoax is an e-mail etiquette no-no of the first degree. First, there are the obvious reasons: If you know a message is a hoax, taking advantage of your more gullible friends is highly impolite. And if you don't realize a message is a hoax, recipients will begin to suspect you're not the sharpest knife in the drawer.

But there are more reasons not to forward hoaxes:

- The ever-expanding list of addresses in the messages header or on a purported "petition" is a gold mine to junk e-mailers, who slap the names on their next round of "Make Money Fast" and "Hot Sexy Teens" spam.

- Hoaxes are often malicious or libelous. One widely circulated chain e-mail claimed falsely that designer Tommy Hilfiger used a racial epithet on *The Oprah Winfrey Show,* doing major damage to Hilfiger's reputation. Don't feel sorry for megacorporations? How about the American Cancer Society, whose reputation suffers every time hoaxers use its name on chain letters about fictitious sick kids?

- They distract from real issues. If all the concerned citizens who forwarded that popular e-mail petition about saving funding for *Sesame Street* wrote his or her member of Congress instead, the National Endowment for the Arts might have enough dough by now to finance a ballet in every back-yard.

- Hoaxes multiply like Viagra-dosed rabbits. If one person sends a message to ten people, who each send it to ten people, by the sixth generation the message has reached a million recipients. If each of those people takes a minute to look at the message, that's almost two years of wasted time.

- Emotionally manipulative hoaxes—like those about desperately ill kids—can be disturbing to children who receive them. Even if you're a seasoned adult skeptic who doesn't believe a word, somehow you still feel bad after reading them.

## WHEN YOU'VE BEEN HOAXED

What should you do when you get a message you suspect—or know—is a hoax? Your first duty, of course, is not to forward it. If the sender is some distant acquaintance, feel free to delete the message and forget about it. But if the sender is a friend, relative, or someone else who should gently be set straight before he embarrasses himself (or a loose cannon who must be stopped before he organizes a boycott of Neiman-Marcus), you need to break the news to him. Politely. Don't reply "That's a hoax, you idiot." Try "I thought you might want to know that message you sent me is a hoax. Here's a link to a Web page about it."

What should you do if you forwarded a message, then found out it was a hoax afterward? E-mail the recipients and tell them. Don't be afraid of cluttering their mailboxes—in this case, it's worth it to stop these hoaxes' insidious spread. If you've learned exactly what was inaccurate about the message, explain it in the note, either in your own words or by enclosing a link to a hoax-busting Web site. And be sure to apologize. If you committed this gaffe in a public forum—say, if you e-mailed it to an entire mailing list or to all your co-workers—you might also consider assuring the person in charge (the list master; your boss) that you're sorry, you've learned your lesson, and you won't do it again.

## HOW TO RECOGNIZE A HOAX

Many hoaxes immediately leap out as improbable—but often, rooting one out takes a close reading and some know-how about hoaxers' typical m.o.'s. And sometimes you have to do a little legwork (well, mousework). First, some general tips:

1. *Be suspicious of any chain e-mail message you get.* Your first inclination should be, "Is this a hoax?" Guilty until proven innocent. Be ruthless.

2. *Be extra suspicious of any message with the sentences "Forward this to everyone you know" or "This is not a hoax."* It's almost certainly a hoax.

3. *Consider the sender—but not too strongly.* A health-news item is more credible if it was sent to you by your friend who's a registered nurse than by your accountant. But the nurse might have been taken in, too.

4. *Examine the message closely.* Are there misspellings or typos? Multiple exclamation points? Some pranksters are good at crafting professional-sounding messages, but many aren't. Does the message cite a source for its information—and is it an organization or media outlet you've heard of? Legit messages often go out of their way to cite sources and include links to Web sites where you can verify the information. Is

there a date attributed to the information? If not, it could be outdated. (If the date cited is April 1, watch out.)

5. *Think about the logic and implications of the message.* If its contents would make headline news, why haven't you heard about it before? (If organ thieves were really drugging vacationers and stealing their kidneys, wouldn't *Dateline NBC* be on the case by now?)

6. *Does the message promise you money or prizes for forwarding it to others, or offer to donate money to a cause for every copy sent along?* If so, it's almost certainly a hoax. Corporations don't "test e-mail tracking systems" by sending cash to citizens at random. Nor do they unleash chain letters to raise funds for charity. (Well, not usually. See "In My Humble Opinion" at the end of this chapter.)

7. *Does the message ask you to send money to anyone?* Run the other way. Pyramid, or Ponzi, schemes (in the classical chain-letter pyramid scheme, you send money to someone at the top of a list while adding your name to the bottom, with the promise that as you climb to the top, later recruits will send you many times what you paid out) are illegal, offline or on.

8. *If you're still not sure about the truth of the message, do a little research. Check the message out at a Web site dedicated to exposing hoaxes, myths, and urban legends:*

   - snopes.com: Folklore researchers Barbara and David Mikkelson maintain one of the Web's most extensive databases of hoaxes and urban legends.

   - urbanlegends.about.com: Another exhaustive catalog of hoaxes that debunks the claims of scores of chain e-mail messages.

   - hoaxbusters.ciac.org: The U.S. Department of Energy's guide to spotting hoaxes.

   - www.cdc.gov: The Centers for Disease Control's Web site includes a page debunking phony health scares.

9. *Check the Web sites of companies or organizations mentioned in the message.* If Nike were really giving away free shoes, the company would likely mention it on its Web site. In addition, many groups targeted by malicious hoaxes post truth alerts on their Web sites. For example, the American Cancer Society maintains a page on its site (www.cancer.org) dedicated to debunking hoax messages that mention it.

10. *Do a search about the topic of the message on a newspaper Web site, a medical-information site, even a general-interest search site like Yahoo! or Google.* You may discover a news article or newsgroup posting exposing it as a hoax.

11. *Ask someone—your office tech-head, a Net-savvy relative, anyone whose knowledge and instincts you trust.*

---

### Embarrassing E-Moment

Many users of the Web-based e-mail service MSN Hotmail have been taken in by a recurring chain e-mail hoax. Purported to come from a "Jon Henerd" of the "Hotmail Admin. Dept.," one version of the e-mail reads: "Hotmail is overloading and we need to get rid of some people and we want to find out which users are actually using their Hotmail accounts. So, within a month's time, anyone who does not receive this email with the exact subject heading, will be deleted off our server. Please forward this email so that we know you are still using this account. If you do not pass this letter to anyone we will delete your account." Anyone out there want to sponsor a "Grammar for Spammers" course?

---

## A BRIEF TAXONOMY OF E-MAIL HOAXES

These pesky critters can be divided into several species. Here's a field guide of their distinguishing characteristics, along with some typical specimens. Since pranksters often aren't all that creative—

substituting a new name for that of a phony sick child, for example—familiarizing yourself with hoaxdom's greatest hits will go a long way toward ensuring you don't get fooled.

## Sick Kids

The tearjerkers of the e-mail hoax world. A small child is desperately ill—sometimes the e-mail purportedly comes from the kid himself—and wants to be immortalized in a chain letter. (Some legacy.) Or, often, the e-mail claims that forwarding it will cause a donation to be made toward the kid's treatment or research.

### A Classic of the Genre: Jessica Mydek

Little Jessica Mydek is seven years old and is suffering from an acute and very rare case of cerebral carcinoma. This condition causes severe malignant brain tumors and is a terminal illness. The doctors have given her six months to live.

As part of her dying wish, she wanted to start a chain letter to inform people of this condition and to send people the message to live life to the fullest and enjoy every moment, a chance that she will never have. Furthermore, the American Cancer Society and several corporate sponsors have agreed to donate three cents toward continuing cancer research for every new person that gets forwarded this message. Please give Jessica and all cancer victims a chance.

Send a copy of this to everyone you know and one to the American Cancer Society at acs@aol.com.

What's wrong with this message? Well, the three-cents-a-forward claim is a tip-off. And isn't the American Cancer Society an organization that seeks donations, not makes them? Still, this classic hoax and its variations fooled so many people that the American Cancer Society (and the Make-A-Wish Foundation, substituted in a variation) had to put disclaimers on their Web sites.

### Embarrassing E-Moment

In 1989, Craig Shergold, a nine-year-old British boy, was diagnosed with a life-threatening brain tumor. To cheer him up, a friend began a campaign to get Craig into *The Guinness Book of World Records* for receiving the most get-well cards. He got his wish: By 1991, he had collected 33 million cards. Even better, he beat the cancer. But his plea made its way to the Net, where it turned into an e-mail chain letter. Shergold, now healthy and in his twenties, regularly pleads for the cards to stop—to no avail. He estimates he's gotten 300 million cards and counting. Shergold donates the proceeds from recycling the paper to cancer research. "They come for every occasion," Shergold told *People*. "Christmas. Easter. Valentine's Day. Although I don't mind the Valentines if there are pictures."

### Phony Freebies

If all the chain e-mail messages that promised you free money or gifts for forwarding them were bona fide, you'd have a thick bankroll, all the M&M's you could eat, and Miller beer to wash them down. And you'd have a full closet, since many of these hoaxes seem to target teen-beloved clothing chains like Gap and Abercrombie & Fitch. (One imaginative e-mail purported to be celebrating the "merger" of Abercrombie and Fitch. The company took that name in 1904.) Most of these messages purport to be testing an e-mail tracking program—a sure sign they're pranks.

### A Classic of the Genre: Nikes for Everyone

Nike is proud to announce that we now not only lead the industry in technology used to develop high quality athletic shoes and apparel, but we have also recently entered into a joint venture with Microsoft. Many of you may have heard about the e-mail tracking program that was recently developed by Bill Gates. Now, Microsoft is allowing us to use this system to find our most reliable customers and offer them great discounts or even free shoes. If you are interested in receiving discounts on much of our newest merchandise, then simply forward this message to at least one person. When you forward the message, we receive a notice telling us your e-mail address and the number of people that you forwarded this message to.

The first 500 people to forward this message to 50 or more people, will receive a free pair of Nike shoes (retail value $119.99 or less). You will be notified by e-mail about how to obtain your free shoes or discount coupons. Thank you for helping us with our first Internet marketing campaign. Please visit our website at www.nike.com.

What's wrong with this message? It's that old "e-mail tracking program" again. Not to mention an implausible vision of corporate largesse, which is easily debunked by visiting Nike's Web site, nike.com, where no reference to the giveaway appeared.

## Petitions

You name the cause, there's probably a petition circulating somewhere in cyberspace for or against it. Trouble is, the information in most of these missives is either outdated or flat-out wrong—and even if it's correct, a cyber-petition is utterly meaningless. Who exactly is going to track how many signatures it gets? And even if someone did bring the petition to the attention of government or corporate bigwigs, there's no way for them to determine if the names are genuine. E-mail etiquette dictates: Don't circulate e-mail petitions, no matter how worthy the cause sounds. There are better ways to raise awareness of an issue you care about.

---

## Net Peace :(

Any petition that asks you to add your name to the end of the e-mail. Those never work. (Okay, I'm cynical.)

---

### *A Classic of the Genre: Petition Hoax*

```
SAVE SESAME STREET!

This is a petition to save Sesame Street.
ALL YOU DO IS ADD YOUR NAME TO THE LIST AT
THE BOTTOM, then forward it to everyone you
know. The only time you send it to the
included address is if you are the 50th,
100th, etc. Send it on to everyone you know.

PBS, NPR (National Public Radio), and the
arts are facing major cutbacks in funding.
In spite of the efforts of each station to
reduce spending costs and streamline their
services, the government officials believe
```

that the funding currently going to these
programs is too large a portion of funding
for something which is seen as "unworth-
while." Currently, taxes from the general
public for PBS equal $1.12 per person per
year, and the National Endowment for the
Arts equals $.64 a year in total. . . . The
only way that our representatives can be
aware of the base of support or PBS and
funding for these types of programs is by
making our voices heard.

Please add your name to this list if you
believe in what we stand for. This list
will be forwarded to the President of the
United States, the Vice President of the
United States, the House of Representatives
and Congress.

If you happen to be the 50th, 100th, 150th,
etc., signer of this petition, please forward to: [address removed]. This way we can
keep track of the lists and organize them.
Forward this to everyone you know, and help
us to keep these programs alive.

Thank you.

What's wrong with this message? For one thing, Congress was
considering cuts in arts funding back in 1996—but this message is
still kicking around the Net. For another, *Sesame Street*—a cash
cow that pays for itself—was never in danger. And finally, the
every-fiftieth-signer scheme makes little sense, if you think about
it. If the forty-ninth recipient sent it to twenty friends, there would
be twenty fiftieth signers.

## Disinformation

Move over, Burger King: The Net is the true home of the whopper. There are phony health scares. (Contrary to one popular e-forward, deodorant does not cause breast cancer—thankfully for those of us who ride the subway in the summer.) False rumors about celebrities or corporations. Financial flimflammery. Political smears. Forwarded news stories whose facts—or authors—evolve as they're passed around. Hysteric warnings about fictitious computer viruses (which we'll address in the next chapter.) And 57 more varieties of hoaxes, urban legends, rumors, inaccuracies, and half-truths. The lesson? With e-mail, suspect everything. Trust no one.

### A Classic of the Genre: Killer Bananas

```
Warning:

Several shipments of bananas from Costa
Rica have been infected with necrotizing
fasciitis, otherwise known as flesh eating
bacteria. Recently this disease has deci-
mated the monkey population in Costa Rica.
We are now just learning that the disease
has been able to graft itself to the skin
of fruits in the region, most notably the
Banana which is Costa Rica's largest
export. Until this finding scientist[s]
were not sure how the infection was being
transmitted. It is advised not to purchase
Bananas for the next three weeks as this
is the period of time for which bananas
that have been shipped to the US with the
possibility of carrying this disease.

If you have eaten a banana in the last 2-3
days and come down with a fever followed
by a skin infection seek MEDICAL ATTEN-
TION!!! The skin infection from necrotiz-
```

ing fasciitis is very painful and eats two to three centimeters of flesh per hour. Amputation is likely, death is possible. If you are more than an hour from a medical center burning the flesh ahead of the infected area is advised to help slow the spread of the infection. The FDA has been reluctant to issue a country wide warning because of fear of a nationwide panic. They have secretly admitted that they feel upwards of 15,000 Americans will be affected by this but that these are "acceptable numbers". Please forward this to as many of the people you care about as possible as we do not feel 15,000 people is an acceptable number.

—Manheim Research Institute

This unappetizing hoax (the Manheim Research Institute does not exist, although later versions substituted the Centers for Disease Control or major U.S. universities as the purported source) spread so widely that the CDC and the International Banana Association had to release statements denouncing it. Come on, folks: Wouldn't killer bananas have made the evening news?

## Embarrassing E-Moment

At a 2000 debate between New York senatorial candidates Hillary Clinton and Rick Lazio, moderator and WCBS-TV reporter Marcia Kramer asked the two for their stands on "Federal Bill 602P," legislation she said was before Congress that would let the Postal Service "bill e-mail users five cents for each e-mail they send." No such bill existed—Kramer had been taken in by a widely circulated hoax e-mail. And Clinton and Lazio? Eager to please voters, both proceeded to state their staunch opposition to it.

## IMHO (In My Humble Opinion):
## Sweet Charity—or Iffy Etiquette?

In their eagerness to take advantage of e-mail as a marketing tool, movie studios, record labels, and other companies have launched e-mail promotional campaigns that resemble e-mail hoaxes too closely for comfort. For example, to advertise the video release of *The Perfect Storm,* Warner Bros. started an e-mail campaign offering to donate five cents to the American Red Cross every time a user forwarded a promotional e-mail to a friend. In this case, the offer was legitimate—since users had to visit the Warner Bros. Web site to forward the message, the company could track the number of recipients.

```
From: "Warner Bros. and The Perfect Storm"

Subject: This E-Mail Helps the American
Red Cross

+=+=+=+=+=+=+=+=+=+=+=+=+=
WITNESS THE CHALLENGES.
EXPERIENCE THE DANGER.
HONOR THE HEROISM.
+=+=+=+=+=+=+=+=+=+=+=+=+=

Warner Bros. would like to honor the
real-life heroes of "The Perfect Storm,"
and we need your help. Every time you
forward this e-mail to a friend, Warner
Bros. will contribute five cents to the
American Red Cross. Help us reach our
contribution goal of $50,000.

To see a rich media version of this
important email and then forward it to
your friends, click on this link:

[link]
```

The intentions of such campaigns are undoubtedly good, but I'm not so sure about their Netiquette. Since such e-mails' wording is so similar to that of many chain-letter hoaxes, they might be mistaken for hoaxes—or, worse, such promotions could lend credibility to hoax e-mails. And encouraging users to flood their friends' mailboxes with commercial messages, even for a good cause, is dubious e-manners. A more polite alternative: A company can set up a Web site—along the lines of the popular the-hungersite.com—and donate a small sum of money to charity for every visit paid. When visitors see the company's good intentions, they'll spread the necessary word of mouth themselves.

# 10
# Viruses: Don't Get Sick, Don't Get Tricked

- *How can I keep myself and my friends safe from computer viruses that spread via e-mail?*

- *What should I do if I suspect I've contracted a virus? Should I e-mail people I've e-mailed and tell them?*

- *How can I spot a virus hoax?*

Computer viruses are nasty. They can destroy files on your computer's hard drive. They can set up programs that swipe your Internet service password. They can hide away until a certain date, then come to life—or do their damage gradually and stealthily. They can even take over your e-mail program and send out hundreds of copies of themselves, wreaking havoc as the computers that handle the e-mail of huge corporations collapse and crash under the onslaught.

At the same time, the hype, fear, and misinformation that swirl around viruses can be as vexing as viruses themselves. Breathless news reports and cheesy cyberthriller movies scare people into thinking that viruses lurk around every corner of the Net (they're actually fairly rare) and that the average user is powerless to halt their evil spread (they're actually pretty easy to avoid). Hoaxers take advantage of gullible users by starting chain e-mail messages warning of nonexistent viruses—which circulate to far more people, and probably waste more total time, than real viruses could ever hope to.

What does all this have to do with etiquette? First, keeping yourself safe from viruses isn't just your own personal business. Since computer viruses spread from person to person, just like the real thing, making sure your computer is virus-free is as much an etiquette must as good personal hygiene. You wash your hands after using the bathroom, right? *(Right?)* You cover your face when you sneeze. The few simple steps you take to avoid computer viruses should be just as automatic.

Second, you owe it to your fellow users to understand some basic facts and fictions about viruses. With a little knowledge, you'll be less likely to spread a virus—and you won't annoy others by helping to spread a hoax or indulging in unnecessary paranoia.

## WHAT IS A COMPUTER VIRUS?

A virus is a piece of executable computer code—a little computer program—that, like its biological namesake, can create copies of itself. While biological viruses infect cells in your body, computer viruses burrow into files on your computer: software programs, files that are parts of the computer's operating system, even some documents. When you run those files, the virus unleashes whatever damage it was designed to do—anything from displaying a silly message to destroying data.

## TYPES OF VIRUSES

You'll hear computer people use all sorts of heavy-duty terms to classify viruses, but they usually reflect three things: What kind of files does the virus infect? What kind of damage is it intended to do? And how does it spread?

### What Files Do Viruses Infect?

- File-infecting viruses: These classic viruses infect computer programs: copies of commercial software, applications downloaded from the Net, software received via e-mail. When you run the program, you unleash the virus.

- Boot-sector viruses: The oldest type of virus targets the files that make your computer start up. If it does enough damage, your PC may not be able to start.

- Macro viruses: Once, data files like word-processing documents were considered immune to viruses. Not anymore. Viruses can now hide away in macros, mini-programs intended to perform useful tasks within Microsoft Word and Excel documents. Particularly easy to spread, macro viruses are gaining favor: Recently, eight of the top ten reported viruses were macro viruses.

## What Kind of Damage Can They Do?

- Benign viruses: Not all viruses carry a payload intended to do something dastardly. Some are simply programmed to display a triumphant message at a certain time. Some never activate at all, just create copy after copy of themselves within a computer's files—which is not exactly benign, since such viruses can eventually clog up your computer's hard drive, sap its speed, and generally make it act pretty much like you do when you have the flu.

- Malignant viruses: These are programmed to do something deliberately destructive, usually erasing or corrupting files on your computer. They rarely announce their presence, preferring to operate stealthily. Viruses called time bombs wait for a certain date to spring into action.

- Trojan horses: Not technically viruses, these are computer programs that appear to be helpful—but hide an unexpected, damaging function. One renowned Trojan horse wittily titled Back Orifice lets whoever sent it to you take over your computer—deleting or stealing files or passwords—by issuing commands over the Net.

- Worms: To spread from computer to computer, classic viruses have to wait for a human to send an infected file to another person. Not worms. These especially creepy crawlies attempt to write you out of the equation—for instance, by taking over your e-mail program and sending out messages, with copies of themselves attached, to all your friends.

## Embarrassing E-Moment

The "I Love You" Virus: This worm spread around the world in no time in 2000—largely because of what geeks call good "social engineering." (That is, its creators knew just how to get humans to help spread it.) It arrived as an e-mail with a subject line reading "I Love You"—often from a friend or business contact. When curious recipients opened the attached "loveletter.doc" Word file, they unleashed the macro virus. If the recipients used Microsoft Outlook as their e-mail program, the virus then sent infected "I Love You" messages to people in their saved address books. It also damaged files on recipients' computers. Experts estimate that the virus spread to as many as 45 million computers worldwide, shutting down many corporations' e-mail networks. And it's still out there, in dozens of variations. Still, you've got to admire the original "I Love You" concept. A virus posing as an etiquette dilemma? Diabolical.

### How Do I Get a Virus?

An infected file has to get onto your system, and you have to open it. The virus can arrive any of several different ways:

- E-mail attachments: Before e-mail became popular, a virus used to have to wait for an unwitting human to give an infected disk to another user—like traveling by the *Niña*, the *Pinta*, and the *Santa María* when compared to the jet speed of today's Net. More than half of infections now come via e-mail attachments—sometimes created by self-propagating worms, sometimes by users who consciously attach files they don't realize are infected.

- Downloads: Software or data files you obtain from the Net can harbor viruses that may infect your computer if you run or open them.

- Disks: Whether oldfangled floppies or newfangled high-capacity storage disks, CDs, or DVDs, disks can also transport infected files.

## PROTECTING YOURSELF (AND OTHERS) FROM VIRUSES

They're out there. They're bad. The good news? Computer viruses are a highly preventable disease. (If anyone figured out a way to make the common cold this avoidable, he'd have a Nobel Prize and a bazillion dollars.) You can keep your computer virus-free—and thereby avoid infecting friends and co-workers—with a one-two punch: anti-virus software and a few safety precautions.

### Anti-Virus Software

Think of anti-virus software like a home smoke detector: Don't bother questioning whether you need it or not. You need it. Get it. Fortunately, these programs, made by a variety of companies, are easy to get your hands on: Your computer may come with anti-virus software pre-installed, or your office computer may have one set up by the tech staff. If not, there are free programs on the Web—or you can shell out a few bucks for one with all the bells and whistles, available online or at a software store.

These programs can be set up to automatically scan your computer's hard drive—or any new file attempting to board it—for anything dangerous. (Yes, they do more than ask the file for ID and ask if it packed its luggage itself.) Once they detect a virus, they sound an alert and assess whether the damage can be repaired. Often, they can successfully cleanse the virus from the file, leaving the file with a clean bill of health—though sometimes the infected file can't be salvaged.

Anti-virus software can't protect you, though, if it's not set up properly. (Or not turned on.) And it does need an occasional bit of TLC to keep its defenses up to date. A few rules:

- Open your anti-virus program and familiarize yourself with what it scans and doesn't scan. Set it up to carry out as many tasks as possible automatically.

- Set it up to scan any disk you put in your computer's disk drive.

- If you can, set it up to automatically scan e-mail attachments as they're downloaded. If the program doesn't offer that option (or if the attachment was compressed, which can make viruses more difficult to detect), manually have your anti-virus software give every attachment a once-over before opening.

- Scan any software you download from the Web, either automatically or manually. (Scan for viruses both before and after you've installed the program—a virus might turn up as the program expands into numerous files during installation.)

- Regularly visit the Web site of the company that made your anti-virus software and download updates. (Or subscribe to updates on disk.) These ensure that the software can detect newly developed viruses—an arms race you don't want to lose.

## Other Precautions

Just because your body has an immune system playing defense against germs doesn't mean you should lick subway poles or gobble month-old egg salad. Likewise, even if you have anti-virus software running, it's a good idea to follow a few everyday rules to keep the bugs at bay.

- *Don't open any e-mail attachment that you're not expecting, from a stranger* or *a friend.* If in doubt about a message from someone you know, write back to the sender and ask what the attachment is. And scan any attachment with your anti-virus software before you open it.

VIRUS MYTH DEBUNKED: You can't get infected by a virus just by *reading* the text of an e-mail message or *receiving* an attachment. You have to *open* the attachment to get infected. So don't panic if you get a suspicious or unexpected attachment. *Don't* double-click on it to see what it does. Just delete it.

**My sister will not correspond via e-mail with me because my Internet access is at the public library. She says her computer will get a virus. Is this true?**

Hmmm. Bet public toilets scare her too. Tell her to have no fear; even if the library computers harbor virtual bookworms, she'll be safe if she follows standard precautions: Don't open unexpected or suspicious e-mail attachments (where most of the nasty critters hide) and scan incoming files or programs with anti-virus software. She should definitely chill if you're e-mailing plain ol' text-only letters—great for sharing family gossip, but unlikely to transmit bugs.

- *If you're downloading software from the Web, stick to sites you can trust.* You're safest using a big commercial software maker's own site or large software clearinghouses that vouch on their site that they check programs for viruses. If you're snagging software from an unfamiliar site or—even more dangerous—swapping it with a stranger, be sure to give your anti-virus software a crack at it before and after installing.

- *Back up your hard drive periodically.* That means making copies of your programs and files and saving them somewhere else: on disk, on a tape drive, on an external hard drive, on a server at work, on a Web backup service. Like other unpleasant chores, it takes time—but if the worst happens and a virus totals your computer, you'll be glad you did it.

### The Name Game

Should you watch out for attachments with certain names? Virus warnings often tell users to beware of e-mail messages with certain subjects or attachments with certain file names. This isn't a bad idea—especially when a worm like the "I Love You" virus first starts spreading like wildfire—but it is a little misleading. Virus writers aren't dumb: Many such e-mail worms can easily mutate (or be altered by enterprising miscreants), changing the subject line or file name they travel under. Within months, "I Love You" had spawned dozens of variations—including one that pretended the infected attachment was software to combat the "I Love You" virus and another that repeated the subject line from the last legitimate message the victim e-mailed to recipients in his address book. So don't stress out about memorizing the various disguises of the latest virus threat. Just keep that anti-virus software running—and stay suspicious of any e-mail attachment.

A few more tips and tricks:

- Some e-mail programs can be set up to open attachments automatically. Make sure yours isn't doing so.

- Also beware of programs that let you "preview" e-mail messages—a way of seeing their contents without having to open them manually. This option may leave you vulnerable to viruses. Turn it off.

- Set up your Microsoft Word and Excel programs to alert you before running a macro and watch out for anything unusual when you open a new file.

VIRUS MYTH DEBUNKED: Usually, nothing happens on the screen when you get a virus. Don't expect a little picture of a bomb or a message saying "Gotcha." A smart virus does its damage in secret—you might not discover it for days or weeks.

---

## Net Peeve : (

People tell me, "I think I got a virus. But I hit 'enter' and it didn't do anything." You shouldn't hit "enter"!

---

## PRACTICE SAFE SENDING

"But enough about me!" manners-minded readers might think. "Isn't etiquette about consideration for other people?" With viruses, keeping yourself safe and keeping others safe are pretty much one and the same. But protecting others should loom large in your mind. For one thing, someone you're sending e-mail to may not be as virus-savvy as you are: You can't assume recipients are running anti-virus software or know not to double-click on that mysterious "loveletter.doc" attachment. For another: If the fear of getting a virus doesn't motivate you to take precautions, the prospect of giving one to someone else ought to. A few rules for safe sending:

1. Keep your own computer virus-free with all the safety steps described in this chapter.

2. Scan program files or documents with anti-virus software before sending them as e-mail attachments.

3. When sending an e-mail attachment, explain in the text of the message exactly what the attachment is.

4. Don't pass along software from a shady source unless you're sure it's safe.

5. Don't share diskettes you haven't scanned for viruses.

## DON'T BE A TYPHOID MARY

If your office or group of friends has a virus problem it can't seem to lick, the problem often boils down to one person who, either ignorantly or willfully, disobeys the virus safety rules. It could be the woman down the hall who brings in disks from home and doesn't scan them; it could be the manager who turned off his anti-virus program because it "took too much time to run." For safety's, duty's, and etiquette's sake, don't be that person.

## REALITY CHECK: HOW SCARED OF VIRUSES SHOULD I BE?

One thing's for sure. You don't want to get infected. One recent study estimated that on average, an office computer stricken by a virus costs companies nearly $2,500 and 45 hours of work. At home, the situation isn't any better, since users often need professional help to recover from an infection.

But viruses aren't anything for average users to lose sleep over—not when there's much more worthwhile stuff out there to worry about. (Car crashes, certainly, and for fans of the exotic, may I recommend mad-cow disease?) It all depends on how you use your computer. If you're an office user who sends and receives a lot of attachments and uses programs such as Word and Excel, you should be very concerned about viruses. Download a lot of software from the Web or like to swap stuff on disk with friends? Be concerned. But if, like many home users, you use your computer primarily to surf the Net and send plain text e-mail messages, you have less reason to worry—though you should still follow all these precautions.

## IF YOU DISCOVER A VIRUS

What should you do if your anti-virus software detects a virus in an e-mail message? Should you tell the person who sent you the file? Should you alert your office's tech staff?

First, nuke the virus. Leave that to your anti-virus software, which will attempt to repair the infected file or, if it can't surgically excise the virus, delete the file. (If it asks permission for either of these tasks, click "OK"—these programs know best.)

Yes, you should inform the sender—unless you suspect that a stranger may have sent you the virus maliciously. If you get multiple messages you think are malicious, report them to your office tech staff or your Internet service provider; otherwise, send the person who sent you the virus an e-mail briefly detailing what happened and sharing whatever information about the virus your anti-virus program gave you. Don't be afraid of deluging the sender with e-mail—better that fifty people warn her that she's propagating a virus than she spreads it to fifty more.

You should also inform your office tech staff if you receive an infected message at work. Don't expect a four-alarm response—after all, if your anti-virus software detected the virus and got rid of it, it did its job. You're safe. If you suspect you've been infected, or if you're experiencing an onslaught of infected e-mail, definitely give the techies a jingle.

**I got hit by the Anna Kournikova e-mail virus, which sent itself to everyone in my address book. Should I warn recipients?**
Yes—better that your pals endure a volley of "Don't open the attachment in my last message!" notes than get aced by a virus. But disinfect with anti-virus software first, lest your warning harbor another bug.

If a particularly nasty virus has put your computer on the disabled list for a lengthy stay, consider warning recipients through another means. If the virus was sent to just a few people, you could call them. If it went to more, you could have a colleague (with a healthy computer!) e-mail them.

---

### Net Peeve :(

When someone sends me the happy99 virus [an e-mail worm], then fifteen minutes later sends me a message saying "Don't open e-mail from me—it's got a virus." And the second message is carrying another copy of the virus.

---

## VIRUS HOAXES

Falling victim to a computer virus can be just as unpleasant as catching the real-life flu. Chain e-mail messages warning about phony viruses, meanwhile, are just as epidemic. They don't do any real damage, but as annoying time-wasters (particularly for technology help-deskers who have to calm periodic panics), virus scares are a sort of virus themselves—and, needless to say, one of many users' biggest Netiquette pet peeves. (For more on other types of Net hoaxes, see Chapter 9, "E-Mail Hoaxes.")

> IF YOU RECEIVE AN E-MAIL ENTITLED, "HOW TO GIVE A CAT A COLONIC," DO NOT OPEN IT!!!!!!!!
>
> It will erase everything on your hard drive. Forward this letter out to as many people as you can. This is a new, very malicious virus and not many people know about it. This information was announced by IBM. Please share it with everyone that might access the Internet. Once again, pass this along to EVERYONE in your address book so that this may be stopped. AOL has said that this is a very dangerous virus and that there is NO remedy for it at this time. Please practice cautionary measures and forward this.

Any guesses about whether this is a genuine virus warning? Seems easier than the $100 question on *Who Wants to Be a Millionaire*: It's a hoax. But chain e-mail messages such as this one fly around the Net by the millions, clogging in-boxes, wasting time, and stirring up needless fear.

How can you tell if an e-mail warning about a virus is bona fide? Here's an easy answer: If you have to ask, it's not. Well, probably not. The U.S. government, Microsoft, AOL, anti-virus software makers, and other respectable organizations do not rely on chain e-mail messages to warn users about viruses. In fact, the only ways a warning about a real virus should land in your e-mail are:

- You subscribe to an e-mail newsletter about computer viruses put out by the government, an Internet security company, or related organization.

- Your company's tech squad sends a warning to employees.

- An official representative of your Internet service provider sends a warning to users.

- Someone hears about a new virus from one of these reliable sources and passes the information along to you.

But the vast majority of breathless messages hitting your in-box are likely to be hoaxes. Fortunately, hoaxes are usually pretty easy to pick out:

Signs of a hoax:

- Asking you to "forward this to all your friends."

- Having been forwarded along by several users before it got to you.

- Typos, misspellings, and grammar errors.

- Dropping vague references to important-sounding organizations to sound more official: "A new virus has just been discovered that has been classified by Microsoft (www.microsoft.com) and by McAfee (www.mcafee.com) as the most destructive ever!" A virus hoax that recently landed in my in-box screamed, "Yesterday, in just a few hours, this virus caused panic in New York, according to [a] news broadcast by CNN (www.cnn.com)."

- Describing the virus's effect in vague or implausible terms. Remember, you can't get infected by a virus by simply reading the text of an e-mail message—you must open an infected attachment. So a warning that just reading a message with a certain title will erase your hard drive is guaranteed to be a tall tale.

- Not including contact information or links to more details. Bona fide organizations that send out such warnings always include a link to a Web site with more information about the virus and the name and title of the person responsible for sending the warning.

## The Granddaddy of Virus Hoaxes

Perhaps the most successful virus hoax was Good Times, a warning that swept the Net in the mid-nineties and still, Ebola-like, breaks out on occasion.

> Happy Chanukah everyone, and be careful
> out there. There is a virus on America
> Online being sent by E-Mail. If you get
> anything called "Good Times", DON'T read
> it or download it. It is a virus that will
> erase your hard drive. Forward this to all
> your friends. It may help them a lot.

What does a real virus warning look like? No organization is responsible for alerting individual computer users to viruses. (That's why most of those e-mails you get are hoaxes.) However, Internet security companies and a few government organizations do provide information about new viruses on their Web sites or in e-mail newsletters they send to subscribers. Someone might pass along information from one of these newsletters to you. But beware: Hoaxsters have become adept at imitating the style of these virus alerts.

## Virus Hoax Encyclopedias

If you can't immediately detect a virus warning as a fake, you can check it out on the Web. Several Web sites are dedicated to tracking and busting the Net's ever-multiplying virus hoaxes. Three to bookmark:

Symantec.com: A site run by Symantec, which makes Norton anti-virus software. At the Anti-Virus Research Center, you'll find an exhaustive list of virus hoaxes as well as information about real viruses.

vil.mcafee.com: McAfee.com, another anti-virus software maker, serves up a Virus Information Library with databases documenting hoaxes and genuine threats.

Vmyths.com: Run by an independent virus expert, this site offers an A-to-Z list of virus hoaxes and commentary about virus hysteria.

What should you do if someone sends you a hoax virus warning? Deleting it and forgetting about it is a perfectly acceptable option. But if the sender is someone you know well, respond and break the news to him—gently and politely: the message and any similar ones he might get in the future are probably hoaxes and should not be forwarded. Send him a link to one of the above Web sites so he can check future messages for himself. Don't be afraid such a reply is rude. You'll be sparing the sender future embarrassment—and all his correspondents much annoyance.

**A co-worker insists on forwarding every virus hoax she gets to the entire staff. What should I do?**

Unless you're pals, it's best not to confront her yourself—she might take your advice the wrong way or, worse, not pay you any attention. Instead, without naming names, ask your office's technology manager or another supervisor to send all employees a message explaining that such messages are hoaxes and should not be forwarded. As with real viruses, a little prevention goes a long way.

Rob Rosenberger, who runs Vmyths.com, a Web site about virus hoaxes and myths, suggests sending the following message to all employees once a year.

To all employees:

We have experienced another rash of hoax virus alerts spreading around the company. These hoaxes are disguised as "helpful" emails with a warning about a dangerous new computing threat. These emails are *hoax chain letters* which make the sender look stupid. They waste employee time and spread false information.

Stupid employees may forward hoax alerts

with my blessing. If you're *not* stupid, and
you receive an email warning of any type,
forward it to the "Computer Security"
email account. Our experts will investigate it and notify you if any further
action is required.

Needless to say, etiquette demands slightly more tactful wording (no one likes a snooty techie)—but, minus the references to
employee stupidity, this message could save everyone a great deal
of aggravation.

*Final note:* A joke parodying virus hoaxes warned of the
dreaded Honor System virus: "An e-mail will say 'This virus works
on the honor system. Please forward this message to everyone
you know, then delete all the files on your hard disk. Thank you
for your cooperation.'"

# 11

## I Do Not Like That Spam I Am

- *How can I keep junk e-mailers from getting my address?*
- *Is there a way to block spam from my mailbox?*
- *How can I fight back against spammers?*

I do not like that e-mail spam.
I do not like it, Sam I am.
I do not click it with my mouse
I do not want it in my house!
Why do I get that e-mail spam?
Tell them to can it, Sam I am!

As a Samantha—Sam for short—I spent my elementary-school years getting called "Sam I Am" by clever classmates and hating every minute of it. With the above, I consider myself avenged against Dr. Seuss.

Dr. Seuss had many redeeming qualities. Spam, however, has none. *Spam* is Net lingo for unsolicited advertising e-mail—the electronic equivalent of junk mail or telemarketers who try to sell you time shares during dinner. If you've been on the Net for long, you're probably all too familiar with spam's come-on subject lines:

DO YOU LIKE HOT SEX?

STOP SMOKING IN 7 DAYS GUARANTEED

EARN UP TO $1000 OR MORE PER WEEK!

LIVE TEEN SEX SEE IT NOW!!

YOUR INFO REQUEST

E-mailers can get dozens of such messages a week, so it's no surprise that spam is many users' number-one e-mail beef (or should that be pork?). It's also harder to kill than a cockroach infestation. Many spammers forge their e-mail addresses or change them every time, so it's difficult for Internet service providers or individual users to block their barrages. And forget about replying "Take me off this list!" To unscrupulous spammers, that's just confirmation that they've reached a working e-mail address—and encouragement to send more spam.

## WHY IS IT CALLED SPAM?

According to legend, spam got its name from a Monty Python sketch about a restaurant that specialized in Spam luncheon meat. On the menu, as recited by waitress Terry Jones: "Well, there's egg and bacon; egg sausage and bacon; egg and Spam; egg bacon and Spam; egg bacon sausage and Spam; Spam bacon sausage and Spam; Spam egg Spam Spam bacon and Spam; Spam sausage Spam Spam bacon Spam tomato and Spam; Spam Spam Spam egg and Spam; Spam Spam Spam Spam Spam Spam baked beans Spam Spam Spam or Lobster Thermidor à Crevette with a mornay sauce served in a Provencale manner with shallots and aubergines garnished with truffle pâté, brandy and with a fried egg on top and Spam." Meanwhile, hearing the magic word, a troop of Vikings drowned out all other conversation by singing lustily: "Spam Spam Spam Spam. Lovely Spam! Wonderful Spam!" So early Netizens adopted the name spam for the onslaught of unwanted ads drowning out other conversation on the Net.

Actually, spam does have a formal name: unsolicited bulk e-mail (UBE) or unsolicited commercial e-mail (UCE). As if the world needed more TLAs (three-letter acronyms). But just about everyone—even governmental organizations—just calls it spam.

And what of the innocent processed pork product at the center of it all? Hormel Foods, maker of the foodstuff Spam, doesn't object to the transformation of its trademark into Net slang, though it requests that references to e-mail spam appear in lowercase letters. (Hormel did, however, sue when the movie *Muppet Treasure Island* introduced a character named Spa'am, high priest of a tribe of wild boars. Hormel lost.)

Actually, Netizens have a strange love-hate relationship with Spam the foodstuff. You'll find many Web pages dedicated to haikus (yet another strange Net obsession) about the mystery meat:

Formless, spreadable
beneath contempt. Oity Me!
I am deviled SPAM.

While there's no magic way to eradicate all spam, the tide is turning in the battle against it. There's plenty you can do to defend yourself—and even help Internet service providers shut spammers down. But first, let's talk about why sending spam is an e-mail etiquette felony.

It's easy to see why advertisers are tempted to send bulk e-mail. Sending e-mail to tens of thousands of addresses is far cheaper than sending junk mail or hiring telemarketers. Lists of e-mail addresses can be bought for pennies a target, and plenty of services will handle the whole process for just a few cents more. Since spam is so cheap, advertisers can turn a profit if just a few among thousands of recipients respond to the offer—indeed, even if 99-plus percent of targets delete the message in disgust.

Spam might be profitable, but it's certainly not ethical. A few years ago, when many e-mail users paid per-minute fees for their connections to the Internet, the chief problem with spam was easy to explain: Every junk e-mail costs users money to read and delete. Today, although most of us pay flat per-month fees for our Internet access, spam still takes money out of our pockets, albeit indirectly—and it does more than monetary damage.

## PAYING FOR SPAM

- Spam costs you money. Some estimates conjecture that up to a third of all e-mail sent on the Net is spam. Companies and Internet service providers have to buy more computers and faster Internet connections to deliver and store all those extra messages—and hire more staff to battle spam. One large Internet service provider estimated that spam-related costs added 10 percent to customers' bills.

- Spam slows down the Net. All those messages use up bandwidth—that is, they can clog up the pipes that transmit Internet data and overtax the computers that sort it. So surfing the Web takes longer and other e-mail is delivered more slowly.

- Spam eats up storage space. Many e-mail users, particularly on Web-based e-mail services like MSN Hotmail and Yahoo! Mail, are allowed limited online storage space for messages. Go a few weeks without clearing out the spam, and you can easily find yourself over the limit.

- Spam is often a scam. Bulk e-mailers often tout phony get-rich-quick schemes, lure users into stock swindles, or peddle fraudulent products or services.

- Spam can be offensive. Those HOT SEX! spams often are sent to kids—and to plenty of adults who don't care to read them either.

- And finally, spam wastes users' time—and those seconds add up.

## SPAM BASICS

### How Can I Identify Spam?

Usually, you'll know it when you see it. Subtlety isn't most spammers' strong suit. Most of the time, all you need is a glimpse of the subject line: Spammers are fond of words and phrases like "hot," "free," and "make money fast." They're also partial to capital letters (ouch! our ears!) and enough exclamation points to gag a Valley

Girl. Open any message and you'll see more of the same: a cheesy come-on for some shady product or service, complete with more capital letters, exclamation points, and atrocious grammar.

Some spammers have begun turning to stealthier subject lines, trying to fool you into opening messages labeled "hi" or "info you requested." Upon opening, most of these messages also offer up the usual instantly identifiable come-ons. But beware the slightly smarter spammer, who might craft a professional-looking but phony news-service article touting some over-the-counter stock or a message purporting to be from your Internet service provider that asks you to "confirm" your password. Be suspicious of any e-mail sent from an unfamiliar address—and don't ever give personal information to a stranger.

A few more tricks: Always look at the sender's e-mail address before opening a message. If you don't recognize it, be on guard. Much (though certainly not all) spam nowadays is routed through overseas e-mail addresses. Look for two-letter country codes—like .uk or .fr—at the end of the sender's address in place of .com, .org, or .net. Finally, you can tell if the message was sent out in bulk by checking whether your name appears in the "To:" line. If it doesn't, the message was sent to others besides you—a warning sign of spam.

## Spam Safety

Been spammed? Safety first. Don't reply, even to complain or request to be taken off the spammer's mailing list. If the return address isn't fake, you'll just be confirming that your e-mail address is live, working, and prime for more spam. Don't open any attachments. They could be anything from pornography to a virus-infected file. Don't click on any Web links in the message. You'll likely wind up someplace highly unsavory—or at a site set up to scam you. Don't call any phone numbers listed in the message, even if the message gives the number as a hotline to be removed from the mailing list. One popular spam scam is to entice users to call offshore numbers that bill them for exorbitant charges. And for the sake of fellow Netizens everywhere, don't buy anything. For the spammer, just one sale can justify tens of thousands of junk e-mails. And you're almost certainly getting ripped off.

**I got e-mail from someone whose name I didn't recognize. Should I write and ask who he or she is?**

Be careful—it could be a salesman or scammer using a friendly come-on. If a mysterious correspondent doesn't bother to introduce himself, don't reply.

### Top Spam Scams

The Federal Trade Commission released a list of fraudulent offers most likely to arrive in consumers' mailboxes. The "Dirty Dozen":

1. Fraudulent business opportunities that trumpet huge earnings without much work—often illegal pyramid schemes

2. Solicitations to become a spammer yourself

3. Chain-letter pyramid schemes that ask you to send money to names on a list, replace one of the names with your own, then forward the list. These schemes are illegal, and nearly all participants lose money.

4. Work-at-home schemes such as stuffing envelopes or assembling crafts

5. Health and diet scams, such as miracle weight-loss pills and cures for impotence or hair loss

6. Phony get-rich-quick schemes such as newsletters describing how to make unlimited profits trading money on world currency markets

7. Promises of free goods for joining a club and signing up others (the old pyramid scheme, yet again)

8. Phony investment opportunities (either outright scams or pyramid schemes)

9. Offers for cable descrambler kits (they usually don't work, and even if they do, they're illegal)

10. Solicitations for "guaranteed" loans or credit, on easy terms. (The loans turn out to be useless lists of lenders who will turn you down if you don't meet qualifications; promised credit cards never come through.)

11. Offers to erase accurate negative information from your credit rating. (There's no legal way to do it.)

12. Offers that claim you've "won" a fabulous vacation for a very low price. (You'll have to pay through the nose for upgrades and other hidden fees.)

### *Embarrassing E-Moment*

In 2001, an employee at *The New England Journal of Medicine* accidentally forwarded a junk e-mail with the subject CASH COW, promoting a get-rich-quick scheme, to 80,000 doctors, journalists, and consumers who subscribed to the publication's online mailing list.

## IS IT REALLY SPAM?

Not all commercial messages that land in your mailbox are spam—i.e., *unsolicited* advertising. You may also get promotional messages or newsletters that you signed up for, perhaps without noticing, when you visited, registered at, or bought products from a Web site. ("Opt-in" marketing—asking users to check a box to sign up for promotional messages—is considered the ethical approach. But many Web sites nevertheless employ "opt-out" marketing: You get the promotional messages if you *don't* check a box requesting *not* to receive them. This underhanded tactic is poor corporate Netiquette, but common nonetheless.)

Fortunately, such messages are usually easy to distinguish from spam. They come from a reputable company or Web site you visited. And they almost always explain up front, or in a tagline at the end, what the message is, who it is from, why you're getting it, and how to unsubscribe. After all, reputable companies don't want their messages mistaken for spam.

To unsubscribe from such lists, follow the given instructions carefully. (They usually involve visiting the company's Web site or sending a message to a specific e-mail address.) To avoid getting on such lists in the first place, be extra wary when you're registering or shopping at Web sites. Watch out for buttons or checkboxes that ask whether you want to receive "updates about the site" or "messages from our sponsors." Scour these forms like Johnnie Cochran looking for a loophole.

### Embarrassing E-Moment

A December 2000 study of top online shopping sites found that several had become spammers: They continued to send customers unwanted e-mail even after customers had followed instructions to unsubscribe from their newsletters. Offenders included drugstore.com, Staples.com, and VictoriasSecret.com.

**Is spamming illegal? I offer a legitimate product for sale (I own a jewelry company), not some get-rich-quick scheme. I wanted to send e-mail out in bulk to advertise.**

A growing number of states have laws imposing various regulations on unsolicited e-mail ads, and sending junk e-mail may also violate your Internet service provider's policies. But most important, it's an etiquette felony: Can that spam.

## DON'T BE A SPAMMER

Maybe you're looking for a cheap way to advertise your business. Maybe you even got spam telling you about all the money you can make by becoming a spammer yourself. An unscrupulous bulk e-mailer might even falsely claim that your advertising message will be sent only to e-mail users who signed up to receive ads. Don't fall for it. If the sheer rudeness of spamming doesn't dissuade you, consider the following:

- You'll earn the enmity of thousands of Netizens, all of whom have the perfect platform to spread bad word of mouth. (Not to mention retaliate with angry e-mail and phone calls.)

- You'll destroy your business's credibility. No legitimate company looks good turning to a technique often employed by scammers and porn peddlers.

- You'll violate your Internet service provider's rules. Almost every ISP forbids users from sending spam. You'll lose your Internet access—and if other ISP's catch wind of your spamming tendencies, you might have a tough time finding another to take you on.

- You might wind up in court. An increasing number of state laws forbid some of spammers' shadier practices or let Internet service providers sue spammers who violate their rules. (More on this in a few pages.)

*Warning:* The term *spam* doesn't apply just to e-mail sent to a list of random strangers. Any unsolicited commercial messages on the Net may be considered spam—and earn its originator the well-deserved wrath of fellow users. Don't post ads to Web site message boards, Usenet newsgroups, e-mail mailing lists, or chat rooms. If you believe your product or business will strongly interest a certain group—for example, you've just written a book about the topic being discussed—look for the group's posted ground rules, check with someone in charge, or listen in on the discussion for a few weeks to find out whether such messages are welcome. After battling spam day in and day out, Netizens can be exquisitely sensitive about any intrusive commercial messages, even the most well-meaning.

I wrote a book about chess for children, but it's carried by precious few bookstores. In an effort to call it to the attention of others, I looked up on the Internet the e-mail addresses of chess clubs and players and invited them to visit my Web site. I got a response from one man saying this was "trolling the Net" and all but illegal, so I stopped doing it. Was he correct?

Better put the messages in check, mate. Sending unsolicited commercial e-mail, especially to individuals but also to organizations or companies that don't expressly welcome such pitches, is a Netiquette no-no. (E-mailing a well-crafted query to a bookstore or a magazine that reviews chess books, however, would be more acceptable—it's their business to field such requests.) To be a more polite self-promoter, try taking out an ad on a chess Web site, seeking out Net message boards or newsletters that allow commercial messages, or building up your Web site with some useful, free-to-all services—how about adding listings for children's chess clubs or an e-mail newsletter with weekly chess tips?

## NEWSLETTER NETIQUETTE

Spam is a scourge. But e-mail newsletters that users can choose to receive can benefit companies and customers alike. (Just ask Banana Republic, whose e-mail sale alerts efficiently relieve me of my clothing budget.) Companies, however, must mind their manners. A poorly conceived or poorly run newsletter can leave a decidedly spam-like aftertaste in customers' mouths. A few corporate-citizenship tips:

- Keep the sign-up process straightforward. Subscribers should have to "opt in": provide their e-mail address specifically for the newsletter or check a sign-up box during registration at your Web site. They shouldn't have to check a box to opt out of mailings. And inform subscribers exactly what they're getting into: Does "Sign up for our newsletter!" mean they'll be getting weekly updates about what's on your site or occasional brief messages about big changes?

- Explain at the beginning of every message what the list is and how recipients can unsubscribe. Use a brief note like this: "Welcome to the weekly shoppingsite.com sale alert. You subscribed to this newsletter at shoppingsite.com. To unsubscribe, visit http://www.shoppingsite.com/newsletter/unsubscribe or reply to this message with the word 'Remove' in the subject line."

- Make unsubscribing super-simple. Give customers a direct link to a Web page where they can unsubscribe. Provide an option for unsubscribing via e-mail for those who don't want to fire up their Web browsers.

- Provide something useful. Rather than just exhorting subscribers to visit your site or buy your stuff, deliver some news they can use right in the e-mail. Touting your Web clothing boutique? Try a short article on five new ways to tie a scarf.

- Customize the messages subscribers get. This can be as simple as letting users pick whether they want to hear about sales in the women's department, the men's department, or both—or as complex as Amazon.com's system that lets customers sign up for e-mail alerts when their favorite authors or musicians release new works.

- Like to use photos and funky formatting in your newsletters? Give subscribers the option for a plain-text version. Not everyone wants to wait for all that artwork to download.

---

## Net Peeve :(

Mailing lists that don't include information on how to unsubscribe.

---

### Embarrassing E-Moment

All those Floridians who didn't vote for president in the 2000 election might not have been befuddled by confusing ballots. They could have just been sick of spam. During the campaign, the Democratic National Committee asked supporters to become "e-Precinct Leaders" by promising to pass along weekly DNC e-mails to ten undecided voters they knew. The Republican National Committee had its own eChampions program, whose participants agreed to send along messages to as many friends as possible. The GOPers ran into a few bugs: At one point, people who never signed up started getting flooded with eChampion e-mail—up to 400 copies of the same message. The RNC said someone had hacked into its server. Could it be . . . Nader?

## CAN THAT SPAM!

Sick of spam? You *can* fight back. Believe it or not, after years of battling back and forth, the good guys are beginning to win the war against spam. The strategy: An ever-improving defense—and a newly energized offense. The defensive lineup consists of filtering and blocking systems that make mincemeat of spam before it reaches your mailbox. The offense is a battalion of state laws that regulate spam—and let Internet service providers sue the pants off some spammers.

**I'm disgusted every time I open my e-mail and find unwanted advertisements. Is there any way to get rid of these? I only want e-mail from my family.**

Hey, advertisers, knock it off! Spam is rude!

Telling spammers off might feel good, but it probably won't help, so let's consider some other tactics. The most drastic is to set up your e-mail program to block all messages from senders other than those you designate. Some programs will automatically filter bulk mail into a separate in-box. An alternative: Get a second e-mail address. Give the main one only to family and friends, and use the other (Hotmail.com and yahoo.com offer free accounts) for shopping or registering at Web sites. Then check the junk-magnet address once in a while to pluck out anything important.

But first, let's talk about strategies that help keep you on the sidelines altogether—that is, ways to keep spammers from getting your e-mail address in the first place.

You might get a ton of spam, while your friend, who uses the same Internet service provider, receives very little. Is she just lucky? Maybe. But more likely you've unwittingly made your e-mail address more available to spammers. To put together their caches of addresses, spammers can't just pick up the phone book. Instead, they use special software to harvest addresses from around the Net. Some ways they can grab your address:

- When you visit a chat room

- When you post a message to a Usenet newsgroup or a message board on a Web site

- If your e-mail address is listed in a Web e-mail address directory

- If your Internet service provider lists it as part of a member directory

- If you subscribe to an e-mail mailing list

- If your address is listed on your Web site (or on someone else's)

- If an unscrupulous company you've provided with your address sells its mailing list

- If you forward an e-mail chain letter

Diabolical, huh? Don't panic. There's a simple way to avoid making yourself vulnerable to spammers. Get a second (or third or fourth) e-mail address and use it when you engage in high-risk activities like chatting or posting to a message board. You can sign up for a free Web-based e-mail account at MSN Hotmail or Yahoo! Mail. Or if you're on America Online, create another screen name. Give your main personal e-mail address only to family and friends, and use the other address for everything else. You can check your spam-bait mailbox less frequently to clear out the junk, and make sure nothing important is hiding amidst it. (In fact, many heavy Web surfers find it worthwhile to have three personal e-mail addresses or screen names: one strictly private one for family and friends, one for medium-risk activities like registering at Web sites and online shopping, and one for sure spam magnets like chatting.)

A few other tips for protecting your address:

- When you sign up for an Internet service provider, create a free Web-based e-mail account, or register at any online site, don't fill out any form that makes your name, e-mail address, and information about yourself available to other members of the service. Such membership directories are gold mines for spammers. If you've already posted information about yourself—such as by creating a Member Profile on America Online—you can often delete it.

- Get your name off of Web e-mail address directories. Visit the sites to check if you're listed and find instructions for removing your name. Some of the most popular directories: bigfoot.com, InfoSpace.com, people.yahoo.com, Switchboard.com, and whowhere.com.

- On some public e-mail mailing lists, any member can request a complete list of subscribers. You can often block your address from being given out. Check the instructions you got when you subscribed to the list to find out how.

- When posting to Web message boards or Usenet discussion groups, some users try to fool automatic e-mail address harvesting programs by tinkering with the e-mail addresses they give: jane@doe.com becomes jane@no-spam.doe.com. If Jane wants fellow users to be able to e-mail her, she tells them in her signature to remove the "no-spam" in her address.

## BLOCK THAT BOZO!

Once you've taken precautions to protect your e-mail address, your next line of defense against junk e-mail is to activate your e-mail program's or Internet service provider's spam-blocking system. Different systems work in different ways, but all have the same goal: Identify incoming spam and prevent it from reaching your in-box. Many systems use sophisticated filters that look for messages from known spammers, combinations of words frequently used in spam, and other distinguishing characteristics (like the mechanisms spammers use to forge their e-mail addresses). Another spam-fighting method is filtering out all messages that aren't addressed directly to you.

These systems aren't perfect. The occasional spam may slip through—or a system may accidentally think a legitimate message is spam. That's why these systems don't immediately delete suspected spam. Instead, they route it to a folder especially designated for junk e-mail. (With some systems, these messages are automatically deleted after a set period of time). You can browse through the folder to make sure nothing important wound up there. If something important did, you can take steps to ensure it's routed to your in-box next time.

Most e-mail programs and ISPs also offer other spam-fighting options. You can choose to block e-mail from senders or domain names you specify. Or you can opt to accept e-mail only from a list of senders you supply—a drastic but effective way to avoid spam (and surprise e-mails from long-lost lovers).

Most ISPs and corporations also work behind the scenes to shield users from spam. Many subscribe to a blacklist of known spammers called MAPS. They also take spammers to court and devote research to keeping up with spammers' slippery techniques. Pay a visit to your ISP's Web site for its latest recommendations on how to give spam the slip.

Some popular e-mail programs' and service providers' spam defenses:

*Microsoft Outlook*: Use the Rules Wizard to activate this program's filters for suspected junk e-mail and adult-content e-mail, which look for suspicious phrases like "extra income" and "over 18." You can route flagged messages to any folder you designate. You can also use the Rules Wizard to block mail from specific senders or mail that is not directly addressed to you.

*America Online*: Go to keyword: Mail Controls to block e-mail from designated senders or domain names or allow e-mail from only designated senders or domain names.

*Yahoo! Mail*: Users are automatically protected by Spamguard, which routes suspected spam to a folder titled Bulk Mail. Messages remain in the Bulk Mail folder for at least thirty days, then Yahoo! automatically deletes them. (You can also delete them yourself.) If you discover a non-spam message incorrectly routed to the Bulk Mail folder, you can use filters to direct it to your in-box in the future—or click on a link to forward the message to Yahoo!, which will evaluate whether it was mistakenly classified as spam. You can also use Yahoo! Mail's filters to block mail from specified senders.

*MSN Hotmail*: Go to Options to turn on the Inbox Protector, which filters suspected spam to a folder called Bulk Mail. This method may also screen out legitimate bulk mail, like mailing-list messages or messages sent to a group of recipients via "Bcc." You can enter the names of senders whose mail you want to receive on a Safe List. Hotmail also allows users to block messages from specified senders.

*EarthLink*: This Internet service provider claims the spam-blocking service with the best name: Spaminator, which is automatically turned on for every new user. Suspected spam gets sent to a Spam Storage folder on EarthLink's Web site, where it sticks around for three weeks before being deleted. While reading through your nabbed spam, you can choose to resend any message to your in-box or, if you believe it was mistakenly classified, send it to the Spaminator for analysis. You can also use your own e-mail program to set up filters or blocks.

If your e-mail program or Internet service provider doesn't offer a spam-blocking system, you can pick up anti-spam software on the Web. Try SpamKiller (www.spamkiller.com) or Spam Buster (www.contactplus.com) or visit a spam-fighting Web site like Abuse.net or www.cauce.org for more links.

## HELP STAMP OUT SPAM

When it comes to battling spam, the best offense is a good defense. Filtering, blocking, and protecting your e-mail address are effective methods to minimize the spam in your in-box. But playing all defense all the time can leave frustrated users itching to fight back. There are a few tactics you can try to turn the tables on spammers. They're not always effective; spammers are slippery. And some of these methods require advanced Net savvy. But give them a try if you're sick of suffering in silence.

- *You can report spammers to their Internet service providers.* Most ISPs strictly forbid spamming and will boot offenders off their services. You can usually report spam coming from a specific domain name by forwarding the message to abuse@[domainname].com. For example, if you've been spammed by someone with the address spammer@yahoo.com, forward the message to abuse@yahoo.com. A Web site called SpamCop (spamcop.net) can examine an e-mail, determine the network where it originated, and automatically send a complaint letter to the sender's ISP in your name. Spammers, of course, often forge their addresses, but there's a chance the wronged ISP may be able to track them down.

- *You can sometimes report spammers to your own Internet service provider.* Not all ISPs encourage this—check your ISP's policy. (If you're getting spam at work, check with your tech department about whether and to whom you should report it.) America Online recommends that its members report all spam by forwarding it to TOSspam@aol.com. (You can also report spam at keyword: Notify AOL.) AOL boasts that its legal eagles have taken more than forty spammers to court.

- *You can report some types of spam to the U.S. government.* If you believe a spam is fraudulent, deceptive, or unfair, you can alert the Federal Trade Commission by forwarding the e-mail to uce@ftc.gov or filling out an online complaint form at www.ftc.gov. The FTC enters complaints about Internet, telemarketing, and other types of consumer scams into a database available to law-enforcement agencies worldwide. You can also bring deceptive spam to the attention of your state attorney general's office.

DON'T: Use nasty tactics—like flooding a spammer's mailbox with messages—to attempt to exact revenge. Two wrongs don't make a right—and in all likelihood, the spammer has either abandoned the address or forged it in the first place, so your assault would only inconvenience an innocent victim or ISP.

Anti-spam measures have made life more difficult for spammers—slightly. One veteran spammer recently told the *Wall Street Journal* that is costs him at least $1,000 to send out 1 million messages—up from $400 two years ago.

## SPAM AND THE LAW

A growing number of states—sixteen at this writing—have passed laws regulating spam in various ways. Most ban one or more of spammers' nastier habits, such as forging return addresses, ignoring recipients' requests to unsubscribe, sending adult-oriented spam to children, and violating their Internet service provider's anti-spam policies. In addition, some state laws let Internet service providers sue spammers for damages.

While a number of spammers have been successfully sued or shut down under these laws, some legal experts think the regulations may eventually face tough going in court, since the Constitution grants the U.S. Congress, not the states, authority to regulate interstate commerce. And so far, spam battlers haven't gotten any help from Capitol Hill: While a few federal anti-spam bills have been introduced in Congress, none has been passed into law. In the court of etiquette, however, spam continues to be a first-degree felony.

**I work as a corporate recruiter and regularly e-mail job openings to potential candidates. Is this considered spam?**

Headhunters don't always play by Marquis of Queensberry rules—but if recipients didn't request these mailings, they're spam: bad manners, bad business, and possibly illegal. Switch to a newsletter wanderlusting workers can voluntarily sign up for.

# 12

## Spy Games: E-Mail Privacy

- *Is my employer spying on my e-mail at work?*
- *How can I keep my e-mail safe from hackers?*
- *Encrypted, anonymous, and disappearing e-mail*

Not worried about the privacy of your e-mail? Three names that should send a chill down your spine: Michael Smyth, Monica Lewinsky, and Bill Gates.

First, meet Mr. Smyth: In 1995, the Pillsbury employee was fired after supervisors intercepted e-mail messages he sent a co-worker in which Smyth allegedly threatened to "kill the backstabbing bastards," referring to sales department managers, and called a planned holiday party the "Jim Jones Koolaid affair." Smyth sued for his job back, claiming that company policy stated that e-mail was confidential. But in one of the first federal court decisions to address employee e-mail privacy, a judge ruled that "the company's interest in preventing inappropriate and unprofessional comments or even illegal activity over its e-mail system outweighs any privacy interest the employee may have." Lesson: At work, your employer has the right to monitor every e-mail you send.

As for Monica: Prosecutor Kenneth Starr's investigators retrieved scores of deleted e-mail messages from Lewinsky's home and work computers, providing some of the most damning—and embarrassing—evidence of her affair with President Clinton, including the unforgettable quote "The big creep didn't even call me on V-Day." Lesson: Just because you delete an e-mail doesn't mean it's gone.

And Billionaire Bill: The Microsoft mogul won't soon forget the power of e-mail, either. During the software giant's block-buster antitrust trial, government prosecutors subpoenaed internal e-mails sent by everyone from Gates on down to low-level employees. Some of those messages became key smoking guns in court. One Microsoft senior executive sent this internal e-mail about the battle with rival Netscape for dominance in the Web browser market, in which Microsoft was accused of competing unfairly by integrating its browser program with its popular oper-ating system: "It seems clear that it will be very hard to increase browser market share on the merits of [Microsoft browser] IE 4 alone. It will be more important to leverage the OS asset to make people use IE instead of [Netscape browser] Navigator." In his own taped deposition, Gates claimed not to remember having sent several e-mail messages attributed to him, including one ask-ing: "Do we have a clear plan on what we want Apple to do to undermine [rival computer company] Sun?" Lesson: Even private conversations can become future public statements.

How private is your e-mail really? "About as private as a post-card," goes the phrase security experts love to cite. (Ever since I heard that, I've tried to write something mildly salacious on post-cards just to liven them up for the looky-loos.) The analogy is apt. At work, your e-mail may be monitored by your employer. E-mail sent from work or home can be unexpectedly outed by a crimi-nal or civil legal action. And while it's a federal crime for any unauthorized third party to intercept private e-mail, that doesn't mean no one will try—whether it's a crime of technical skill (you're targeted by a malicious hacker) or a crime of opportunity (a nosy neighbor notices you forgot to sign off of your Hotmail account before leaving the cybercafé).

How to safeguard your e-mail's privacy? The most important step is to realize just how little privacy you have, especially in the workplace. We'll talk about rules to stay out of trouble, as well as strategies to keep e-mail safe from unauthorized snoops and a few high-tech solutions to privacy problems.

"You already have zero privacy—get over it."

—A favorite saying of Scott McNealy, CEO of Sun Microsystems

## *IS YOUR BOSS BIG BROTHER? E-MAIL PRIVACY AT WORK*

Is your company spying on your e-mail? You'd better believe it. And by that I mean two things: First, more and more companies are monitoring their employees' e-mail—some routinely, some only in specific cases when they suspect wrongdoing. And second, even if you suspect your bosses aren't playing Big Brother, it's far wiser to assume they are anyway. ("Hey, I haven't been fired yet!" is dangerous, though popular, reasoning.) Your company may not be actively monitoring your e-mail, but your old messages— retrievable from your computer's hard drive or from backup tapes many companies maintain for years—could suddenly come back to haunt you in a variety of situations.

Who's watching? According to a 2000 survey by the American Management Association, 38 percent of major U.S. firms monitor their employees' e-mail—that's a jump from 27 percent in 1999.

- 6.8 percent constantly monitor employees' e-mail

- 4.6 percent do it routinely, but not all the time

- 13.5 percent do it occasionally

- 13.9 percent do it only in specified instances, such as for performance evaluations or disciplinary investigations

Isn't spying on people's e-mail illegal? Not at work it's not. As of this writing, your e-mail privacy rights at work, under U.S. law, are nearly nonexistent. The reasoning: Your employer pays for your computer, your Net connection, and your time—in other words, they own your increasingly desk-chair-shaped rear end.

Most companies don't even have to inform employees that their e-mail is being monitored, although there are exceptions. A few states have laws requiring that companies disclose their monitoring practices, and federal agencies and some unionized companies have to tell employees too. In the AMA survey, nearly 90 percent of companies conducting monitoring disclosed that fact to their employees—good news on the honesty front—but that still means 10 percent didn't.

> **Survey Says**
> *According to the American Management Association survey, 78 percent of major firms monitor at least one form of their employees' communications.*
>
> - *54.1 percent monitor Internet use (such as Web surfing)*
>
> - *44 percent monitor telephone use (such as numbers called and time spent on the phone)*
>
> - *38.1 percent monitor e-mail*
>
> - *14.6 percent videotape employees*
>
> - *11.5 percent monitor the content of telephone conversations*

What are they looking for? The snoops are pretty much like you—they're just trying to cover their butts. About the scariest thing a corporate bigwig can imagine is a sexual harassment or civil rights lawsuit—in which a stack of pornographic or racist e-mails being swapped by employees can make very compelling evidence. In addition, in heavily regulated industries like the financial services sector, surveillors watch for employees engaged in illegal activities such as insider trading or defrauding customers. Finally, some companies might be looking for workers sending out résumés, badmouthing their bosses, or just sending too much personal e-mail.

### Embarrassing E-Moment

One of the first times e-mail was used as evidence in a sexual harassment suit came in 1995, when copies of e-mail messages with jokes such as "25 reasons beer is better than women" were used to buttress a claim against Chevron Corporation. The company settled for $2.2 million.

According to the American Management Association survey, more than half of major firms had disciplined employees for misusing e-mail, while 16 percent had fired employees. What infractions are grounds for a pink slip? In a 2000 survey conducted by *CIO* (Chief Information Officer) magazine, 90 percent of tech executives said sexual harassment via e-mail was a fireable offense, 84 percent said sending pornography could bring the ax, and 80 percent said employees could be fired for compromising trade secrets.

### Embarrassing E-Moment

In 1999, the New York Times Company fired twenty-three employees—most in a Norfolk, Virginia, administrative office—for sending e-mail it deemed "inappropriate and offensive." The messages reportedly included gags about women and men and—stop the presses—blond jokes.

How exactly do companies monitor e-mail? There's probably not a room in the basement where a bunch of squinting speed-readers peruse your every message. Instead, most companies use software that flags certain words—like sexual terms, racial epithets, executives' names, words like "résumé," financial lingo like "shares" or "short"—in certain contexts. The programs—as sophisticated and customizable as your company cares to pay for—might then call the message to the attention of a human being.

## OLD E-MAIL DOESN'T DIE—OR FADE AWAY

Relatively few companies constantly monitor employees' e-mail, but a disciplinary problem or legal action can place messages you've already sent or received under scrutiny. You already know that your e-mail program's "delete" button is deceptive. Given access to your computer's hard drive, a talented techie can revive the dearly deleted. (You can use special software to wipe your hard drive clean of message remnants, although such programs still might not foil an expert in computer forensics.)

In addition, most companies make their own backup tapes of all incoming and outgoing e-mail messages, storage files over which you have no control. How long does your employer keep these files around? Perhaps months, perhaps years. In some industries and in government offices, a minimum time is required by law. And while most companies might be diligent about making tapes, not all are diligent about electronically shredding them when they can. So for the purposes of privacy, consider your e-mail to have been granted eternal life.

### Embarrassing E-Moment

Sam Campana, a former mayor of Scottsdale, Arizona, had the questionable habit of calling 911 from her cellular phone when she got lost to request driving directions from the operator. The city's police chief sent Campana e-mail warning her that this was not a proper use of 911. When the local press requested copies of officials' e-mail under state and federal sunshine laws, reporters turned up the message—and Campana topped the nation's punchlines for a few days.

This wealth of forever-after e-mail has, of course, become a bonanza for the legal profession. In civil and criminal cases, lawyers can now sift through reams of their targets' messages in search of smoking guns. Is this a healthy development? Probably not. If everything we write in e-mail can and will be used against us in a court of law, e-mail becomes a much less useful communications tool—forget about brainstorming or idle interoffice banter. "The preservation and discovery of computer-deleted material has forced companies and prudent individuals to severely curtail the practice of using e-mail for all but the most innocuous materials," James M. Rosenbaum, a U.S. District Court judge in Minnesota, wrote in an article in *The Green Bag*, a legal journal, proposing a six-month statute of limitations on exhuming old e-mail. Such a rule, he wrote, "acknowledges that anyone is entitled to make a mistake and to think a less than perfect thought." But for now, alas, the e-mail paper trail is cold, hard legal reality—just ask Bill Gates or Monica Lewinsky.

### Embarrassing E-Moment

One of the first public figures to stumble over old e-mail was Reagan aide Oliver North. His secretary Fawn Hall worked overtime shredding paper documents, but North forgot about backup tapes of e-mail messages he had deleted. In 1987, hundreds of e-mail messages helped implicate North in the Iran-Contra scandal.

### Embarrassing E-Moment

Bill Gates isn't the only ubergeek to have been tripped up by old e-mails. E-mail sent by the teenage founder of Napster, Sean Fanning, and his fellow execs gave the record industry a boost in its bid to shut down the Internet music-swapping service for copyright violations. In one exchange, a chat-room moderator wrote to Fanning, "Admitting we know Napster is used for the transfer of illegal MP3 files, might not be the best thing to do." Replied Fanning: "Excellent point . . . you should all be very aware of what you say." He then added: "It appears my hypocrisy knows no bounds."

## IT PAYS TO BE PARANOID: RULES FOR E-MAIL AT WORK

- *Be very, very careful what you write on your corporate e-mail system to recipients inside or outside the company.* Don't send any message, joke or not, that the most sensitive soul could construe as pornographic, racist, sexist, or demeaning to any individual or group. (Yes, that rules out just about any joke people over the age of eight will find funny, but you should be trading jokes on your own time anyway—it's a job, not open mike night at the coffeehouse.) Don't use any off-color language. Don't flirt. Don't job-hunt. Don't complain or gossip about a boss, client, co-worker, or underling. Don't discuss anything unethical or illegal. Don't discuss any sensitive personal information: an illness, your finances, your love life. And when discussing ticklish business situations, don't say anything you wouldn't want to own up to in court.

  Experts are fond of the warning "Don't say anything in e-mail you wouldn't say to _____ ." I can't settle on just one way to end this sentence, so fill in the blank with your pick:

your boss

your mother

your worst enemy

*The New York Times*

a nun

---

### Embarrassing E-Moment

Shortly after the March 1991 beating of motorist Rodney King, Laurence Powell, one of the LAPD officers later tried for the beating, sent out a message via a police computer system: "Oops. I haven't beaten anyone so bad in a long time." A transcript of the message was used in court against Powell.

- *Avoid sending personal e-mail from work, or keep it to a minimum.* If your workplace is the sort that frowns on personal phone calls, better follow the same rule for personal e-mail and avoid it entirely. If your company's rules are more relaxed, it's still best not to conduct your entire social life from your desk. Stick to a few personal messages a day sent during your lunch hour or after hours. And don't discuss anything you wouldn't want your bosses to know about.

- *If you don't have an Internet account at home to use for personal e-mail, get a free Web-based e-mail account.* Yahoo!, MSN Hotmail, and Excite are among companies that offer free e-mail addresses you can check using the Web. Your e-mail messages will be sent by and stored on the Web site's computers. But beware: If your company is using a program that records everything you type at your office computer, it will see your Web-based e-mail, too. And of course, if it's monitoring your Web habits, it will find out if you park at Hotmail.com for hours.

- *Learn all you can about your company's surveillance.* You should always assume your company is watching. But it can't hurt to do a little snooping about how closely your e-mail is being monitored, what the spies are looking for, what methods are being used, and how long backup tapes are kept around. Find out your company's official position on e-mail monitoring. Then make friends with one of your office's technology staffers and see what he or she knows about what's really going on. Or simply call your company's human-resources department and ask. You never know what a bored bureaucrat may reveal.

### Survey Says
*58 percent of workers in a survey said they are not worried about their employers monitoring their e-mail use, but 79 percent said they keep a separate account for personal e-mail.*

*Source: Vault.com*

## MONITORING AND MANNERS

**At work a client e-mails us raunchy jokes. How can I get him to stop without losing his business?**

Forget losing the client—your company could lose its shirt in a sexual-harassment suit, so stanching the raunch takes priority. (And, law aside, you and your colleagues shouldn't have to read sleaze.) Which is the perfect excuse to use with the Neanderthal client: Tell him your lawyer has put the kibosh on the blue stuff.

When I wrote this answer, several readers wrote in to say my advice might risk offending the client. "You'll catch more flies with honey than you will with vinegar," one wrote. I stand by my answer: Appearing to condone raunchy jokes in the workplace is just too dangerous nowadays. If you're super worried about offending him—or really do get a kick out of his material—you could ask him to switch to your personal e-mail address.

> ### Survey Says
> *46 percent of workers say they have never received sexually explicit or otherwise improper e-mails at work, while 25 percent say they receive such messages "sometimes" or "often." 14 percent of workers say if they got such an e-mail, they would forward it to friends or coworkers.*
>
> *Source: Vault.com*

What about accidental e-mail? I once was e-mailed an extremely unfunny racist dirty joke by a stranger in some far-flung division of my company who had obviously entered the wrong e-mail address. I didn't want to rat on the poor bozo, but nor did I want to appear to be trading in contraband, just in case anyone was watching. I replied (without including the original message), telling the guy that he had the wrong address and not to e-mail me such material again. And I saved a copy of my reply. I never heard from him again, or from any corporate watcher. But it never hurts to be paranoid.

## Embarrassing E-Moment

In 2000, the Midland, Michigan–based division of Dow Chemical fired fifty employees for sending inappropriate messages. The offending e-mails reportedly included an animated image of President Clinton singing about Monica Lewinsky and a silhouette of the cartoon *The Flintstones'* Fred, Barney, and Wilma getting cuddly in a ménage à trois.

## A WORD ABOUT WEB SURFING

This book focuses on e-mail, not the Web, but I can't let this chapter go by without a warning about surfing the Web at work. Even more companies watch where employees surf—54 percent, according to the American Management Association survey—than monitor employees' e-mail. Most companies don't mind if you occasionally check up on sports scores, but spend office hours trading stocks, planning your vacation, or surfing porn sites and you may find yourself out of a job (and a Net connection). And don't surf any sites—medical resources, job-hunting sites, political organizations, personal ads—that might inadvertently reveal information you don't want your employer to know.

## IMHO (In My Humble Opinion): Surveillance Etiquette

The blunt realities of workplace e-mail surveillance lead to rules that are more about self-preservation than proper etiquette. (Although paranoid employees do tend to write pretty polite e-mails.) But perhaps etiquette rules should apply to the watchers themselves. Is there a polite way for employers to go about invading employees' privacy? Well, maybe not, but the practice isn't going away, so here are some suggestions about how employers can mind their manners.

- Inform employees if they are being monitored. Doing this surreptitiously simply isn't playing fair.

- Issue a clear policy about what kinds of e-mails are and aren't allowed. Is any personal e-mail sent from a work computer grounds for discipline? Is forwarding jokes or chain letters banned? Let your workers know—don't keep them guessing.

- Use the least intrusive levels and methods of surveillance for the job. If you're monitoring for insider trading, customize your surveillance program to check for words like "buy," "sell," and "merger," not idle complaints about low-level managers. If you suspect that an employee is goofing off, first check the amount of time he spends on the Web, not the sites he visits.

- Don't embarrass employees. It's enough to note that an employee's message was "personal" in a disciplinary report—not to write up details of her argument with her boyfriend. Set a strict confidentiality policy so those privy to workers' e-mail don't start gossip.

- Give as few people as possible access to employees' e-mail—every tech staffer or manager shouldn't be able to snoop. Have someone other than an employee's direct manager supervise surveillance or examine the employee's e-mail for disciplinary purposes and bring the manager into the loop only when a violation is confirmed.

## WHO ELSE MIGHT BE WATCHING?

Your employer might not be the only snoop eavesdropping on your e-mail. If law-enforcement organizations suspect you of wrongdoing, they can get a warrant to seize your e-mail from your Internet service provider or retrieve files from your computer's hard drive. And then—attention, *X-Files* fans!—there are the technologies developed by the government's super-snoops. The FBI can wiretap computer communications, gobbling up information sent to and from a target's computer. The National Security Agency, meanwhile, boasts Echelon, a global wiretap program that reportedly eavesdrops on billions of international e-mails, phone calls, and other communications, looking for words like "bomb," "President," or "narcotics" in suspicious contexts. Is this a problem if you're a law-abiding citizen? Probably not (though ever-suspicious European officials have accused these programs of being out to swipe corporate secrets). But they're a chilling reminder that e-mail is anything but private.

---

### Embarrassing E-Moment

In 1997, Timothy McVeigh, a much-decorated senior chief petty officer in the U.S. Navy, saw his seventeen-year career destroyed by an e-mail that led superiors to suspect he was gay. The trouble started when McVeigh (no relation to the Oklahoma City bomber) wrote to the wife of a shipmate from his personal e-mail account. The wife was alarmed by McVeigh's e-mail address, boysrch@aol.com, shorthand, she guessed, for "boy search." She looked up the sender's American Online member profile. There, he described himself as "Tim" from "Honolulu." Under marital status, it read "gay." A navy investigator called AOL and confirmed that "Tim" was, in fact, McVeigh—a disclosure that breached AOL's confidentiality policy. A court ruled that the navy had violated its own "don't ask, don't tell" policy in pursuing the case, and McVeigh reached a settlement that allowed him to retire. His suit against AOL also ended in a settlement.

---

Then, of course, there are those who spy on e-mail illegally. The danger can take on many guises, from sophisticated cyber-criminals who try to steal corporate secrets to, more often, mischievous teens who have just enough technological skill to con naive users out of their passwords. And users who share their computers with others can leave their e-mail wide open to prying eyes simply by being absentminded.

ETIQUETTE TIP: In some high-tech circles, it's bad form to call a miscreant who breaks into someone else's e-mail accounts, Web sites, or computers a hacker. The word *hacker* originally referred to an elite computer-programming enthusiast—or, as defined by *The New Hacker's Dictionary*, "A person who enjoys exploring the details of programmable systems and how to stretch their capabilities, as opposed to most users, who prefer to learn only the minimum necessary." Those who back this definition of *hacker* insist that people who use their computer skills for evil should be termed crackers. While the old-school hackers have pretty much lost the media battle—when someone breaks into a high-profile Web site, you can bet the headlines will call him a hacker—if you find yourself among a bunch of gray-bearded techie types, watch your language. After all, hackers built the Net.

## SNOOP-PROOFING E-MAIL

- Take precautions against viruses (see Chapter 10, "Viruses"). Anti-virus software and other properly prudent measures, like not opening unexpected e-mail attachments, can keep you safe from Trojan horses (virus-like programs that can give senders access to your computer) and other efforts to compromise your computer's security.

- Pick a hard-to-crack password for your e-mail account (and any other sensitive computer information). Make your password difficult to guess: Don't use any common English word, and especially don't use popular passwords such as "password," "love," "God," "sex," or variations on your name. A combination of letters and numbers makes the best password.

- Change your password frequently—every 30 to 120 days, security experts recommend.

- Don't give your password to anyone, be it your best friend or someone claiming to be a representative of your Internet service provider. (The latter is a common online scam, so common that America Online now puts a warning on chat-room screens: "Reminder: AOL staff will never ask you for your password.")

- Make sure you sign off your e-mail account when you leave a computer you share with others, such as a terminal in a classroom or a public library. Quit the Internet access program or

Web browser you're using. (If you've been browsing the Web, it's also a good idea to clear the program's cache, which stores a list of sites you've visited.) When signing on to your account, don't select any option that stores your name or password on the computer. If you use your own computer but others have access to it when you're away—such as during your lunch hour at work—use a screen saver that requires anyone seeking to use the computer to enter a password.

---

"I don't do any e-mails, because I don't think e-mail's secure. You know, everybody laughed when we had all this e-mail controversy. The Republicans wanted Al Gore's e-mails and mine. I've sent a grand total of two e-mails. I e-mailed John Glenn in space. And I e-mailed some Marines and sailors on a ship at Christmas. That was it."

—President Bill Clinton, to *Vanity Fair* magazine, December 2000

---

### Embarrassing E-Moment

Former CIA director John Deutch was stripped of his security clearances in 1999 for storing classified national security secrets on an unsecured home computer that was used to receive and send e-mail (as well as access pornographic Web sites).

## PUMPED-UP PRIVACY

Are we losing the battle for e-mail privacy? The snoops get ever more sophisticated, but e-mailers have a few technological weapons in their arsenal.

*Encrypted e-mail:* If you're concerned about your e-mail being intercepted in transit—you're e-mailing sensitive business infor-

mation, perhaps, or maybe you just enjoy playing James Bond—
you can encrypt it. Encryption programs scramble your message
using a secret code. Your intended recipient has a key that can
decode the message. Anyone else would see an unreadable (and,
if the encryption is strong enough, uncrackable) string of letters,
numbers, and symbols. Some e-mail programs come with built-in
encryption features. If yours doesn't, head for the Web site
www.pgp.com, where you can download the popular, powerful
encryption program modestly called Pretty Good Privacy. You can
integrate PGP into common e-mail programs such as Microsoft
Outlook and Eudora; read the online manual carefully to learn
how to install and use this valuable (and free, if you're downloading it for personal use only) technology.

*Anonymous e-mail*: It's easy to imagine situations in which
you wouldn't want anyone to be able to connect an e-mail message to your real-life identity. You might want to use e-mail to
blow the whistle on wrongdoing at your company. You might
want to contribute to an e-mail mailing list—perhaps a support
group for battered women or people with mental illnesses—without your employer or other people you know offline finding out.
The bad news: Even if your e-mail address doesn't betray your
real name, it's fairly easy for someone to use the header information—all that gobbledygook at the top of e-mail messages—to
trace a message back to you. The good news: The Net offers services that let you go incognito. Anonymous remailers strip your
message of any identifying clues, then send it on its way. The easiest to use are Web-based remailers: Just visit a Web site and type
in your message. Try searching Yahoo! for "anonymous e-mail" for
a current list of such services. Of course, if your employer is monitoring your Web surfing, better use anonymous e-mail services
from home or a public computer.

*Anonymous e-mail etiquette*: It's critical to good e-mail etiquette—and to the survival of these invaluable services—that you
not abuse anonymous remailers by using them to commit illegal
acts, make defamatory comments, threaten or harass anyone, send
junk e-mail, or spread hate speech. (Anonymity doesn't render
you immune to the law—law-enforcement agencies or a plaintiff

in a civil case can get a court to order the remailer to turn over its records, if it keeps them. Even if it doesn't, there may be ways to track you down.) Don't use anonymous e-mail to play a practical joke or to tease anyone, either. Such messages can scare recipients—and, as Mom would put it, anonymous e-mail is not a toy.

*Disappearing e-mail*: "This message will self-destruct in five seconds...." For *Mission: Impossible* fans—and e-mailers who hate the idea of leaving a permanent record—a few software companies have been developing ways to stamp an expiration date on e-mail. These features, mostly targeted at corporations (listening, Microsoft?), have only recently started entering the market: Check out Disappearing Inc. (www.disappearing.com) for a feature that works with almost any e-mail program. You can also use "shredder" software (included with computer utility packages from makers like McAfee and Symantec, or look for free programs on the Web) to ensure that e-mail you delete is really deleted—although elite experts in retrieving deleted messages may be able to outsmart some of these programs. And remember, the person you sent the e-mail to has a copy.

### Embarrassing E-Moment

Some describe the Bill Clinton–Monica Lewinsky sex scandal as a low point in presidential morality. Others decry it as the result of the politics of personal destruction. The rest of us can just remember it as one long national Embarrassing E-Moment. Consider . . .

- Prosecutors also seized the computer of Lewinsky's friend Catherine Allday Davis, a former college classmate. E-mail Davis sent to Lewinsky, including thoughts about her husband, was published, over the objections of Davis's lawyer, in an appendix to the Starr report.

- According to the Starr report, Lewinsky showed President Clinton an e-mail describing the effect of chewing Altoid mints before performing oral sex. Lewinsky was chewing

Altoids at the time, but the president replied that he did not have enough time for oral sex.

- And, of course, we got a once-in-a-lifetime window into the world of e-mail chitchat, courtesy of Lewinsky and Linda Tripp. (Didn't these two have *work* to do?") A few more samples:

```
From: Lewinsky, Monica, OSD/PA
To: Tripp, Linda, OSD/PA
Subject: RE: Afternoon
Date: Tuesday, February 04, 1997 2:15 PM
Priority: High
```

```
Thank God for you! Oh Linda, i don't know
what I am going to do. I just don't under-
stand what went wrong, what happened? How
could he do this to me? Why did he keep
up contact with me for so long and now
nothing, now when we could be together?
Maybe it was the intrigue of wanting some-
thing he couldn't have (easily) with all
that was going on then? Maybe he wanted
to insure he could have variety and phone
sex while he was on the road for those
months? AAAAHHHHH!!!!! I am going to lose
it! And, where is Betty's phone call?
What's up with all this s——? oh, well.
bye.

msl
```

From: Tripp, Linda, OSD/PA
To: Lewinsky, Monica, OSD/PA
RE: hi, ya
Wednesday, March 05, 7997 11:34 AM


Are you asking me if the tie is really pretty? It is positively gorgeous. I am knot (ha!) particularly into ties, but from my exposure to you, I am developing an interest. Yours was stupendous, no kidding, clean, crisp, texture, color, pattern, bright, without being at all over the top . . . a total hit.

# 13

# *Netiquette for Kids*

- *What rules should kids follow to avoid risks on the Net?*
- *Is it unethical for me to spy on my teenager's Web surfing?*
- *What's the polite way to ask someone for homework help via e-mail?*

My mother had a standard line when she didn't want me to drive someplace by myself. "But I'm a good driver," I'd protest. "I trust you," she'd reply, "I just don't trust the other drivers out there."

Many parents feel the same way about their children using the Internet. They know the Net is a terrific educational resource and a fun way for kids to socialize. They trust their kids. But they worry about the dangers their kids face from other people on the Net—dangers that young surfers, like beginning drivers, may not expect, recognize, or know how to defend themselves against. Predators attempt to seduce or trick vulnerable kids: Web sites tempt them with prizes in return for personal information; spammers bombard them with advertisements for porn sites. No child is invulnerable: Your daughter might be well behaved, trustworthy, and computer-savvy enough to juggle four chat sessions, two e-mail replies, and an honors history paper simultaneously. But if she weren't naive, reckless, or just plain stupid on occasion, she wouldn't be a kid.

So the most important e-etiquette rules regarding kids are safety rules—the do's and don'ts parents must ensure that their children learn and follow. But these aren't the only rules for the junior Net set. Just like in the real world, kids online can be cruel, rude, or annoying to other children (anyone care to remember junior high school gym class?) or to grown-ups, sometimes without realizing the consequences of their actions. So, like adults, wired kids have to learn to mind their manners online. (At least on the Net no one knows you have your elbows on the table.)

Finally, there's the issue of proper etiquette between parents and children. (No, going through labor didn't give you an automatic etiquette exemption, though it does grant you considerable leeway.) How can parents guard their children's safety while respecting their children's freedom and privacy? How should children show respect for their parents' rules, time, and property? Every family will come up with its own approach. But when it comes to kids and the Net, respect—for rules, for parents, for children, for others on the Net, for danger—is a crucial family value.

## WHAT DO KIDS DO ONLINE?

Believe it or not, surveys show that kids use the Internet for homework research more than for any other activity. Of course they're not necessarily poring over the *Encyclopaedia Brittanica* Web site solo: E-mail, chat, and instant-messaging are the next most popular pastimes for teens, while preteens prefer game-playing.

> **Survey Says**
> *52 percent of teens say they have sent e-mail to a stranger or received e-mail from a stranger.*
>
> Source: *2000 Web Savvy and Safety survey sponsored by Microsoft*

## FIRST STEPS

The most important thing a parent can do to make sure kids follow online safety and etiquette rules? *Be* a parent. Some parents tend to ignore or become overly paranoid about their kids' online activities. The Net is not exempt from real-world dangers or real-world rules—and it's not exempt from real-world parenting. Talk to your children about what they're up to online and who their friends are. If you're not online, have your kids show you around. More tips for making the Net part of family life:

- Work out a set of house rules regarding the Net—everything from safety do's and don'ts to the amount of time a child may spend online—together with your child. (You're the ultimate judge, but if your kid objects to any of the rules, she should have a chance to petition the court. If she starts filing *amicus* briefs from the ACLU, though, you're out of your league.) Consider listing the rules in a printed contract you and your kid both sign—with kids, rules have a way of going in one ear and out the other. (Probably because the relevant brain cells are taken up with song lyrics.)

- Put the computer your child uses to surf the Net in a family room, not the child's bedroom. Ask him what he's up to every once in a while, or look over his shoulder after asking permission. (Yes, ask permission—an important sign of trust and respect that will also teach your child to respect others' privacy. If he panics or hides the screen every time you stop by, however, it's time to have a serious talk.)

- Surf with your kids. Before you let them out on the Net solo, take them on training-wheels spins; once they're wired, every once in a while, have them give you a tour of sites and chat rooms they like to visit. Ask for a peek at their instant-message buddy list, too.

- Talk with your kids about the dangers on the Net in detail. The more kids know about a problem, the more likely they are to take it seriously and overcome the grip of "it'll never happen to me" syndrome. Share your worries, and ask your kids what they worry the most about. Ask them about risky situations they've already faced and how they deal with them: Have they ever been invited to a private chat room by a stranger? Do they get pornographic spam? Have they ever accidentally visited a Web site that made them uncomfortable? You might be surprised by the risks your kids regularly face online—and by how they capably deal with them.

- Be honest about any monitoring you do of kids' online activities. There are several ways for parents to peek in on kids, from using a child's password to read his e-mail to installing software that secretly records all of his Net moves. Surreptitious snooping should be an absolute last resort, as it will demolish your kids' trust in you. Remember that kids may also access the Internet somewhere you can't monitor, like school or a friend's house.

**I'm thirteen. I got into trouble with the Internet and my mom took it away from me. I want her to trust me again. What can I do?**

Bringing home straight A's and volunteering to scrub the bathroom wouldn't hurt. More to the point (assuming your "trouble" didn't reach the level of, say, hacking into the Pentagon): Your mom could use software to monitor your Net moves, but a simpler, less sneaky solution would be for you to offer to move the computer to the family room (if it's not there already) and go online only when she's there to peek over your shoulder occasionally. Which you will promise not to whine about.

> **Survey Says**
> *63 percent of parents say they check to see whom their teens are e-mailing, but only 22 percent of teens believe their parents are doing that. 14 percent of teens say they have an e-mail address their parents don't know about.*
>
> Source: *2000 Web Savvy and Safety survey sponsored by Microsoft*

## DANGERS AND DEFENSES

The Net may not be as dangerous as scaremongers, politicians, and ratings-hungry TV newsfolks often make it out to be. Pedophiles don't lurk in every chat room. Hard-core pornography is fairly difficult to "stumble" across accidentally. But it's just as unwise to underestimate the very real risks children face—and the importance of understanding the dangers, taking precautions to minimize risks, and knowing what to do if a child encounters trouble. Here's an overview of the chief aspects of the Net's dark side, along with safety tips for kids and their grown-ups.

*Note*: Online safety for kids is a subject worth its own book—and there are several good ones available for parents who want to learn more about specific threats, kid-friendly sites, and software to keep children safe. (One of my favorites: *The Parent's Guide to Protecting Your Children in Cyberspace*, by Parry Aftab, a lawyer and director of cyberangels.org, the online arm of the Guardian Angels organization.) There are also several Web sites worth bookmarking and exploring:

- www.cyberangels.org: A site with detailed safety education information and a large volunteer staff that can help kids and parents report and cope with problems.

- www.missingkids.com: The Web site of the National Center for Missing & Exploited Children offers a tipline for reports of child exploitation and child pornography.

- www.wiredkids.org: A nonprofit project that offers information about safety and using the Internet effectively for kids, parents, teachers, and schools.

## Predators

A pedophile who seduces or befriends a child online and lures him or her into a real-world encounter is the worst nightmare of almost every parent of a wired kid. These incidents are very rare—but not rare enough.

### Rules for Kids

- Never give out personal information about yourself to anyone you meet online. This includes your last name, age, gender, birthday, e-mail address, street address, telephone number, school name, parents' names, or anything else someone could use to identify you or locate you offline.

- Don't fill out a profile or join a member directory offered by your Internet service provider, instant-messenger service, or any Web site. You may not realize it, but your name, age, hometown, and any other information you enter are made public to anyone using the service or site.

- Never telephone or accept a phone call from anyone you meet online unless you ask your parents first. (Many parents ban phone contact and in-person meetings altogether.)

- Never arrange an in-person meeting with anyone you meet online unless you have permission from a parent.

- Ask your parents before sending your photo to someone you meet online. Never post it in public.

- Don't keep online secrets from your parents. Tell them about any new friends you exchange e-mail with.

- If someone e-mails you something or says something online that makes you uncomfortable, tell a grown-up immediately.

### Rules for Parents

- Talk to your kids about who their online friends are.

- Make sure children know that people online may not be who they say they are. Talk to them about the danger of cyber-predators.

- Have kids stick to special kids-only chat rooms, which are monitored by adults. Consider banning children, especially younger ones, from using chat rooms at all.

- Be alert for warning signs, like a child receiving mysterious phone calls, letters, or gifts or becoming secretive about his or her computer use.

### If It Happens

- If your child has been sexually solicited or sent sexually explicit images by someone who knows he or she is under eighteen—or if your child is missing and you suspect a cyber-predator is involved—call your local law-enforcement agency, the FBI (the local field office is in the phone book), and the National Center for Missing & Exploited Children's CyberTipline (1-800-THE-LOST or www.missingkids.com), which shares tips with law-enforcement agencies. To preserve evidence, don't touch anything on your computer unless a qualified cybercrime investigator tells you to.

- If you or your child are sent child pornography, contact the FBI or National Center for Missing & Exploited Children.

## Cyberstalking

A child may receive a stream of threatening or harassing e-mail from a stranger who may threaten to hurt him or her in real life. Stalking can be triggered by an online argument or a rebuffed flirtation—or a stalker, who might be an adult or another child, might target a victim at random.

### Rules for Kids and Adults

- Don't respond to any e-mails, instant messages, or message-board postings that are obscene, suggestive, threatening, or insulting, not even to say "Stop it." Tell a grown-up about any message that makes you uncomfortable.

- If you get more than one harassing message from the same address, save the messages and tell someone.

- Again, never give out personal information to anyone you meet online.

### If It Happens

- Report any harassing or abusive e-mail message to your Internet service provider and the sender's Internet service provider. Forward the message with a brief note explaining the situation, to "abuse@" the domain name of the sender's address. For example, if the message came from badguy@yahoo.com, forward the message to abuse@yahoo.com. (America Online uses a different address: It asks that users forward abusive e-mail to TOSEMail1@aol.com or report it by visiting keyword: Notify AOL.) The ISP can track down the sender (if he's not faking his return address) and take action—like kicking him or her off the service.

- Block future e-mail from the sender's address. AOL, Yahoo! Mail, and MSN Hotmail let you add names to a list of blocked senders; most other popular e-mail programs let you set up filters to route incoming messages from that address to the trash.

- If a cyberstalker threatens to hurt your child in real life or indicates he knows your child's offline identity, call the cops. You can also contact an organization like cyberangels.org for additional support.

### Inappropriate Material

Porn gets all the press, but it's just a start. Kids can seek out or inadvertently stumble across a variety of material parents may not want them to see: Web sites advocating bigotry; discussions of drug use; information about buying guns or building bombs; sites offering online gambling, hoaxes, and misleading information.

### Rules for Kids

- Tell your parents if you stumble across a site that makes you uncomfortable.

- Don't guess at a Web site's address. Some porn sites (like the infamous whitehouse.com) use Web addresses that are slight variations on names of popular sites. Find sites through a Web directory like Yahoo.com or the kid-friendly Yahooligans.com.

- Be skeptical of information you see on the Web, especially anything you see on a site you're not familiar with. Don't ever spread a rumor or follow any advice you see on the Web unless you confirm it with a trustworthy source of information.

### Rules for Parents

- Talk with your kids about what types of sites they should and should not visit, and why. Encourage them to come to you if they happen on a site they're unsure about or that makes them uncomfortable.

- Encourage kids to start their surfing sessions on kid-friendly search sites or sites listing Web destinations appropriate for children, such as yahooligans.com. Ask Jeeves for Kids (ajkids.com), and B. J. Pinchbeck's Homework Helper (school.discovery.com/homeworkhelp/Bjpinchbeck).

- Consider using blocking software or parental controls to screen out inappropriate sites. (See p. 241).

## Spam

The upstanding citizens who bombard e-mailboxes with unsolicited advertising can't tell which addresses belong to children. So kids often get bombarded with graphic come-ons for porn sites, along with the usual scams and flimflams.

### Rules for Kids

- Learn how to recognize spam. (Like most e-mailers, kids perfect their spam-spotting skills pretty quickly—thanks to ample practice opportunities.) If you get e-mail from a stranger who seems to be trying to sell something, that's spam. Just hit "delete." You'll learn to spot spam from its subject lines, which shout about "FREE!!!" stuff, ways to make money fast, miracle cures, and other stuff kids (and sensible grown-ups) have little use for. (Beware of trick subject lines, like "hi" or "information you requested." They might fool you into opening the e-mail, but you'll figure out it's spam soon enough.)

- If you get sex-related spam—the sort advertising pornography or other so-called adult material—tell your parents. Don't worry, you're not getting such messages because you did anything wrong, or because anyone is interested in harassing kids. The spammer probably just doesn't know—or care—which of the thousands of addresses on his list belong to children and which to adults. Just delete this stuff, but tell your parents about it. For one thing, you don't want them discovering it on their own: Non-Net savvy parents, shocked to find X-rated come-ons (usually not illustrated, thank goodness) in their kids' mailboxes, can often get the wrong idea, suspecting that their children have been visiting porn sites. (Attention, parents: Kids don't have to do anything to land on spammers' address lists. Kids, show your parents this section as a get-out-of-grounding-free card.) And your parents can help you figure out strategies to avoid or block out spam.

- Never reply to spam—not even to tell the sender to knock it off—or follow instructions given in the message for getting yourself off the spammer's mailing list. You'll just confirm that your address is alive and working—and probably get more spam.

- Never follow any Web links contained in spam. You could wind up someplace you shouldn't (and most likely wouldn't want to) be.

- And of course, never take any spammers up on their offers (most of which don't appeal to kids anyway). The stuff advertised in spam is usually a scam of some sort—it could even be illegal. Leave this stuff to gullible grown-ups.

### Rules for Parents

- Teach kids to recognize spam. Show them a few examples from your mailbox, and make sure they know to ignore and delete it.

- Show kids how to take precautions to make sure spammers don't get their hands on their e-mail address in the first place (see Chapter 11, "I Do Not Like That Spam I Am.")

- Activate any special spam-fighting features in your kids' e-mail program or on their Internet service (see Chapter 11)—these can be remarkably effective in putting a stop to most spam.

- Don't worry too much about spam. Like adults, kids quickly become adept at ignoring and deleting it. If kids get X-rated spam, have a talk about it but don't overreact. Your kids are probably savvier than you imagine at sending trash right to the trash.

## Information Gathering

Many Web sites attempt to collect personal information about kids for marketing purposes, encouraging them to provide details about themselves and their families by means of registration forms, surveys, quizzes, contests, and bribes such as coupons. (One Web site registration form even asked kids whether their parents owned mutual funds. I pity any elementary-schooler who actually knew the answer.) While adults can make informed choices about coughing up private data online, kids can't—which is why a federal law now requires sites to obtain a parent's consent before collecting any information from children younger than thirteen.

### Rules for Kids and Parents

- Ask your parents before providing any personal information to a Web site.

- Check out Web sites' posted privacy policies (also required by law if they gather any information from kids younger than thirteen) to see what they do with the information you give them.

- Report any Web site that solicits information from a kid younger than thirteen without requiring a parent's permission to the Federal Trade Commission at www.ftc.gov or 1-877-FTC-HELP.

## Hackers

Miscreants seeking to break into a computer or Internet account can find easy targets in kids, whose passwords can be simple to guess or easy to con out of them. Kids who aren't careful about e-mail attachments could also easily have their computers infected with a virus or a Trojan horse program.

### Tips for Kids

* Don't open any e-mail attachment from a stranger. Scan any e-mail attachment from someone you know with anti-virus software.

* Don't share your e-mail password with friends and don't tell it to anyone who asks you online, even if they pretend to be someone official.

* Think up a hard-to-guess password. Don't make it something someone who knows you could guess, like your pet's name or your birthday. Try a combination of letters and numbers, and use your imagination.

### Tips for Parents

* Make sure your child's computer has anti-virus software installed, with as many automatic options as possible turned on.

## Meanies

Some people on the Net are simply not very nice—and they may not know they're corresponding with children. Insults, flame mail, and mean-spirited pranks can devastate kids.

### Tips for Kids

* Don't respond to any mean or insulting messages, and leave any online conversation that takes a nasty turn.

- Tell a parent about abusive e-mail or messages. You or your parents can report them to the offender's Internet service provider (see "Cyberstalking," p. 234) and possibly get them kicked off the service.

### Tips for Parents

- Keep kids away from the more Wild West–like reaches of the Net: Usenet newsgroups, unsupervised Web message boards, and unmonitored chat rooms.

When you don't want to give away personal information about yourself to someone you're chatting with, is it better to lie—even though lying is wrong—or just to tell them you don't want to say?

Lots of people pretend to be somebody else online; talking to strangers in an online chat room is more of a fantasy game than a situation that demands honesty. If kids aren't old enough to know the difference (or to pick a fake name and stick to it), they shouldn't be chatting unsupervised. If you're not the imaginative type, though, it's perfectly fine to tell someone you'd rather not say—or to change the topic quickly.

### JUST SAY YES

Some Web sites help keep kids safe. Children's search sites make sure kids' Web searches don't send them to sites unsuitable for young eyes. Many companies, organizations, and individuals create lists of especially good sites for kids. And some sites and Internet services set up chat rooms and message boards for kids, with adults monitoring conversations and strict rules about what participants can and can't say, do, or reveal. A few sites to bookmark:

### Kid-Friendly Web-Searching Sites

- Yahooligans (www.yahooligans.com)

- Ask Jeeves for Kids (www.ajkids.com)

### Lists of Good Web Sites for Kids

- The American Library Association's Cool Sites for Kids (at www.ala.org)

- B. J. Pinchbeck's Homework Helper, a list of sites created by a kid (school.discovery.com/homeworkhelp/bjpinchbeck)

### Monitored Chat Rooms and Message Boards

- AOL's "Kids Only" area (keyword: Kids Only)

**My young daughter tried to go to the White House Web site and got a porn site instead. Where can I go to complain about this?**

Porn peddlers snapping up Web addresses that are variations or misspellings of other popular sites might be sleazy, but it's not necessarily illegal, so complaining to the folks at www.whitehouse.gov (the real White House site) won't do much good. But it's easy to avoid such surprises: Instead of guessing at a site's address, consult a Web directory like Yahoo.com—or, for your daughter, the expressly kid-friendly Yahooligans.com.

### BLOCKS AND LOCKS

While there's no substitute for good parenting, parents can also use technology to help keep kids safe on the Net. Many Internet service providers and several software programs on the market let parents control what kids can see, say, and do on the Net. Options in most of these programs include:

- Blocking kids from accessing Web sites in various objectionable categories, such as nudity, drug use, violence, and hate and intolerance, with sites classified either by human surfers or by software that automatically examines sites for objectionable words or images.

- Restricting kids to visiting only pre-approved sites

- Blocking e-mail messages containing objectionable phrases, attachments, or pictures

- Allowing kids to send and receive e-mail to and from only specified addresses

- Barring kids from accessing chat rooms, instant messages, or discussion groups

- Preventing a child from entering his name, phone number, or other specified information on the Net

- Regulating the amount of time a child can spend online

Most programs allow parents to customize the controls so they can choose categories and activities to block according to the child's maturity and the family's values. These programs aren't perfect. Filters don't always catch objectionable sites, and they often block out innocuous sites or sites some parents feel children ought to be able to access, such as Planned Parenthood's Web site. (Fortunately, most of these programs are more sophisticated today than they were a few years ago, when one popular service, which banned any site with the word *breast*, came under fire for blocking sites that discussed breast cancer or cooking chicken breasts.)

*What to look for:* Popular commercial blocking software programs include Cyber Patrol, CYBERsitter, Net Nanny, and SurfWatch. Internet service providers often offer free versions of one of the above programs or develop their own system of parental controls. (America Online's system, which offers appropriate settings for three age levels or lets parents create customized settings, is available at keyword: parental controls.) Each program works differently—in the options it offers, in how it determines which sites to block, in the number of children it can be set up for, in cost—so investigate a few to find the one that's right for your family.

Is using blocking software proper parental etiquette? I think it's fine for preteen or younger kids, who could easily blunder into unsuitable material or risky situations if left to surf unsupervised. For the youngest surfers, strict controls—especially options blocking them from accessing risky areas such as unsupervised chat rooms as well as features restricting them to preapproved sites and e-mail correspondents—are a good precaution. An even better approach, though, is not to let young children surf solo. A parent sitting next to a preteen at the computer or keeping a watchful eye out nearby is a more effective safeguard than any software.

Once kids become more mature (and, as any parent knows, kids of the same age vary widely in their maturity levels), they can handle more independence—and they may begin to resent nannyware-insisting parents' lack of trust. If you use blocking software, consider lifting restrictions as your kid shows the appropriate degree of responsibility. (Hmmm . . . maybe "Pick up your laundry for a month and we'll talk" would be a good approach.) It's important for parents to remember that blocking software isn't perfect. Savvy kids may be able to get around some restrictions, or kids can easily access the Net someplace other than their home computer. Technology is no substitute for good parenting—or good preparation.

### Survey Says

*About two-thirds of wired parents say they have made rules for their kids about going online. The rules they set:*

*96 percent require that their kids not give out personal information*

*89 percent restrict areas their kids may visit*

*86 percent limit the amount of time their kids may spend online*

*78 percent require that their kids finish their homework before logging on*

*78 percent ask that kids check with an adult before going online*

**53 percent require that an adult be present when the child goes online**

Source: The America Online/Roper Starch
Worldwide Adult Cyberstudy 2000

**Survey Says**
*30 percent of parents say they sometimes deny their kids access to the Internet as punishment.*

Source: The UCLA Internet Report: "Surveying the Digital
Future," UCLA Center for Communication Policy

## MY MOTHER THE SPY

Some software offers Mom and Dad the opportunity to play Big Brother. Some of the popular site-blocking programs discussed above allow parents to access a list of sites children visit or see periodic snapshots of the computer screen. Other software makers sell programs that can surreptitiously record every keystroke and click a child makes. (Titles include Spector and Disk Tracy.) There are also lower-tech ways to snoop, like opening the history or cache file of your kid's Web browser—files that record the most recent sites visited. (Savvy kids often know how to cover their tracks with these last methods, though.)

In most cases, spying on kids' Net moves, particularly those of older teens, without telling them falls outside the bounds of good parental etiquette. It's a violation of privacy—and trust—on a level with reading their diaries or tapping their phones. Every family situation is different, of course, but it's wise to think of these programs only as an absolute last resort if you believe your child is in danger. Or you might consider using such spyware with your child's permission, perhaps as a condition of letting a kid who has violated your rules on multiple occasions back onto the Net. Remember, of course, that determined kids can access the Net in places you can't monitor, such as in school or at a friend's house.

## BEING ON YOUR BEST E-HAVIOR

For kids, knowing how to stay safe online is an important part of Internet etiquette, but it's also important to know how to be polite. Just like on the playground (anyone else here still have scars, physical or emotional, from elementary-school dodgeball games?), kids on the Net can annoy or hurt other children and adults alike—on purpose or without realizing the damage they're doing. Some e-mail and related e-etiquette tips for kids:

### Basic Training

- *Remember that once you send an e-mail, you can't erase it.* Take a minute to think about how the person you're sending it to will feel when he or she reads it. Don't ever send e-mail when you're angry.

- *Remember that anyone you send a message to might forward it or show it to someone else.* Don't pass along gossip or say anything mean or untrue about another person in e-mail. In fact, don't say anything in e-mail you wouldn't want your parents, school principal, best friend, or worst enemy to hear. (Actually, it's a good idea to picture one or more of the above people before you hit "send.")

- *Be careful if you're making a joke or being sarcastic in an e-mail message.* Sometimes it's hard for a reader to figure out you're being humorous. Try using a smiley :-) or Net lingo like <g> (grin) or <jk> (just kidding) to help people know you're being silly.

- *On the other hand, e-mail isn't a chat room.* Don't use too many smileys, exclamation points, abbreviations, and invented spellings like "kewl." And don't type in all-capital or all-lower-case letters. In chat this kind of speedy shorthand writing is fine and dandy, but in e-mail it'll give readers a headache.

- *Don't e-mail strangers uninvited, and don't keep e-mailing anyone who doesn't respond or asks you to stop.*

## Forwarding Follies

- *Don't forward any personal message—or tell anyone about its contents—unless you have the sender's permission.* E-mailers intend many messages to be private, even if that means not telling your friends about that flirty note you got from the new cute guy in class.

- *Don't forward jokes or other e-mail tidbits to friends or family members unless you know the people you're sending them to want to receive them.* Other people may not have the time or the desire to read them—or they may not share your sense of humor.

---

### Net Peeve : (

I worked as a camp counselor one summer, and when I got back to college the kids I supervised started including me in their chain letters and jokes—forwards appropriate only for nine-year-olds, like messages where you'd scroll down to see a picture of a Beanie Baby made out of letters and numbers.

---

- *Never forward chain e-mail messages, the kind that say "send this to five friends or else."* Even if the e-mail says something bad will happen to you if you don't forward it or promises a reward if you forward it, these messages are just pranks that waste people's time. (Hokum about messages causing bad luck sometimes upsets young children—yet another reason chain letters should go straight to the trash.)

---

### Net Peeve : (

Kids need to understand that there's a professional e-mail address and a fun e-mail address. My nieces and nephews send me messages like "You'll be cursed if you don't forward this message" at work—that's uncool.

---

- *Beware, too, of hoaxes and false rumors that travel by chain e-mail.* Kids are particularly vulnerable to scary or heart-tugging e-hoaxes (for more about how to identify a hoax, see Chapter 9, "E-Mail Hoaxes"). Don't believe anything you read in a chain e-mail—and don't become part of the problem by helping a hoax to spread.

**My grandson got an e-mail claiming that for every friend he forwarded it to, McDonald's and Pizza Hut would donate $1 to help treat a child with epilepsy. As a gullible eleven-year-old, he is following directions. Do I smell a rat? How should I break it to him and his friends?**

Your sniffer is spot-on. Chain e-mails that promise rewards for forwarding are almost always hoaxes, and pranksters particularly love to concoct heart-tugging tales about sick kids. It's smart to check up on any forwarded e-plea at a hoax-busting Web site like snopes.com, which debunks a version of the message you describe. Show your grandson that listing and teach him to help stop the spread of such whoppers by not forwarding any e-mail unless an adult okays it (and by avoiding chain letters, which is good advice for gullible grown-ups, too).

- *Keep other people's e-mail addresses private.* Don't give your friends' or relatives' e-mail addresses out to other people without their permission. When you send e-mail to several people who don't know each other, use blind carbon copies so they don't see each other's names and addresses.

- *Don't send a large e-mail attachment to someone without asking him or her first.* Attachments can cause problems for people with slower Net connections or limited storage space for e-mail.

### Social Scenes

- *Learn the rules of the road in an e-mail mailing list, message board, or chat room before you speak up.* Read any posted rules, then hang out awhile to get a sense of how the group operates. Find out whether you are expected to stick to a certain topic, and if there are any topics or questions that are prohibited (in many kid-friendly chat rooms, questions such as "Where do you live?" or "What's your phone number?" are no-nos).

- *Don't criticize other people for breaking the rules (unless they're safety rules, in which case you should alert a supervisor).* Someone in charge will fill them in—you'll just sound like a snob.

- *Don't start an online argument, use bad language, or violate any posted behavior rules.* You might find yourself kicked off the group—or even off your online service.

## Hack Attack

- *Don't break into or snoop through another person's e-mail account or computer.* Don't share your password with friends—and don't try to guess anyone's password or break into their computer another way. That's called hacking (or cracking) and it's illegal; it can land even kids in big trouble.

### Embarrassing E-Moment

In September 2000, a sixteen-year-old Miami boy known as "c0mrade" was sentenced to serve 6 months in a juvenile detention center for breaking into NASA and Department of Defense computers, stealing software and more than 3,000 e-mails. It was the first time an underage hacker was given a jail sentence. Another requirement of his sentence: writing letters of apology.

## School Rules

- *Don't e-mail or instant-message your teachers outside of school hours unless you have their permission.* Just because they're online doesn't mean they're available for round-the-clock homework help or want to be added to your joke-forwarding list. While college instructors and some grade-school teachers often make themselves available to students via e-mail, respect their generosity and time by following any guidelines and, generally, by sticking to urgent schoolwork-related matters. (A college instructor I know decided to start signing on to AOL under a different screen name after her students began instant-messaging her with questions that could easily wait for the next class, or sometimes just to ask, "What's up?" She also wasn't wild about her students knowing her predilection for Net surfing between 2 and 4 A.M.)

- *Don't ask strangers for homework help unless they expressly invite questions from students.* Out-of-the-blue questions from kids pop up every day on scholarly e-mail discussion groups and in the mailboxes of just about any Netizen with a Web site detailing expertise in a homework-susceptible field. (If Albert Einstein were around and e-mailing today, you can bet he'd be sorting through a mailbox full of messages like "Dear Albert, I have to write a report about the solar system. Can you please send me some information about it? The report is due Tuesday. Thank you very much, Kayla.") If you're hitting the books and the books are winning, some kids' sites offer live homework helpers who answer questions via chat or e-mail. And chances are you can find answers at one of the Web's many reference sites: Check out the search sites and lists of student-friendly resources listed in this chapter.

- *If an expert welcomes questions from students, show you've done some homework already before asking for help.* Asking a very general question ("Can you send me some information about mastodons?"), a question whose answer can easily be found elsewhere ("How big was the average mastodon?"), or a question that appears to be asking the recipient to do your homework for you ("Please tell me why mastodons became extinct in approximately 500 words") wastes the correspondent's time—and decreases your chances of getting an answer. Wired scholars will usually be happier to answer questions relating directly to their specific research or expertise (which, of course, you should know before contacting them) or recommend books, articles, or other resources where you can learn more about their field.

---

## Net Peeve : (

I'm a professor in Georgetown University's cyberculture studies program, and I maintain a Web site that includes class syllabi, reading lists, and links to other academic resources—as well as my e-mail address. I get e-mail from everyone from high school students to grad students asking me the most general questions and expecting immediate answers. I get questions like, "I'm writing a paper on the influence of technology on culture. Please respond by this afternoon." Or they send me a huge 200K attachment with a note saying "I'm writing this paper. It's due next week. Can you look it over?" And they barely introduce themselves—the message is signed something like "Dan."

I don't mind answering questions—I love that younger students can break through the hierarchies. But they need to learn better etiquette. You should send e-mail that's no more than a screen long—twenty-five lines or so. Define who you are and what you're doing. And show you've done your homework. Mention other books or papers you've looked at. Make it clear you know who you're talking to and what you're looking for.

---

- *Don't take anyone else's work you find on the Net and present it as your own.* The Web is full of shady sites offering ready-made term papers—and being able to copy and paste from online news articles or encyclopedia entries tempts some lazy students to borrow large chunks of others' writing without bothering to identify the source or even change any of the wording. This is plagiarism, and it's unfair to other students, your teacher, and ultimately to yourself, since you cheat yourself out of the opportunity to learn.

It's also a ticket to trouble. Teachers are savvy about spotting Web plagiarism. They can use search sites to compare suspicious passages in your paper to text on millions of Web pages. They surf the term-paper sites. They swap tips. Crime doesn't pay.

In schoolwork, treat information you get from trustworthy Net sources the same way you'd treat information from a book, magazine article, or other offline resource: Paraphrase information or use quotes of no more than a few sentences, and always give the name of the source.

Taking someone else's online creations is wrong outside of school, too. For example, you should not copy text or photos from someone else's Web site onto your own Web site or into an e-mail message without permission from whoever created the text or photo. (That includes commercial Web sites as well as people's personal sites. Companies that own popular movies and TV shows often take a dim view of people copying images or articles from official sites for their unofficial fan sites—lawyers don't like sending cease-and-desist letters to kids, but they will if they have to.) An easy way to stay safe: When you see something you like on the Net, e-mail friends a link to it or put a link on your Web site— don't send or post a copy of it.

### Embarrassing E-Moment

"I had a student who plagiarized an entire report on smart urban growth from an obscure Internet site. Poor guy, he had the misfortune to submit the report as a final paper to a professor who is publishing in that exact area (me!), and so he was caught against all odds. If he had only cited the site, I would have happily given him an 'A' for doing such complete and relevant research, but . . ."

## SHARING A KEYBOARD

"Dad, can I borrow the car?" Those six words can make any parent's heart clutch. (What they'll do to his clutch it's better not to contemplate.) Parents and kids should be just as cautious if they share a computer, as many families do. One very important rule: Once kids are old enough to e-mail unsupervised, they should have an e-mail address and mailbox separate from their parents'. (Many services let you set up additional screen names for family members, and some schools assign kids their own e-mail addresses and even Internet service accounts. Or kids can sign up for a free Web-based e-mail service.) Giving kids free rein in their parents' in-boxes—and letting them send mail out under their parents' names—is just asking for trouble. Another caution for parents: Don't let kids e-mail or surf on an Internet account you use for business. If your only Internet access is through work, it's time to ante up for a personal account. You don't want any juvenile mishaps or misbehavior to jeopardize your job. A few more rules for sharing the driver's seat:

- *Don't snoop.* Kids should know to stay far away from their parents' e-mail (parents, don't tempt fate—use a password your kids can't guess, and don't write it down anywhere obvious). Parents, once you've decided your kids should be able to e-mail unsupervised, stay out of their in-boxes too. And try to resist snooping through other files, like online downloads.

- *Set up rules for kids about downloading (large e-mail attachments or files from the Web can eat up your computer's storage space) and installing software (which can cause all sorts of mayhem if not done properly).* Make sure you have anti-virus software up and running.

- *Set up separate sets of Web bookmarks.* And parents as well as kids should watch where they surf—or learn to cover their tracks. If you don't clear your Web browser's cache or history file, anyone else using the computer may be able to tell what sites you've visited recently. (Even if they're not out to snoop,

Web browsers usually show links to recently visited sites in a different color.)

**Somebody sent an instant message (IM) to my dad while he was in the bathroom. Should I have answered it for him?**

There's no need for you to play secretary. IMers understand that people step away from their PCs—the sender can always zap an e-mail if he's about to log off. And since the IMer thinks it's your dad at the keyboard, you might see something not intended for your eyes before you can explain who you are. (You wouldn't dream of impersonating your dad, right? Talk about mischief potential.)

# Appendix A
## Geekspeak Glossary

*Parlez-vous* geekspeak? E-mailers' passion for TLAs (three-letter acronyms) and ever more baroque abbreviations can leave newbies yearning for a Berlitz class. Lingo seeps into e-mail from all of the Net's numerous dialects: chat-room shorthand, online gaming terms, Usenet parlance, tech-industry buzzwords, old-school hackerese. This guide to more than 150 terms should help you interpret mystery messages—but remember, it's rude to use lingo to show off. Only use it in e-mail if you're sure your recipient speaks the language.

| Abbreviation | Definition |
| --- | --- |
| $0.02 | my two cents |
| aamof | as a matter of fact |
| adn | any day now |
| afaik | as far as I know |
| afk | away from keyboard |
| asap | as soon as possible |
| a/s | age/sex |
| a/s/l | age/sex/location |
| aysos | are you stupid or something? |
| bbiab | be back in a bit |
| bbl | be back later |
| bcc | blind carbon copy |
| bcnu | be seeing you |
| bf | boyfriend |
| bfd | big freakin' deal |
| bfn | bye for now |
| bg | big girl |
| bion | believe it or not |
| brb | be right back |

| | |
|---|---|
| btdt | been there done that |
| btw | by the way |
| bwdik | but what do I know? |
| byam | between you and me |
| bykt | but you knew that |
| cc | carbon copy |
| c4n | ciao for now |
| cmiiw | correct me if I'm wrong |
| cu | see you |
| cul, cul8r | see you later |
| cula | see you later, alligator |
| cwot | complete waste of time |
| cya | see ya |
| darfc | ducking and running for cover |
| dhyb | don't hold your breath |
| diik | darned if I know |
| dob | date of birth |
| f2f | face-to-face |
| faq | frequently asked questions |
| fbow | for better or for worse |
| fitb | fill in the blank |
| fwiw | for what it's worth |
| fya | for your amusement |
| fyi | for your information |
| fym | for your misinformation |
| g | grin |
| gbu | god bless you |
| gd&r | grinning, ducking, and running |
| gd&rf | grinning, ducking, and running fast |
| gd&w | grinning, ducking, and weaving |
| gf | girlfriend |
| gfete | grinning from ear to ear |
| gg | good game or gotta go |
| gigo | garbage in, garbage out |
| gj | good job |
| gl | good luck |
| gmta | great minds think alike |

| | |
|---|---|
| hak | hugs and kisses |
| hhok | ha-ha, only kidding |
| hhos | ha-ha, only serious |
| hth | hope this helps |
| iac | in any case |
| ibtd | I beg to differ |
| ic | I see |
| idk or idn | I don't know |
| ily | I love you |
| ime | in my experience |
| imho | in my humble opinion |
| imnsho | in my not-so-humble opinion |
| imo | in my opinion |
| impe | in my personal experience |
| inpo | in no particular order |
| iow | in other words |
| irl | in real life |
| iswym | I see what you mean |
| iwalu | I will always love you |
| iykwim | if you know what I mean |
| j/k | just kidding! |
| jas | just a second |
| jff | just for fun |
| jic | just in case |
| jtlyk | just to let you know |
| k | okay |
| kiss | keep it simple, stupid |
| kit | keep in touch |
| kma | kiss my ass! |
| kwim | know what I mean? |
| kyfc | keep your fingers crossed |
| l | laugh |
| lmk | let me know |
| lol | laughing out loud, lots of laughter, lots of luck, lots of love |
| lthtt | laughing too hard to type |
| mgb | may god bless |

| | |
|---|---|
| mhoty | my hat's off to you |
| motas | member of the appropriate sex |
| motd | message of the day |
| motos | member of the opposite sex |
| motss | member of the same sex |
| mtfbwy | may the force be with you |
| myob | mind your own business |
| nbd | no big deal |
| nc | no comment |
| nfw | no freakin' way! |
| noyb | none of your business |
| nrn | no reply necessary |
| ntim | not that it matters |
| ntw | not to worry |
| ntymi | now that you mention it |
| oic | oh, I see |
| omg | oh my god! |
| omik | open mouth, insert keyboard |
| onna | oh no, not again! |
| os | operating system |
| otfl | on the floor laughing |
| otl | out to lunch |
| otoh | on the other hand |
| otooh | on the other other hand |
| paw | parents are watching |
| pc | personal computer or politically correct |
| pita | pain in the ass |
| pos | parents over shoulder |
| posslq | person of the opposite sex sharing living quarters |
| pov | point of view |
| rbtl | read between the lines |
| rl | real life |
| rofl or rotfl | rolling on the floor laughing |
| roflastc | rolling on the floor laughing and scaring the cat |
| roflmao | rolling on the floor laughing my arse off |
| rtbm | read the bloody manual |
| rtfaq | read the frequently asked questions |

| | |
|---|---|
| rtff | read the freakin' faq |
| rtfm | read the freakin' manual |
| rtm | read the manual |
| scnr | sorry, could not resist |
| so | significant other |
| swak | sealed (or sent) with a kiss |
| sys | see you soon |
| teotwawki | the end of the world as we know it |
| tftt | thanks for the thought |
| tgal | think globally, act locally |
| thx, tx | thanks |
| tia | thanks in advance |
| tic | tongue in cheek |
| tla | three-letter acronym |
| tmi | too much information |
| tobal | there ought to be a law |
| tobg | this ought to be good |
| tos | terms of service |
| tptb | the powers that be |
| ttbomk | to the best of my knowledge |
| ttfn | ta-ta for now |
| ttyl | talk to you later |
| ttyt | talk to you tomorrow |
| ty | thank you |
| tyvm | thank you very much |
| vbg | very big grin |
| wb | welcome back |
| wmmows | wash my mouth out with soap |
| wtb | want to buy |
| wtf | what the f——? |
| wtg | way to go! |
| www | World Wide Web |
| wygiwypf | what you get is what you pay for |
| wysiwyg | what you see is what you get |
| yaba | yet another bloody acronym |
| ygiagam | your guess is as good as mine |
| yglt | you're gonna love this |

| | |
|---|---|
| ykya_w | you know you're a [fill in the blank] when… |
| ymmv | your mileage may vary |
| ynk | you never know |
| yw | you're welcome |
| yysw | yeah, yeah, sure, whatever |

# Appendix B
# Country Codes

Where'd that e-mail come from? If the sender's e-mail address ends with a two-letter code rather than a top-level domain such as .com or .edu (see Chapter 2, "Replying Right and Coping with E-Mail Overload," for a discussion of e-mail addresses), it came from a domain name registered in another country. It didn't necessarily come from a resident of the country: Some small countries with catchy country codes (like Tuvalu's .tv) sell domain names to all comers while spammers sometimes route their messages through foreign computers to evade tracking.

**The country codes:**

| | |
|---|---|
| .ad | Andorra |
| .ae | United Arab Emirates |
| .af | Afghanistan |
| .ag | Antigua and Barbuda |
| .ai | Anguilla |
| .al | Albania |
| .am | Armenia |
| .an | Netherlands Antilles |
| .ao | Angola |
| .aq | Antarctica |
| .ar | Argentina |
| .as | American Samoa |
| .at | Austria |
| .au | Australia |
| .aw | Aruba |
| .az | Azerbaijan |
| .ba | Bosnia and Herzegovina |
| .bb | Barbados |
| .bd | Bangladesh |

| | |
|---|---|
| .be | Belgium |
| .bf | Burkina Faso |
| .bg | Bulgaria |
| .bh | Bahrain |
| .bi | Burundi |
| .bj | Benin |
| .bm | Bermuda |
| .bn | Brunei Darussalam |
| .bo | Bolivia |
| .br | Brazil |
| .bs | Bahamas |
| .bt | Bhutan |
| .bv | Bouvet Island |
| .bw | Botswana |
| .by | Belarus |
| .bz | Belize |
| .ca | Canada |
| .cc | Cocos (Keeling) Islands |
| .cf | Central African Republic |
| .cg | Congo |
| .ch | Switzerland |
| .ci | Côte D'Ivoire (Ivory Coast) |
| .ck | Cook Islands |
| .cl | Chile |
| .cm | Cameroon |
| .cn | China |
| .co | Colombia |
| .cr | Costa Rica |
| .cs | Czechoslovakia (former) |
| .cu | Cuba |
| .cv | Cape Verde |
| .cx | Christmas Island |
| .cy | Cyprus |
| .cz | Czech Republic |
| .de | Germany |
| .dj | Djibouti |
| .dk | Denmark |

| | |
|---|---|
| .dm | Dominica |
| .do | Dominican Republic |
| .dz | Algeria |
| .ec | Ecuador |
| .ee | Estonia |
| .eg | Egypt |
| .eh | Western Sahara |
| .er | Eritrea |
| .es | Spain |
| .et | Ethiopia |
| .fi | Finland |
| .fj | Fiji |
| .fk | Falkland Islands (Malvinas) |
| .fm | Micronesia |
| .fo | Faroe Islands |
| .fr | France |
| .fx | France, Metropolitan |
| .ga | Gabon |
| .gb | Great Britain (UK) |
| .gd | Grenada |
| .ge | Georgia |
| .gf | French Guiana |
| .gh | Ghana |
| .gi | Gibraltar |
| .gl | Greenland |
| .gm | Gambia |
| .gn | Guinea |
| .gp | Guadeloupe |
| .gq | Equatorial Guinea |
| .gr | Greece |
| .gs | South Georgia and South Sandwich Islands |
| .gt | Guatemala |
| .gu | Guam |
| .gw | Guinea-Bissau |
| .gy | Guyana |
| .hk | Hong Kong |
| .hm | Heard and McDonald Islands |

| | |
|---|---|
| .hn | Honduras |
| .hr | Croatia (Hrvatska) |
| .ht | Haiti |
| .hu | Hungary |
| .id | Indonesia |
| .ie | Ireland |
| .il | Israel |
| .in | India |
| .io | British Indian Ocean Territory |
| .iq | Iraq |
| .ir | Iran |
| .is | Iceland |
| .it | Italy |
| .jm | Jamaica |
| .jo | Jordan |
| .jp | Japan |
| .ke | Kenya |
| .kg | Kyrgyzstan |
| .kh | Cambodia |
| .ki | Kiribati |
| .km | Comoros |
| .kn | Saint Kitts and Nevis |
| .kp | Korea (North) |
| .kr | Korea (South) |
| .kw | Kuwait |
| .ky | Cayman Islands |
| .kz | Kazakhstan |
| .la | Laos |
| .lb | Lebanon |
| .lc | Saint Lucia |
| .li | Liechtenstein |
| .lk | Sri Lanka |
| .lr | Liberia |
| .ls | Lesotho |
| .lt | Lithuania |
| .lu | Luxembourg |
| .lv | Latvia |

| | |
|---|---|
| .ly | Libya |
| .ma | Morocco |
| .mc | Monaco |
| .md | Moldova |
| .mg | Madagascar |
| .mh | Marshall Islands |
| .mk | Macedonia |
| .ml | Mali |
| .mm | Myanmar |
| .mn | Mongolia |
| .mo | Macau |
| .mp | Northern Mariana Islands |
| .mq | Martinique |
| .mr | Mauritania |
| .ms | Montserrat |
| .mt | Malta |
| .mu | Mauritius |
| .mv | Maldives |
| .mw | Malawi |
| .mx | Mexico |
| .my | Malaysia |
| .mz | Mozambique |
| .na | Namibia |
| .nc | New Caledonia |
| .ne | Niger |
| .nf | Norfolk Island |
| .ng | Nigeria |
| .ni | Nicaragua |
| .nl | Netherlands |
| .no | Norway |
| .np | Nepal |
| .nr | Nauru |
| .nt | Neutral Zone |
| .nu | Niue |
| .nz | New Zealand (Aotearoa) |
| .om | Oman |
| .pa | Panama |

| | |
|---|---|
| .pe | Peru |
| .pf | French Polynesia |
| .pg | Papua New Guinea |
| .ph | Philippines |
| .pk | Pakistan |
| .pl | Poland |
| .pm | Saint Pierre and Miquelon |
| .pn | Pitcairn |
| .pr | Puerto Rico |
| .pt | Portugal |
| .pw | Palau |
| .py | Paraguay |
| .qu | Qatar |
| .re | Reunion |
| .ro | Romania |
| .ru | Russian Federation |
| .rw | Rwanda |
| .sa | Saudi Arabia |
| .sb | Solomon Islands |
| .sc | Seychelles |
| .sd | Sudan |
| .se | Sweden |
| .sg | Singapore |
| .sh | Saint Helena |
| .si | Slovenia |
| .sj | Svalbard and Jan Mayen Islands |
| .sk | Slovak Republic |
| .sl | Sierra Leone |
| .sm | San Marino |
| .sn | Senegal |
| .so | Somalia |
| .sr | Suriname |
| .st | Sao Tome and Principe |
| .su | USSR (former) |
| .sv | El Salvador |
| .sy | Syria |

| | |
|---|---|
| .sz | Swaziland |
| .tc | Turks and Caicos Islands |
| .td | Chad |
| .tf | French Southern Territories |
| .tg | Togo |
| .th | Thailand |
| .tj | Tajikistan |
| .tk | Tokelau |
| .tm | Turkmenistan |
| .tn | Tunisia |
| .to | Tonga |
| .tp | East Timor |
| .tr | Turkey |
| .tt | Trinidad and Tobago |
| .tv | Tuvalu |
| .tw | Taiwan |
| .tz | Tanzania |
| .ua | Ukraine |
| .ug | Uganda |
| .uk | United Kingdom |
| .um | U.S. Minor Outlying Islands |
| .us | United States |
| .uy | Uruguay |
| .uz | Uzbekistan |
| .va | Vatican City State (Holy See) |
| .vc | Saint Vincent and the Grenadines |
| .ve | Venezuela |
| .vg | Virgin Islands (British) |
| .vi | Virgin Islands (U.S.) |
| .vn | Vietnam |
| .vu | Vanuatu |
| .wf | Wallis and Futuna Islands |
| .ws | Samoa |
| .ye | Yemen |
| .yt | Mayotte |
| .yu | Yugoslavia |

| | |
|---|---|
| .za | South Africa |
| .zm | Zambia |
| .zr | Zaire |
| .zw | Zimbabwe |

# About the Author

SAMANTHA MILLER answers *People* magazine readers' e-etiquette questions in the "Internet Manners" advice column, which appears on the Web site PEOPLE.com. (Have a question? E-mail it to manners@people.com.) A senior writer at *People* and a longtime Net addict, she has written cover stories on subjects such as Jennifer Aniston and America's most eligible bachelors as well as features on personalities in technology, business, and entertainment. A graduate of Princeton University, she lives in Brooklyn, New York.